The Power
of Geographical
Enquiry

The Power of Geographical Enquiry

How to build an engaging, evidence-led secondary geography curriculum

David Rogers

BLOOMSBURY EDUCATION
LONDON OXFORD NEW YORK NEW DELHI SYDNEY

BLOOMSBURY EDUCATION
Bloomsbury Publishing Plc
50 Bedford Square, London WC1B 3DP, UK
Bloomsbury Publishing Ireland Limited
29 Earlsfort Terrace, Dublin 2, D02 AY28, Ireland

BLOOMSBURY, BLOOMSBURY EDUCATION and the
Diana logo are trademarks of Bloomsbury Publishing Plc

First published in Great Britain, 2026 by Bloomsbury Publishing Plc

This edition published in Great Britain, 2026 by Bloomsbury Publishing Plc

Text copyright © David Rogers, 2026

Cambridge OCR material in this publication is reproduced under licence and remains the intellectual property of Cambridge OCR

David Rogers has asserted his right under the Copyright,
Designs and Patents Act, 1988, to be identified as Author of this work

Bloomsbury Publishing Plc does not have any control over, or responsibility for, any third-party websites referred to or in this book. All internet addresses given in this book were correct at the time of going to press. The author and publisher regret any inconvenience caused if addresses have changed or sites have ceased to exist, but can accept no responsibility for any such changes

All rights reserved. No part of this publication may be: i) reproduced or transmitted in any form, electronic or mechanical, including photocopying, recording or by means of any information storage or retrieval system without prior permission in writing from the publishers; or ii) used or reproduced in any way for the training, development or operation of artificial intelligence (AI) technologies, including generative AI technologies. The rights holders expressly reserve this publication from the text and data mining exception as per Article 4(3) of the Digital Single Market Directive (EU) 2019/790

A catalogue record for this book is available from the British Library

ISBN: PB: 978-1-80199-494-1; ePub: 978-1-80199-492-7

2 4 6 8 10 9 7 5 3 1 (paperback)

Cover design by Laura Neate

Typeset by Lumina Datamatics Ltd
Printed and bound in Great Britain by TJ Books, Padstow, Cornwall

To find out more about our authors and books visit www.bloomsbury.com
and sign up for our newsletters

For product safety related questions contact productsafety@bloomsbury.com

Acknowledgements

Geography is about connections, and this book is the result of many meaningful ones. It has been shaped by the expertise, guidance and kindness of many people. I am indebted to colleagues and friends who shared their wisdom, offered critical feedback and inspired me with their own commitment to geographical enquiry. Their insights have sharpened my thinking and ensured that this work reflects the richness of our subject.

I am grateful to the professional words of Alan Parkinson, Jo Coles and Kate Stockings in helping to shape early drafts, and the incredible team at Bloomsbury for the gentle encouragement. Thank you to Matt Podbury, Richard Allaway and the dedicated members and staff of the Geographical Association for the 'campfire conversations' that have provided both encouragement and the space to test ideas.

My passion for geography teaching was ignited by Jeff Stanfield. He's the reason I took on the geography department at Priory School, where I can honestly say we made a difference. That geography team of Mo, Jo, Sam, Lisa, Alec and Jonathan, with their commitment to the young people of Portsmouth and trust in my judgement, is where these ideas originated. I owe a particular debt to the students I have taught over the years, whose curiosity and questions reminded me daily of the purpose of geography.

I would also like to acknowledge the work of organisations outside education whose commitment to supporting mental health and preventing suicide has saved me during the dark times. My thanks go to 'Attain run cap' and 'bigmoose', whose dedication to saving lives continues to make a profound difference.

Finally, this is for Henry. You will always be first.

Table of contents

Foreword 8
Introduction 10

PART 1 The 'what', 'why' and 'how' of geographical enquiry 19

1 What underpins enquiry in the curriculum? 21
2 What is – and what isn't – enquiry? 35
3 What is the point of enquiry? 55
4 How does enquiry link to educational research? 83
5 What does progression in enquiry look like? 103
6 What are the features of an enquiry curriculum? 117

PART 2 What does enquiry look like in the secondary classroom? 139

7 How do we ask geographical questions? 141
8 How do we gather information? 161
9 How do we develop critical evaluation of information? 193
10 How do we enable students to communicate their learning? 225
11 How do we critically evaluate the enquiry process? 243
12 Conclusion: How does enquiry enable great geographers to change the world? 259

Afterword 266
Bibliography 268
Appendix 1: Example enquiries that lead to change 281
Index 298

Foreword

Enquiry has been a statutory part of the National Curriculum for geography since 1991, but if you asked 20 geography teachers to describe what it is, you would probably receive 20 different responses. For some, it is an approach to learning that is applied to everything that is taught; for others, it refers to open-ended 'enquiry questions'. Some might associate it with fieldwork but not classroom teaching, whilst for others it is a lens through which to see the world differently.

If you asked the same 20 teachers to say who developed the idea of enquiry in geography, they would mention the same name: Margaret Roberts. David has dug deep into his own teaching experience(s), and his personal perspectives on this pedagogical technique act as a useful companion piece to the current edition of Margaret's book (Roberts, 2023). It adds to a small but growing body of work on this important aspect of geography teaching.

Margaret's thinking was very much influenced by those with whom she worked. Teaching is a collegiate profession, and this book puts David within your departmental purview. David has distilled key messages from numerous workshops he has led at conferences in the UK and overseas on this topic, and from his experience of leading a geography department in a challenging south coast school to become a department known for its creative practice. His ideas are provocative and will make you think. They may be of particular value to those new to teaching, who are still forging their professional identity, or to ITE (initial teacher education) departments.

Enquiry engages students in disciplinary practice, allowing them to be participants in the construction of geographical knowledge. This is knowledge as praxis, and central to curriculum-making in geography. David's book could form the basis for discussions in your department. He tackles misconceptions about enquiry and connects it to current research thinking in education. I often refer to a Dylan Wiliam quote from 2012: 'every teacher needs to improve, not because they are not good enough, but because they can be even better' (Wiliam, 2012). David's book offers strategies that you will find helpful, provocations that will make you think harder, stories you can take inspiration from and strategies you could implement immediately.

Margaret Roberts is adamant that classroom encounters and curriculum resources must be authentic, and does not disguise the fact that she draws on experts to help her in areas about which she is less confident. David explores what an enquiry curriculum could look like and how progression can be built in – an area with which many departments grapple. The ideas presented in David's book are practical and feature concrete examples. David provides points of reflection that would make useful discussion points, and plenty of links to additional reading you might want to investigate.

As with all education books, you may disagree with some of what David has to say, but it should make you reconsider your own practice where enquiry is concerned. David takes each stage of enquiry and unpicks it with practical examples, concluding by considering how great geographers can change the world, demonstrating the power of geographical enquiry.

Pinning lessons to big geographical questions will give you opportunities to develop critical and creative investigations that promote student agency. Enquiry should be at the heart of what you do in the classroom, and David's book will help you focus on developing powerful teaching experiences that lie at the intersection between the subject, the everyday experiences of the students with whom you work and your own ever-evolving subject knowledge. Your students deserve nothing less.

Alan Parkinson
Vice President Education, Royal Geographical Society
Head of Geography, King's Ely Prep

Introduction

In this book, I aim to weave academic perspectives with the pragmatic knowledge of working in several *interesting* coastal strip secondary schools in southern England. I hope to provide practical tips for implementing an enquiry approach within British secondary schools. Geography is a huge subject and, as Alan Parkinson (2020) notes, we shouldn't expect to be an expert in it immediately.

The approach in this book can be summed up by the following diagram:

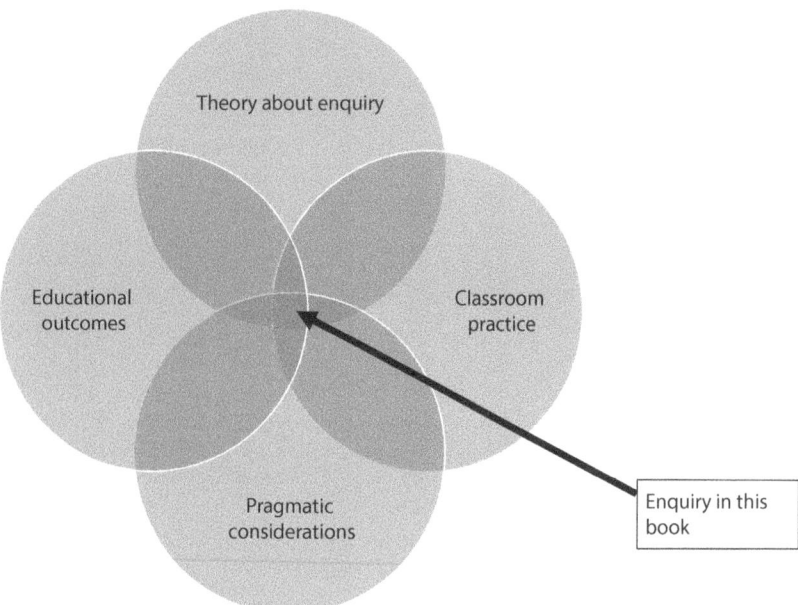

Figure 0.1: Enquiry definition in this book

This is how I see enquiry, based upon two decades of successful – and unsuccessful – classroom practice in coastal schools on the south coast of England. What follows is the product of the application, reflection upon that application and how it links to educational research. It's based upon the fantastic work of other dedicated and passionate advocates and researchers of geography teaching, whom I have tried to acknowledge throughout. I hope that the stories contained within this book give you permission to teach through enquiry. The purpose of this book is to give the reader the background and ideas to shape what enquiry teaching means in your context with your team and your young people.

> **Definitions**
>
> **Enquiry approach:** A single definition of the enquiry approach is difficult to pin down as it must be contextualised to individual institutions. In this book, the enquiry approach is a pedagogy that involves students learning how to be geographers as they investigate geographical issues by asking questions, critically engaging with evidence and geographical information, making sense of it and then communicating their conclusions. Enquiry can be purely teacher-led, ending at known learning points, student-led or anything in between.
>
> **Discovery learning:** A student-centred approach to education where learners construct their own knowledge by exploring, experimenting and solving problems themselves.

Enquiry is not exclusive to geography; it is difficult to define and, in recent years, has been linked – wrongly – to discovery learning. These factors perhaps contribute to Ofsted finding that 'in most schools, geographical enquiry was either ignored completely or mistaken for asking pupils to research topics themselves' (Ofsted, 2023a). This book argues that an enquiry approach is not only vital to providing students with an understanding of the distinctiveness of geography but also a crucial framework upon which to organise learning. The view in this book is pragmatic, weaving the academic research together with workload, accountability and other demands of being a teacher.

As the nature of geography, its knowledge and teaching vary between people, I am not attempting to provide a definitive guide to enquiry. I do, however, give my view on the subject. It is how I approached enquiry as a geography teacher, a geography leader and a senior leader. It is how I would approach it today. There are many excellent sources of information around the development of the wider geography curriculum, cognitive science and instructional design, and I have pointed towards these where relevant. I have aimed to link these together and provide an account that weaves together my experience of working for two decades in challenging secondary schools with the 'ideal' geography that academics advocate teaching.

Whilst I have included examples of content and ideas from a range of sources, including my own practice, I firmly believe that the content covered in a particular institution is for that geography team to decide. If our discipline is impossible to become an expert in its entirety, then we need a mechanism and set of tools with which we can discover, learn, remember and evaluate new information. Enquiry provides that toolbox.

To me, enquiry *is* teaching geography. It is our distinctive and premier pedagogy. I hope that this book provides you with the opportunity to pause and think hard about what you teach and how you teach it to those individuals in your institution. What content do you choose to cover? With what narratives do you weave through and connect different parts of our subject?

There are three key principles I have stuck to that reflect what I believe teaching is for.

1. **These are stories:** I am not an academic. Whilst I have endeavoured to think about and be shaped by the perspectives and contexts of others, all I can really do here is include a narrative of the things I have done, seen and heard that have ended up in fantastic educational outcomes. What I put here is thus a narrative of what has worked for me. It may work for you, need some tweaks or not suit your context or perspective at all.

2. **Sometimes I am deliberately provocative:** Linked to these being a narrative about the teaching adventures that I have gone through, my aim here is to provoke thought that will lead to better teaching, and therefore learning, of geographical content and skills. Sometimes that may involve being deliberately provocative to create some cognitive dissonance. I invite you to talk to your colleagues, whether in your school or further afield, in a respectful dialogue. We can disagree well. Reach out and talk to me if you need clarification, agree or think I'm totally wrong. I see that as a professional dialogue that leads to better outcomes for young people, rather than something to run away from.

3. **I believe in the campfire culture of teaching:** This links to the professionalism and collegiate nature of teaching. I know that there are single-person departments, and they can still be connected through

the brilliant work of the Geographical Association (GA) and Royal Geographical Society (with the Institute of British Geographers) and through social media. The professional judgements of teachers, based upon their knowledge of the geography curriculum, the pedagogy of geography, their context and their knowledge of the young people in the classrooms, is paramount. Teaching is a social enterprise, not a robotic delivery mechanism. Campfire culture relates to those moments when colleagues get together and talk about students, curriculum, assessment, teaching and learning. It goes back to my early days as a mountain leader whilst at university, where I gained my thirst for teaching others. At the end of each day, all the instructors got around the stove and 'washed up that day' – our way of evaluating and reflecting on the day's events. We based our narrative on data from that day and included the plan going forward. In the context of geography teaching, this could be department meetings, an end-of-day catch-up as a team or a conversation via social media or a group WhatsApp.

Yes, there is much out there to point the way towards great geography teaching; however, the decisions of expert geography teachers taken in a collegiate manner is the only way in which to apply anything to your situation.

Activity

Take a moment and consider the world since 2020. Write a list of world events that have had an impact on geography.

It is worth noting that during the writing of this book, the world landscape constantly shifted. By the time you read this, some information will be outdated. This is why the enquiry process is so powerful: it enables us and our learners to effectively learn, whilst global events shift around us, changing the content of our subject. During the time of writing, there have been countless disasters and conflicts raging around the world and there have also been events that have inspired hope and optimism. In just over five years, the UK has had four prime ministers. In a book about enquiry, it is worth pausing here and reflecting on the following.

> **Activity**
>
> Write a list of events that have occurred in the last 12 months.
>
> - Would they match with a colleague?
> - Map the location of these events. Is your list representative of the world?
> - How have these events impacted on you?
> - How do these events shift, change, link or add to current geographical knowledge?
> - Do they impact the young people whom you teach?

These are questions that geographers ask. As geographers, we should encourage students to ask such questions, to pause and think and to apply their knowledge to new situations.

The world is changing, and the curriculum is always under review by its political masters. This said, after over two decades in the geography classroom, it is possible to keep up by adopting an enquiry approach. In addition, whilst the landscape seems to shift rapidly, the underpinning knowledge and concepts shift at a slower rate. Enquiry provides the framework upon which we can hang the changing world as we ensure that the subject is not fossilised.

How to use this book

This book has two parts. The first sets out the theory and background of geography and enquiry teaching. The second delves into each stage of enquiry in depth. I have endeavoured to weave practical examples and points of reflection throughout. My intention is to give you the permission to develop and provide your own geography curriculum, based upon the enquiry approach and educational research.

Part 1 begins with **Chapter 1**, which considers the wider curricular aims and types of knowledge before defining enquiry. It situates enquiry within the wider context of geography education, demonstrating how it develops students' substantive, procedural and disciplinary knowledge.

Chapter 2 introduces the enquiry approach in geography, emphasising its dual role as a teaching method and core part of disciplinary knowledge. I present my own model of the enquiry approach, based upon 20 years of teaching and blended with the work of great geographers. The concept of the geographical rucksack is introduced, highlighting the role of students' prior knowledge and experiences. The chapter concludes by challenging some of the established misconceptions that have built up around the enquiry approach.

In **Chapter 3**, I explore the current state of enquiry-based learning in secondary school geography, examining both the challenges and opportunities it presents. The case for embedding enquiry at the heart of the curriculum is made, showing how it can deepen student understanding, foster critical thinking and support anti-racist and decolonial approaches.

Chapter 4 begins with defining educational research, before examining how it can inform geography teaching, whilst acknowledging its limitations. The importance of teacher agency and professional judgement is highlighted, if research-informed strategies are to be adapted effectively for the enquiry classroom. This chapter considers the role of schemas, cognitive conflict and elaboration in supporting deep learning, emphasising how enquiry encourages students to connect new knowledge to prior understanding. This chapter summarises some of the most useful research and its implications for geographical enquiry.

Chapter 5 explores how enquiry can be systematically developed and sequenced to ensure clear progression in students' knowledge, skills and thinking. It examines what it means for students to 'think like geographers', linking together both substantive and procedural knowledge. The role of the teacher is highlighted at every stage. A model of progression is presented that moves from simple closed enquiries to open enquiries with little teacher input.

Chapter 6 highlights how enquiry acts as the golden thread that runs through the geography curriculum, shaping not only what is taught but also how students learn to think, question and connect knowledge. It emphasises the importance of a curriculum built and owned by expert teachers, contextualised to local needs and responding to the dynamic nature of the subject. Rather than a static product, the curriculum is presented as a living framework that evolves.

Part 2 considers what enquiry can look like in the secondary geography classroom. To do so, we zoom into lesson sequences and individual activities, as well as the components of the enquiry model. Each chapter provides an explanation of each stage of enquiry and what progression looks like in that area. **Chapters 7 to 11** focus on the five areas of geographical enquiry from the model presented in Chapter 2, giving a more detailed exploration of the relevant part of the enquiry model plus practical examples.

I conclude in **Chapter 12** by arguing that an enquiry approach *is* geography in schools, and the world of the algorithm and artificial intelligence (AI), geography and enquiry can all be used to inspire curiosity, giving students the qualities and qualifications that they need for the next stage in their lives.

To help to illustrate this, several enquiry examples are provided in **Appendix 1**, designed to help shift the preconceptions for young people, as well as show how they can engage in changing and shaping issues.

There are a few features in this book to help to guide your reading and learning:

- **In this chapter:** This is a short summary of what each chapter contains.
- **Activity:** These are suggested activities for you to use alone or with your geography team. They are practical ways of learning about the enquiry process. Consider completing them on your own, with colleagues or with your classes. If you are leading a geography team, they could be used throughout an academic year with developing enquiry as the department continuing professional development (CPD) focus during department meeting time
- **Reflection:** Enquiry needs us to stop and think hard. Reflection boxes are 'pause points' to give you thinking time before reading on. They are intended for you to complete on your own; perhaps take a walk in nature as you ponder, create a mind-map or look to the further reading. There is no need to specifically write anything down or share any thinking with others.
- **Key takeaways:** These boxes end each chapter, providing a short summary of what you have read. They are written to be easy to share with senior colleagues.
- **Definitions and examples:** I have included definitions of key words and terms plus expanded examples where needed.

For some readers, I am sure that what follows will seem to encompass *all* of geography teaching. If it does, that is because I see enquiry *as* geography teaching. To me, they are the same.

Each of us is our own person and I have included the influences that made me the person and educator that I am today. You will have your own view of enquiry and how it can be developed in your classroom. I am giving you permission to try new things, and I would encourage you to keep the individual personality that is you within your teaching.

Developing and embedding an enquiry approach took me five years to achieve, plus three years before examination outcomes increased rapidly and rose above the school averages. Great geography cannot be implemented quickly.

PART 1

The 'what', 'why' and 'how' of geographical enquiry

This part will look at the 'what' and the 'why' of enquiry. The reader will discover that the professionalism and decisions of expert teachers are at the heart of the geography classroom, as both curriculum-makers and teachers. What is clear is that there is no single, 'correct' way to approach using enquiry in the geography classroom, and taking a binary approach will ultimately be futile.

There is no agreement about what enquiry is, so it is what you make it as you contextualise the approach to your classroom. There are several powerful arguments for taking an enquiry approach. Educational research is reviewed with the conclusion that it only gives us the fundamentals of cognitive science and psychology. What it doesn't do is present us with applied studies in the geography classroom. Educational research and the enquiry approach are aligned.

This part ends by presenting a model of progression in enquiry, before giving some examples of what a curriculum based upon enquiry could look like.

I hope that this part leaves you informed and buoyant. Great, high-quality geography teaching that results in young people leaving with excellent qualifications and qualities depends on expert teachers making sound decisions. These decisions are about what approach to take, what pedagogy should be employed and what content should be taught.

1 What underpins enquiry in the curriculum?

> **In this chapter**
>
> This chapter defines what geographical enquiry is and why it is essential in schools. It situates enquiry within the wider context of geography education, demonstrating how it develops students' substantive, procedural and disciplinary knowledge. The chapter highlights the importance of careful geographical concepts informed by curriculum design, and how enquiry serves as both a tool to organise the curriculum and a pedagogical approach. By fostering curiosity, critical thinking and a broader understanding of diverse perspectives, enquiry equips students to engage meaningfully with the world and develop as informed, capable geographers.

The wider school and curriculum context

Geography is a fantastic, fascinating and fallible discipline. Its body of knowledge is vast, contested and forever changing. It can inspire curiosity and awe, whilst also creating divisions and anxiety about the future. It has the potential to include and exclude narratives and groups of people. Geography's real power lies in its ability to allow those who engage with its knowledge and concepts to understand the world so that they may change it for the better.

Teaching geography is about taking the complex and often crazy world around us and helping to make it manageable, understandable and knowable for novice geographers. This is easier said than done, as the same bland content statement from a curriculum document or examination specification will rarely lead to the same curriculum, lesson or outcomes.

As a teacher and curriculum leader, I was also constrained, like many of you, by time. What we can accomplish as *school* geographers, whilst fundamental, is limited. Should we focus on imparting a broad range of geographical knowledge or study less in greater depth? Whilst I believe that this is a departmental decision, constrained within the nature of external examination specifications and the National Curriculum, it does provide perspective about what we can achieve.

To teach geography is rewarding and challenging. Steve Puttick suggests that teaching geography demands that 'teachers be *geographers* in education' (2023, p. 1). To me, this means that we think and act like geographers, teaching the children in our classrooms the geography that they can handle, rather than being informed by a list of generalised content. This should be within a contextualised curriculum that has been created by teachers, using examples to deeply explore our key and organising concepts.

Whilst a full exploration of the geography curriculum and nature of the subject is beyond the scope of this book, before we consider what enquiry is in relation to school geography, it is important to review the aims of the geography curriculum, the different types of knowledge, the terminology used to describe it and the key and organising concepts that make geography a distinctive subject.

What is the point of geography?

Before considering what enquiry is, it is worth briefly considering wider curriculum and geography department contexts. The geography programmes of study for Key Stage 3 begin with the following sentence:

> *A high-quality geography education should inspire in pupils a curiosity and fascination about the world and its people that will remain with them for the rest of their lives.'*

(DfE, 2013a, p. 1)

This means that geography in schools must be far more than the transmission of substantive knowledge and facts. We are tasked with developing young people who ask questions and critically engage with information. Geography teachers should not present 'facts' from one viewpoint. For example, when developing knowledge about places, we must convey the idea that the same place can be defined and experienced by different groups of people in different ways. To present geographical knowledge as something that is purely transmitted, for students to 'know more and remember more', is to potentially reinforce only one aspect and viewpoint of geography. There is a tension between what teachers value, the lived experiences of students and the accountability pressures. These are difficult to juggle.

The aims of school geography are ambitious and span many other school subjects. Before we can develop a curriculum, we need to work out the point of it. One aim will be linked to external examinations. Part of geography's potential is to develop informed and engaged citizens. The box below explores the wider aims of a school geography department.

> **Activity**
>
> What are the aims of your curriculum?
>
> Review the overarching curriculum documents for your setting. These could be exam specifications, your country's national curriculum or your school's overarching curriculum aims. Focus on the aims of the geography curriculum. How are these reflected in your department and classroom?
>
> Write a list of your aims for geography. Should they apply to all ages in your institution?

If the point of school geography is to 'inspire in pupils a curiosity and fascination about the world and its people' (DfE, 2013a, p. 1), then one of the purposes of enquiry is to provide a range of lenses through which young people can understand their world and their place within it. One reason for this, I argue, is so that geographers can go on to make the world better – or, in other words, become informed and active citizens. They can do this by becoming problem-solvers, understanding the problems we face and the interconnected nature of the world.

It is worth remembering that we are restricted by the nature of school geography. It is right that we strive for the very best outcomes in external examinations for young people. In addition, as mentioned, we have time constraints. As a curriculum leader of geography, I saw Key Stage 3 students once every week. This meant that a young person could have been to well over 25 different lessons by the time I taught them again. This is where building upon what students already know is vital. When teaching unfamiliar knowledge, we can connect it to understanding explored through real and relevant concepts, as well as linking to students' own personal experiences (Ofsted, 2021). In this world, those experiences are often dictated by algorithms, kids getting information from their peers, the Trump conspiracy cycle and AI selection – more of this later.

Example

Priory School is an inner-city 11–16 secondary school with very limited outside space and 1,250 students on roll.

What does geography at Priory School aim to do?

I arrived at Priory School as a fresh-faced and optimistic head of geography. Before embarking on developing the subject, it was important for me to establish some overarching aims – to come up with and define the 'why?' of the department.

These aims were developed in subject meetings and linked to the overarching aims of the national and local curricula. They were communicated through posters in every geography classroom and used to guide curriculum development. They applied across Key Stages 3 and 4. It was inherently accepted that we needed to deliver great results in external examinations. We aimed:

- to stimulate a sense of wonder about places
- to help students to make sense of the complex and sometimes crazy world around them
- to inspire and show students how they can change their world
- to help students to explore *their* geography
- to give students the skills and knowledge to make it in the future – whatever their choices are.

As I shall argue later, these aims justify the choice we made to use the enquiry approach in every lesson.

Activity

Examine the aims of Priory School geography presented above. Where does diversity, equity and inclusion (DEI) fit in within these aims? Do they need to be expanded to reflect this more explicitly? Rewrite these aims to reflect your observations.

Ofsted's subject report (2023a) found that the development of procedural knowledge (otherwise known as skills) was not planned for. Enquiry offers a framework upon which to base the development of geographical skills. Many colleagues find the terminology around knowledge confusing, and therefore think that it is either skills *or* knowledge. This is incorrect. We must have skills *and* knowledge. The box below defines the types of knowledge found in the geography classroom.

Definitions

Types of knowledge

The distinction between the different forms of knowledge is a pragmatic one and definitions are themselves conflicted and contested. These definitions are offered as an aid to geography departments and teachers in considering the development of their curriculum.

Disciplinary knowledge: Knowing how we know

This relates to how geographical knowledge has been established and how it continues to evolve and change. These are the big ideas and methods that geographers have used to make sense of the world. It's how geographers think, work and make use of geography. Disciplinary knowledge includes the key concepts, skills, methods and approaches of geographical enquiry, including how geographers use maps and geographic information systems (GIS) to understand geographical phenomena in different locations. We could also explore how geographical models are created and how well they can generalise and predict when applied to different locations.

It is worth noting that whilst we should aim for students to learn about how geographical knowledge is created, the actual creation of new disciplinary knowledge is beyond the scope of school geography.

Procedural knowledge: Knowing how to (skills)

For geography, this is knowing how to work like a geographer and is part of the disciplinary knowledge of the subject. It includes qualitative and quantitative enquiry (both within and outside the classroom) and how geographers develop arguments and perform analysis. It includes both the values and the moral and ethical dimensions involved. Whilst the enquiry approach can't in itself be considered procedural knowledge, it certainly provides a vehicle for its development.

Throughout this book, I use geographical skills and procedural knowledge interchangeably.

Substantive knowledge: Knowing the established facts and key concepts (the 'content')

This is problematic, as substantive knowledge is often thought of as 'established facts'. I prefer the idea of 'accepted facts', because geographical knowledge changes. When I started teaching, it was accurate to say that China was the most populated country in the world; however, in 2023, India's population surpassed China's. Similarly, places change and, as 'one of geography's responsibilities is to reveal the world as it is – not as it was' (Brace, 2024a), examples and case studies change.

Having said that, we can consider substantive knowledge to be the range of contextual and specific knowledge of the world around us, including locational knowledge, tangible features such as rivers, mountains, cities and landscapes, and abstract features such as economic systems and community beliefs.

In geography, this substantive knowledge must be contextualised for the local area within which we teach and based in places. It must be carefully linked to students' experiences of geography. It is also important to understand that it will always be changing, and it is unlikely that colleagues will agree fully about what should or shouldn't be included. In practice, this often means that school geography curricula are based upon what appears in A level or GCSE specifications and then 'pulled down' to lower years. Whilst I do not always agree that what is included in an exam specification is what should be taught, this is an appropriate approach.

For the purposes of this book, I will use the term 'content' to represent substantive knowledge.

(Definitions adapted from GA, 2022, p. 4)

> **Activity**
>
> Examine your own curriculum and identify the different aspects of knowledge. Are they explicitly mentioned in the curriculum document? Are they a key part of sequences of lessons?

With the rise of the 'knowledge curriculum', it is a common misconception that enquiry does not fit. Again, this is false: as will be argued later, an enquiry approach is vital both to develop the aims of geography and in ensuring that young people get to grips with the different types of knowledge. Any approach that devalues skills also means that procedural knowledge is not developed.

Furthermore, when we consider that 25 per cent of marks at GCSE and up to 30 per cent at A level are reserved for skills and techniques (Ofqual, 2017), we neglect the development of skills at our peril. Indeed, I would argue that procedural knowledge should form part of every lesson, and the enquiry approach assists us in this. Whilst guidance will inevitably change, I cannot see an examination landscape in which procedural knowledge (including fieldwork) is not a significant aspect of the examined subject. It also means that procedural knowledge must be a key aspect of geography teaching for all age groups. As many geographical skills require lots of practice if they are to become automatic and not place undue demand on a person's cognitive load, enquiry again provides an ideal developmental vehicle. We can develop this procedural knowledge, preparing students for examinations, from lesson one of Year 7.

It is clear that for enquiry to flourish and lead to great results and developing qualities in young people, geography teachers and departments must engage in a rich and deep conversation around the curriculum. Without deciding upon the key procedural and substantive knowledge that should be prioritised in your own school, it is almost impossible to develop effective enquiry.

What are the key concepts in school geography?

The Geographical Association (GA, 2022) has produced an excellent framework for organising the school geography curriculum. Whilst one of its aims is to influence national decision-makers, it identifies the key concepts in the subject and articulates the aims and purposes of geography. It also sets out the importance of geographical enquiry.

Brooks (2013) argues that concepts are powerful tools for those who engage in the curriculum-making process, pointing out that concepts are hierarchical, organisational and developmental (written, interestingly, at a time when the English National Curriculum was under review). Whilst the National Curriculum in effect at the time of writing may have neglected to include key concepts at Key Stage 3, they are still very much explicitly mentioned at Key Stages 4 and 5. This means that what is taught during the earlier key stages is influenced and shaped by these. Furthermore, I would argue that it is essential to decide and understand the key concepts that help to inform the curriculum if we are to have an effective geography curriculum.

I write from the perspective of a teacher that has experienced multiple Ofsted inspections, frameworks and different versions of the National Curriculum, and the same enquiry approach was used throughout this change. If anything, it gave me and my colleagues an anchor upon which to navigate the constantly shifting school geography landscape. This is perhaps the challenge that geographers face. Whilst not unique to our subject, the substantive and procedural knowledge shifts often. When this is layered upon the shifting external accountability and National Curriculum (often driven by the political perspective of the time), workload can explode.

A good example of the inertia faced in geography is GIS. Whilst it formed a core part of my undergraduate studies in the early 2000s and is explicitly mentioned in the National Curriculum and examination specifications, almost 25 years on its adoption is still problematic. This is often because of the inertia created and the misconception that technology is not available. Excellent geography teachers like Alistair Hamill (2023) have demonstrated how GIS can be used as a 'from the front' teaching resource, and as most classrooms are equipped with a teacher PC and projector, it is now highly possible to get GIS into the geography classroom using this simple approach.

The GA framework (2022) gives geography hope. Whilst the *content* of the National Curriculum and exam specifications may change during reviews and rewrites, the organising and key concepts remain the same. I saw it as my role as a curriculum leader and teacher, to adapt the current curriculum and its content to my context. Indeed, it is difficult to imagine that geography departments didn't focus on the curriculum long before an Ofsted framework started to ask questions about it.

Definitions

Geography has key and organising concepts. These help us decide what to include in our curriculum and how to structure it.

Geographical key concepts (often known as core concepts)

These are the overarching geographical concepts and ideas of the subject that lie behind all the varied content. They are the most significant and abstract concepts, to which more concrete ideas and examples can be linked. They can be considered the golden threads woven throughout all sequences of lessons, which bind and contextualise all topics, rather than them being unconnected. There is a wide body of literature on this, and which key concepts should be used is frequently contested.

The GA framework presents space, place, Earth systems and environment as its key concepts.

Organising concepts

These are also vital, not only to geographical understanding but also in deciding how to structure a school curriculum. They provide a common language for geographers to communicate about geography and a range of perspectives that can be applied to substantive geographical knowledge. They tend to be more general than core concepts and can be applied to a wide range of geographical ideas.

The GA framework cites the organising concepts of time, scale, diversity, interconnection and interpretation.

(Adapted from GA, 2022, p. 7)

Activity

Visit the GA's curriculum framework (2022) and explore it and the accompanying documents. Would you add any key concepts? Are these concepts 'bumped into' throughout your curriculum or contained within single units? Are key concepts used to organise your curriculum?

In a situation where both teaching and geography are complex, I argue that geographical enquiry provides a framework for teachers to help young people to know and understand geography, whilst setting out a pathway to becoming a geographer, able to think, act and communicate as a geographer would.

A child in Year 5 may well be a novice geographer, in that they learn and think differently to experts. They lack the automaticity of our procedural knowledge, and they lack the experience of thinking about our domain-specific knowledge and how that applies to what they are learning about.

By the time this child arrives at the end of their compulsory geography education, at age 14, they will not be at the level of an undergraduate geographer, but we will expect them to have hopefully learned enough to begin to progress towards subject expertise. They should be able to take the substantive and procedural knowledge that they have been taught and apply it to their own enquiry to explore a novel topic. Certainly, I would argue that an A level student that has chosen geography should be even further along this journey.

What has this to do with curriculum design and geographical concepts? Enquiry provides the basis by which students can become *more* expert – particularly in the development of procedural knowledge, where the more often a skill is used, the more automatic it is likely to become, freeing up working memory to focus on learning new material. Enquiry also demands that students link back to their own prior knowledge.

Enquiry in the national curricula

The inclusion of an enquiry approach is justified by the national curricula that are in place in the UK. The following summarises what each national curriculum has to say about enquiry. The model presented in the next chapter allows geography teachers to meet these aims.

Scotland

Geography sits within social studies in the Curriculum for Excellence (Scottish Government, 2010) and enquiry is explicitly mentioned. Students are expected to develop procedural knowledge, linked to evaluating different sources of evidence. They are also expected to carry out a geographical enquiry linked to climate change.

Northern Ireland

The Northern Ireland curriculum (CCEA, 2007) sets out the importance of enquiry within geography, and it is part of the minimum requirement for every student at Key Stage 3. Geography sits within environment and society in the curriculum. Enquiry is mentioned throughout and offered as a choice between an investigative and enquiry-based approach. The curriculum document states that the experiences in Key Stage 3 should help students to engage meaningfully with real and relevant world issues. Students explore the part that they can play in shaping and protecting the environment around them. This links well to enquiry, as it can be used first to understand the world, then to inform action.

Wales

The Curriculum for Wales (Welsh Government, 2022) mentions enquiry explicitly, and Geography is included within the humanities area of learning. When students explore their own locality and country, they need to use different methods of enquiry, and these include the evaluation of different sources of information. The Welsh curriculum also mentions out-of-classroom learning and that students should communicate their ideas and findings effectively.

England

Whilst the current National Curriculum for Key Stage 3 (DfE, 2013a) does not explicitly mention enquiry, if we consider its opening preamble that 'A high-quality geography education should inspire in pupils a curiosity and fascination about the world and its people that will remain with them for the rest of their lives', (p. 1), it is impossible to see how that can be achieved without enquiry. Simply enabling young people to ask questions about their own lived experiences, make connections from them to abstract concepts and be curious about the information given to them and the world helps them to be active enquirers.

What is enquiry in the context of UK school geography?

During a recent meeting of authors for a textbook series that I edit (Hodder's *Geography for Enquiring Minds*), it became undeniable that the educational landscape, particularly in state schools, has shifted. Quite rightly, there is a focus on using evidence-informed pedagogy. For example, the testing effect (as I encountered it during my teacher training) is now adopted widespread as retrieval practice. State schools operate in an accountability structure. However, even with structural constraints such as national curricula, geography subject orders and Ofsted, the key people that drive geography in schools are still the team teaching it. The leadership of geography at school department level is still the most significant driver of high-quality geography being taught.

Whilst the subject is often divided into human and physical aspects, geography is about the interactions between people and places. It therefore needs to be contextualised, and as such it is difficult to pin down a definition of enquiry that would apply to all places. Indeed, enquiry is often seen as a pedagogical approach or alternatively as a set of skills. Before exploring enquiry in detail, we need to distinguish between enquiry as an organisational tool and as a pedagogy.

Definitions

Is enquiry an organisational tool or a pedagogy? The Ofsted subject research report (2021) provides this useful summary:

- As an **organisational tool**, 'the teacher poses a geographical question and selects the curriculum content that allows students to reach an answer'. Sequences of lessons, individual lessons and whole schemes of learning can be organised in this way.
- As a **pedagogy**, geographical enquiry is more difficult to pin down and is 'any activity that opens up problems and issues', whilst encouraging young people to ask 'questions and begin to find solutions'. This definition is more wide-ranging (Ferretti, 2018, cited in Ofsted, 2021).

I would argue that these are on the same continuum. The former is a useful way to teach novice geographers the fundamental knowledge. A carefully crafted geographical question is a hook into the subject and can link the knowledge to their own experience.

The recent rebranding of familiar terms and the 'knowledge' curriculum has further confused the issue within the context of the time-starved, content-heavy curriculum.

Whilst enquiry is not exclusive to geography, it provides a framework and one of the lenses through which geographical knowledge (procedural, disciplinary and substantive) can be explored by learners to understand their world. Initially, this provides the basis of the fundamental content needed to understand more complex concepts and to pass examinations. Enquiry is an umbrella term encompassing a wide range of activities. Whilst this makes enquiry difficult to pin down, it also gives teachers the permission and opportunity to use it to drive the curriculum in their setting.

As already mentioned, the GA (2022) considers enquiry to be part of our disciplinary knowledge, or 'working like a geographer'.

Roberts (2023) states that 'it's not possible to give one definition of "enquiry" because what an enquiry approach means in practice is related to the specific contexts in which it is developed' (p. 8). Roberts also makes the excellent point that some of Rosenshine's list of teaching strategies (Rosenshine, 2012) are based upon constructivist theories and that the enquiry approach demands that teachers subscribe to the notion that teaching geography is not purely about the transmission of knowledge. Yes, students need to know more and remember more, but they must also not only apply this knowledge to novel examination questions but also use it to connect different topics and ideas.

Definition

Enquiry: The Geography 16–19 project suggests tighter definitions of enquiry as 'a range of teaching methods and approaches by which the teacher encourages students to enquire actively into questions, issues and problems rather than to merely accept passively the conclusions, research and opinions of others'. (Naish et al., 2002 p. 63).

This clearly provides an aiming point for school geography, ensuring that younger students are provided with the knowledge required to meet these challenges. I will present a progression of enquiry that can get us there. For example, this can be achieved through demonstrating how questioning effectively can provide pause for thought. Such thinking is distinctly geographical, whilst, arguably, remembering facts about places and people is not and could even reinforce the misrepresentation of both.

> **Reflection**
>
> What does enquiry mean to you?
>
> Before going further, as enquiry can mean different things to different people, what does it mean to you and your department? Is it purely an organisational tool that provides topic titles, or is it threaded throughout the curriculum to allow young people to question and explore the information presented to them?

Key takeaways

- Enquiry encourages students to explore questions critically, not just memorise facts.
- Geography learning involves three types of knowledge: substantive (facts), procedural (skills) and disciplinary (how knowledge is created).
- Key and organising concepts guide curriculum design and help to link sequences of lessons coherently.
- Enquiry works as both a teaching structure and a pedagogical approach.
- Enquiry helps students to move from novice to more expert geographers.
- Enquiry broadens perspectives, including ethical, moral and diverse viewpoints.

2 What is – and what isn't – enquiry?

> **In this chapter**
>
> This chapter introduces the enquiry approach in geography, emphasising its dual role as a teaching method and a core part of disciplinary knowledge. It presents a model where the enquiry process cycles through questioning, gathering, evaluating and communicating information, with critical evaluation. Enquiry is mainly teacher-led in UK classrooms, but a degree of independence can be introduced. The concept of the geographical rucksack is introduced, highlighting the role of students' prior knowledge and experiences. The chapter explores how enquiry broadens perspectives, challenges biases and integrates human and physical geography. Several misconceptions that teachers hold about enquiry are explored.

The enquiry approach to geography

Enquiry must be contextualised, and whilst there are many definitions to enquiry, these are often oversimplified, restrict enquiry to fieldwork or consider it purely as a skill. Geography departments need to spend some time considering what enquiry is within their own context, and here I present my understanding of what enquiry is and how it sits within a school department and its curriculum.

Enquiry is both an approach to discovering geographical knowledge and a set of teaching approaches. It is fundamental to our subject's disciplinary knowledge and a set of skills. The GA (2024a) considers enquiry to be one of the subject's 'signature pedagogical approaches' (p. 3).

Figure 2.1 illustrates my version of the enquiry approach. It forms the basis of school geography, where all sequences of lessons follow the enquiry approach. To me, enquiry *is* school geography. Here, enquiry is employed as both an organising tool and a pedagogy. Chapters 7–11 will explore each stage in more detail, so for now I offer a brief overview. I also suggest that enquiry is a cycle. It begins with high-quality geographical questions.

As mentioned, enquiry is not discovery learning. As will be explored later in the chapter, teachers can instruct students throughout the process, *as well as* giving them more independence.

Enquiry is part of geography's disciplinary knowledge, as it is how geographers find out what we know. Understanding the process of enquiry is therefore vital if learners are to understand how geographical knowledge is created, and if they are to provide effective criticism of it. This does not mean, however, that learners should formulate their own questions and disappear into the AI-generated answers of the Google search engine.

Taking an enquiry approach and weaving it throughout the curriculum also allows young people to develop and deepen their procedural knowledge. This in turn will lead to better learning, as students become more competent in employing geographical skills – more on this in Part 2.

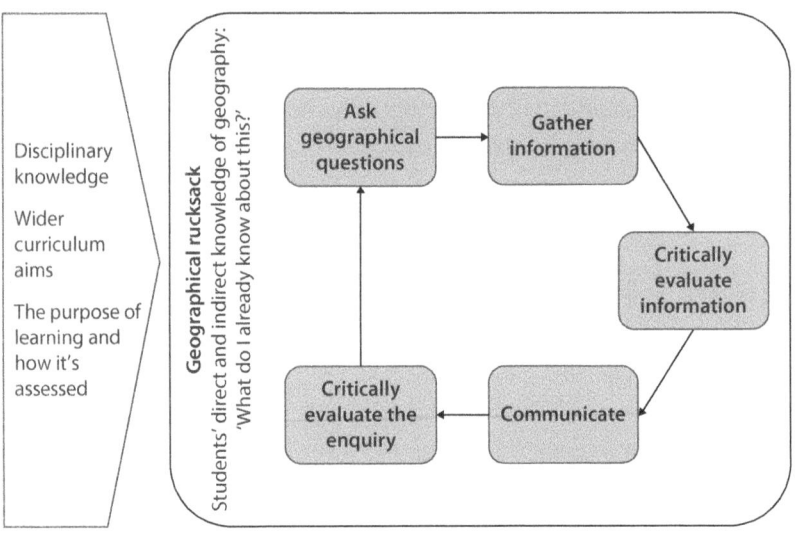

Figure 2.1: The simplified enquiry approach model

An enquiry model for the geography classroom

Figure 2.1, an attempt to combine academic and pragmatic issues, is not a prescribed route. It is a model that I have developed, used and refined during the 20 years I served as a teacher of geography. It is based upon the excellent work of geographers such as Margert Roberts, plus my own ideas and those of the brilliant geography teams with whom I have worked. Like any good enquiry, its implementation was constantly tweaked with feedback from examination outcomes, student and teacher voice and the changing curriculum over the years. A version was displayed in all geography classrooms and referred to often. It is a tool to think about the design of the curriculum and the units within it. Each stage of enquiry can be teacher-led or tackled independently, depending on the age of the class.

Chapters 7 to 11 in Part 2 start with an expanded version of one of the boxes in the model, as we delve into each stage in more depth. Questioning is a core component of each stage.

Definition

Geographical rucksack: This is a term we developed at Priory School to clearly communicate the idea that everyone experiences geography, even if they are passive or unaware of it.

Our geographical rucksack is the informal, collective and individual experiences that we all bring to the formal classroom as our 'geographical rucksack'. It is full of our personal experiences and existing knowledge, which I think of as the direct and indirect knowledge acquired about geographical issues, informing our own ideas and approach as educators. This knowledge is also constructed through the lived experiences of our students, as well as what they have been taught before in formal settings. This will be expanded upon further in Chapter 3.

The enquiry approach in Figure 2.1 provides a framework that geographers can use to begin to understand a complex world within the context of school geography. It helps to form the foundation upon which we can layer concepts and then the detail of the content. Whilst some (e.g. Barton, 2018) have advocated for the ban of all displays in the classroom, so that the blank walls reduce extraneous cognitive load, I argue that this diagram should be both front and centre on the wall and also around the classroom and on mats each lesson. The enquiry diagram is not redundant information; I would refer to it each and every lesson. Explicitly teaching about enquiry allows young people to better understand geography content.

In addition, the personal geographies of both teachers and students inform the perspectives with which we approach any enquiry. Whilst the outcome of an enquiry may be a set of agreed content, especially when constrained by examination specifications or early in the school journey, this approach allows learners to understand how the knowledge is constructed and the issues that lie behind the 'facts'. Furthermore, teachers may choose to provide some concrete examples for students that are age-appropriate.

Whilst I present the enquiry approach as a learning sequence, I agree with Margaret Roberts' framework (2023) in that each stage could occur at any part of the teaching process. The stages are:

- Ask geographical questions.
- Gather information.
- Critically evaluate information.
- Communicate.
- Critically evaluate the enquiry.

The approach presented makes curriculum and planning sequences of lessons more straightforward. Each stage of the approach can be teacher-led, through direct instruction, or allow learners to work more independently or a mixture. For example, a departmental team may set the overarching question to be explored through a set of carefully curated information for students to interrogate. In addition, the question must come first, rather than be retrofitted to content.

In terms of time, it can be completed within a lesson, span a sequence of lessons or a take a whole unit. At Priory School, geography enquiry was explicitly mentioned as part of most lessons and was the organising lens of the curriculum.

Activity

Schedule some department meeting time to audit your existing curriculum against the enquiry approach model presented here.

Enquiry as a lens to widen perspective

I am a white male who was born in the Rhondda Valleys. Whilst in many ways I enjoyed many privileges, I am also the product of my experience, growing up with domestic abuse and experiencing the personal impact of industrial decline. I grew up in a predominately white area and I was – and still am – exposed to the views of others around issues such as migration. Similarly, the students in our classrooms are not empty vessels, devoid of any geographical knowledge or experiences. The outdoors provided an escape for me and school geography provided the knowledge of *why* deindustrialisation was occurring. I was exposed to the global forces of supply and demand and the idea of foreign competition changing the very nature of the places where I grew up.

The reason why I tell you this is that our geographical experiences, both direct and indirect, create the 'lens' through which we pay attention, and therefore impact what we learn. We will also have our own interests and passions, which may influence our curriculum choices as well as our preferred pedagogies. I will explore this in more depth later, but for now I will point out that geography must expose, introduce, challenge and consider different points of views and perspectives to our students *and* ourselves as educators.

Geographical knowledge is created through the lens of whoever writes about it. In this book, I set out to be deliberately provocative to stimulate thought. The Covid-19 pandemic and Brexit have demonstrated that geography is constantly changing. Whilst access to the internet has arguably provided an easy way to keep up to date, it is not equally accessible. Enquiry provides a lens through which geographical knowledge itself is contested, and many concepts and ideas do not fall neatly into classifications. Indeed, the nature of geographical knowledge has often been from a white, Anglo-American/Eurocentric perspective and complicit with colonialism, which we will explore in more detail in Chapter 3.

Activity

Decolonising our language

The language we use in the classroom is important. The terms we decide upon can be problematic. Geography must consider a wide range of views. But what language should we use? For example, the term 'stakeholder' can be offensive to Indigenous people, as it is viewed as a colonialist term: colonising settlers staked their claims on land already occupied by Indigenous peoples.

> What language do you use to describe different groups of people in lessons? What terms are used by the resources that you use, such as textbooks? What are the alternatives? How can we explore these terms and their problems with young people? Consider the alternatives to 'stakeholders' given below:
>
> - interested, affected or relevant parties
> - a list of people's roles (e.g. landowner, community members, Tribal rights and title-holders)
> - participants.
>
> In this book, I try to avoid the use of colonial language, such as 'slums' or 'shanty towns'. Are there any other examples? Why is this important?

In state-funded education, who decides on the knowledge that must be covered? It is often a misconception that national documents make up the curriculum. The curriculum is also not a textbook or exam specification. The curriculum is created by skilful and knowledgeable teachers within geography departments. It feeds into external pressures. National documents and exam specifications may provide the framework, and enquiry provides a set of lenses through which young people can examine real world situations.

For example, most geographical knowledge has been developed through the interests of academics. These academics tend to be male and white and live in the Global North. In addition, our knowledge of geography changes as we get older, learn more and are exposed to different perspectives beyond our own lived experience.

Activity

Pause for a moment. Make a list of the recent developments in school geography within the UK. How have they impacted on your own teaching? This could be in terms of time or extra work or perhaps positive aspects, such as better subject knowledge.

In recent times, our understanding of plate tectonics has shifted (pun intended…), introducing the role of gravitational forces such as ridge pull and slab push. Additionally, our thinking on climate change and its role within the curriculum has continued to develop and gain more importance, as political forces get involved. On top of this, simple facts have changed, such as the UK's fertility rate being at its lowest in 2024, well below the rate needed to sustain natural increase. This is far more fundamental than remembering new storm events.

Whilst splitting our discipline into physical and human is useful when first teaching key content to novice geographers, we must explore how they interact (see Ofsted, 2023a). For example, the built environment changes the microclimate, and tropical storms and tectonic events can have long-reaching implications for settlement patterns and trade.

When I started teaching school geography, I quickly realised that human and physical geography are interconnected. Global development, geopolitics and history have shaped and continue to shape the geography of the world. Geography is also not a discipline that can easily be understood by simply remembering facts.

Example

Consider the concept of place.

Place is defined as a location *plus* meaning. Whilst the location may remain constant, the meaning can shift over time, space and perspective. Indeed, different people of different characteristics will all have a slightly different sense of place. They will all experience and think of the same location in different ways. Therefore, there is no correct answer to what a place *is*. Enquiry gives the space and permission to consider different perspectives and critically evaluate information. Indeed, asking good questions and evaluating information are arguably the most important aspects of enquiry.

National Geographic (n.d.) has an excellent tool that introduces the idea of using different perspectives (see Figure 2.2).

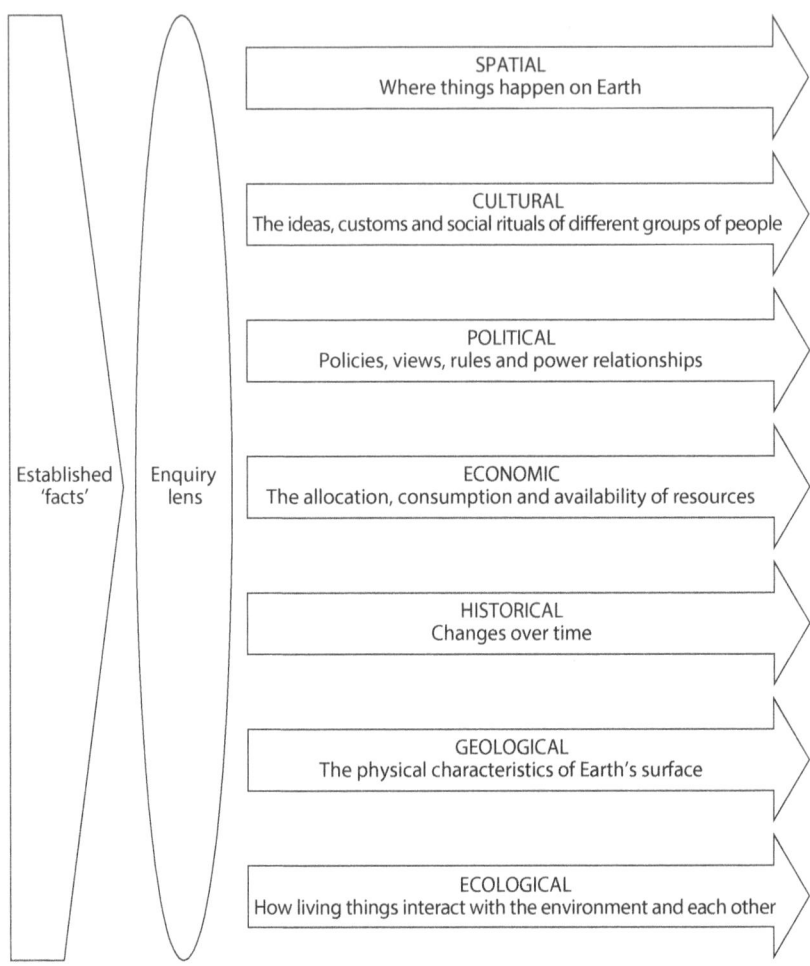

Figure 2.2: The lenses of geographical enquiry (based upon National Geographic, n.d.)

There is a clear tension between the high-stakes accountability of external examinations, 'what we must cover for the mark scheme' and our professional principles to present the world as it is, rather than what is easy for young people to learn and remember. Sometimes this is because we need to cover a case study of an earthquake in a particular classification of country. This develops a simple understanding of the world and does not present the world as it actually is: us and them; rich and poor. (In relation to this, it is worth listening to Episode 74 of the excellent GeogPod from the Geographical Association (2024b), where James Esson is interviewed.) The enquiry approach helps geography teachers to challenge this.

Using enquiry can expand students' experience and perspectives of the places that they study. What are the similarities to their lives? What other perspectives are there? Is this place actually like this? Is this resource and viewpoint reliable and valid? How do we know? I will expand on these ideas throughout this book.

> **Activity**
>
> Think of a geographical fact. I am writing this section around the build-up to Christmas, and the song 'Do they know it's Christmas?' has just been played on the radio. The music is unaltered in 2025 and its well-known lyrics provide a useful starting point for an enquiry. The lyrics present an 'us' and 'them' view of the world and Africa as a barren land – although, as geographers, we know that Africa is not a country but a diverse continent.
>
> Consider the lyrics to this song or another of your choice. What content in the geography curriculum do they link to? Consider the lyrics through each of the lenses in Figure 2.2. How does this change your perception of them? What enquiry questions do you have about them as a geographer? How do they encourage the development of a single story (an oversimplified, often one-dimensional view of a person, place or culture, based upon limited information or stereotypes – see Adichie, 2009)?

Enquiry as an organising tool

If you could indulge me for a moment, I'd like to write about weaving. Weaving exploded as part of Britain's Industrial Revolution. This process fundamentally changed the country and is also intertwined with the extraction of resources, and it was underpinned by colonisation, with all its negative impacts on those colonised countries.

'What has this to do with enquiry?' you ask. Let's consider the structure of woven goods (see Figure 2.3). The warps refer to the lengthwise threads stretched on a loom that form the vertical lines, whilst the wefts are the crosswise threads woven over and under the warps to create the patterns and fabric.

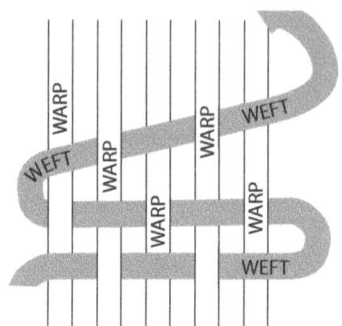

Figure 2.3: Structure of woven goods

The warp threads are the foundation of the woven fabric. If the finished fabric is school geography, the warp represents the key and organising concepts and enquiry. In this analogy, the weft, which can be made of different materials and colours, represents the content. This content continually revisits the warp threads, just as our teaching of geographical content should continually revisit the key concepts and procedural knowledge, which I argue is enquiry.

At the risk of overdoing the analogy, we can add in additional weft threads – perhaps an examination specification. This does not have to remove the other foundations of the subject. The weft can also be manipulated and changed so that different perspectives and ideas are included, creating an ever-more complex pattern.

Disciplinary knowledge and wider curriculum aims inform what we enquire into. When designing a curriculum, we must start from the pragmatic considerations of how the knowledge will be assessed and what it is for. We must also layer in contextual considerations relevant to the individual school and class.

There is no agreed definition of what enquiry is and how it should be employed, although there is a general agreement as to the individual components that comprise enquiry. What I would strongly state is that, in the context of UK geography classrooms, enquiry is not discovery learning.

> ### Reflection
>
> What is enquiry to you? What aspects are you familiar with? What aspects do you need to know more about? What do you agree and disagree with? Are there any that you would add?

What are the seven misconceptions around geographical enquiry?

> **Activity**
>
> Before you read this section, jot down some of the 'truths' that you know about enquiry. Ask around your school; what responses do you get (if any) when you mention the enquiry approach?

Exploring misconceptions is part of many schools' lesson planning, and geography teachers must identify and address them in almost every lesson. This section therefore considers some of the misconceptions that readers may have about geographical enquiry. We have considered *what* enquiry is and *why* it should be used in every geography lesson. Before we move on to the *how*, we need to pause to consider what enquiry isn't. There are many myths around enquiry, many of which apply to teaching as a whole rather than geographical enquiry in particular. Many are linked to the values and perspectives of individuals. From experience, there isn't a simple right or wrong way to teach geography. Expert teaching, which results in good educational outcomes, uses a blend of approaches.

Early in my geography career, I took over a failing department. The curriculum was basic, unchallenged and fossilised. It was seen as an afterthought. I took a failed department and turned it into the highest-performing department in the school, and in the local area, by external examination results, and was awarded the GA's Centre of Excellence distinction. We are in schools to enable young people to gain qualifications, but we are also there to provide a framework and opportunity to develop qualities. The abilities to enquire about alternative perspectives, ask probing geographical questions and critically evaluate sources of information are such qualities.

As geographers, we need to be able to defend enquiry to non-specialist senior leadership team (SLT) members. The increased emphasis on evidence-based teaching, whilst welcome, is to be used with caution. The polarisation of the debate has resulted in several false dichotomies, such as the knowledge versus skills debate, when *both* are needed. You may have non-specialist geographers line-managing your subject. They hold their own misconceptions around what geographical enquiry is, and it is our job, as expert geographers and advocates for the power of geographical learning, to not only counter their doubts but also be the champions of our subject, whose signature pedagogy is enquiry. We are employed as the expert geographers. We are the ones that can demonstrate the power of geographical enquiry, by showing that:

- We can have better examination outcomes *and* high-quality geography.
- We can cover content *and* have deeper, wider, more ambitious curriculum goals.
- We can have direct instruction *and* geographical enquiry.
- We can explore the personal geographies of our students *and* help them to build schemas.
- We can have teacher-led *and* independent enquiry.
- We need to examine the concrete, local and everyday *and* the distant and abstract.

As Dylan Wiliam is often quoted as saying, 'everything works somewhere; nothing works everywhere'. However, what is often missed is that he went on to say that a better question to ask in education is 'under what conditions does this work?' (Wiliam, 2006). Whilst I accept that access to specialist geographers is a challenge in the current recruitment and retention crisis, the professionalism of geography teachers as curriculum-makers is essential.

When performing a simple internet search on the different approaches to teaching, one is presented with over 20 answers, loosely classified into teacher-centred and learner-centred approaches. My argument – and experience – is that teaching actually slides along a continuum of methods, with expert teachers developing the ability to blend together a range of approaches focused on getting the best qualifications and qualities out of young people.

Here are seven of the deadliest myths that choke enquiry and prevent it from flourishing in the classroom. I would remind the reader that what follows is based upon classroom experience and designed to be provocative in places. Some of these are easy to dismiss, whilst others require more explanation and thought.

Misconception 1: Enquiry is discovery learning

Geographical enquiry is not discovery learning, although it does have strong links to constructivist theories. To be explicit, successful enquiry demands direct instruction. In other words, the fundamental geographical knowledge of a topic needs to be expertly taught and explicitly explained by geography teachers. Not only should the components of enquiry be taught and modelled by teachers, but the underlying disciplinary and substantive knowledge need to be secure. Successful independent enquiry relies upon students having extensive and detailed geographical knowledge taught to them by teachers. We can ensure that students both learn the content effectively and store it into their long-term memory, *and* do so through explicit teaching and modelling enquiry.

> **Definition**
>
> **Constructivism:** This is a learning theory that emphasises the idea that individuals construct their knowledge in an active and ongoing process, suggesting that learners create meaning through their experiences and interactions with the environment. It is linked to the teacher being a facilitator and students investigating questions independently.

Whilst there are aspects of constructivism that focus on problem-based enquiry and student autonomy, I argue that it is an end-point. If we consider the progression of students, then they should be moving towards this goal of independent working, but that will most likely be when they leave school after A level. Professional judgement by teachers can introduce elements of choice and student independence but still retain control of the content and skills being learned. It is not one or the other.

Consider the two different types of instruction described in the box on the next page. Whilst the next chapter will examine progression, an A level student would be expected to take part in an independent enquiry, whilst younger students in Year 7 will need more explicit teaching.

> ### Definitions
>
> **Minimally guided instruction:** This is when teachers offer partial or minimal guidance. Learners are expected to discover some or all of the concepts and skills they are supposed to learn on their own. It is often referred to as discovery learning, enquiry learning or problem-based learning.
>
> **Explicit instructional guidance:** This is when teachers *fully explain* the concepts and skills that learners are required to learn. This could be through lectures, modelling, videos, presentations or demonstrations.
>
> (From Kirschner and Hendrick, 2020)

As it is almost impossible to be able to ask a fertile geographical enquiry question without a firm understanding of the substantive knowledge of that topic, explicit instruction is needed. The fundamental knowledge and key concepts in geography do need to be explicitly taught. This avoids the development of misconceptions.

A recent study from Grenell et al. (2024) concluded that young children learn more through direct instruction. Consider the diagram in Figure 2.4. The implication is that for students to be successful in their own independent geographical enquiry, they need a great deal of prior knowledge. This knowledge needs to be explicitly taught to them by teachers. However, there is a stage where that prior knowledge reaches a level that enables learners to make even bigger progress. I suggest that this place is probably arrived at late in the secondary career of young geographers; however, it is essential to do so before A level and the non-exam assessment (NEA). This again reinforces how geography teachers will mainly be employing direct instruction but *within* the enquiry process, making explicit reference to it and allowing the enquiry to contain some elements of choice.

When students end their school geography career, whether at Key Stage 3, GCSE or A level, they need to be able to apply their knowledge to independent work effectively. Indeed, the NEA at A level can be considered one large discovery learning task, so it is essential that if our schools are to enable students to be successful geographers, to understand and learn about their world so that they may go on to change it, geography teachers must ensure that we teach that knowledge through direct instruction.

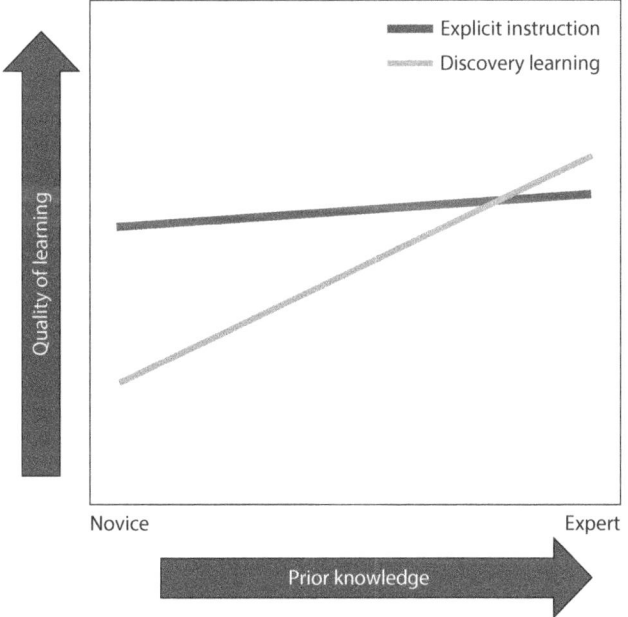

Figure 2.4: Simplified model showing the relationship between prior knowledge and the quality of learning outcomes for two pedagogical philosophies (adapted from Grenell et al., 2024)

Now whilst you may argue that students come to the classroom with a plethora of prior knowledge of their world (the concept of the geographical rucksack, see page 37) – and of course they do – I would argue that is made up of a multitude of experiences that are not automatically seen through a geographical lens by young people. Misconceptions may well have been developed and only one, narrow viewpoint considered. Just because a young person lives in a rural village, it does not mean that they have the substantive knowledge to understand the forces at work that impact that place.

For example, some of my earliest memories are from the miners' strike. I grew up in Maerdy in Rhondda. Whilst I knew that mines were closing, jobs were being lost and deprivation was creeping in, causing migration across South and West Wales, I didn't really know why this was happening. The common answer was 'Thatcher and the Tories'. But that is an oversimplistic and biased viewpoint. It wasn't until secondary school that I was exposed to and started to be able to understand the global processes at work. I was an advocate for dirty coal for years; learning about its contribution to air pollution and the climate crisis changed this. I lived and breathed Wales, but I didn't understand it until I became a geographer.

The knowledge that geography teachers have can be used to teach students directly whilst using the enquiry approach. This means that discovery learning and enquiry are not always the same thing. Whilst older learners may be able to independently follow the enquiry process, their success depends on previous effective teaching.

Misconception 2: Enquiry is group work

One argument that I have come across for not using enquiry is that it requires group work. This is not true. Whilst pragmatic consideration may make group work necessary in fieldwork, enquiry, and the hard thinking it demands, are individual activities. Enquiry work is not group work.

Indeed, if memory is the residue of thought (Willingham, 2009a), then slowing down to consider the messy geographical world is not only essential but also needs individual, paired and group work. Therefore, like most myths around enquiry, this really relates to teaching, rather than being a geography-specific issue. Expert teaching can effectively employ group work by employing several strategies. Indeed, 'group work, as with most things in education, is neither intrinsically good nor bad; it really just depends on how you use it' (Campbell and Bokhove, 2021).

For students to demonstrate how they interrogate a wide variety of data sources, they need to think and work individually. For young people to communicate their learning, they need to craft individual written accounts that can be used to assess their learning and identify where their gaps are and whether any misconceptions have been developed or reinforced. And when done well, a sequence of lessons taking an enquiry approach can lead to incredible, individual extended writing.

I will never forget inviting colleagues to visit geography lessons when I was head of geography. They were convinced that my team was making up the Key Stage 3 data. When they visited, what they saw was an expert team, supported by a great curriculum, teaching young people what they could handle. They had books full of messy thoughts but demonstrated their hard thinking by geographical prose rich with geographical terminology, from lesson one of Year 7.

Misconception 3: Enquiry is something different

As I hope that you are beginning to realise, enquiry is geography's signature pedagogy. When I was a head of department, we developed a curriculum structured around enquiry. Each sequence of lessons:

- was driven by questioning
- included a rich variety of both qualitative and quantitative information from a range of perspectives
- contained the opportunity to critically engage with a variety of datasets
- involved young people communicating their learning
- involved some element of choice.

Most units set out to allow young people to be able to answer a big question or contained pause points. The question came first, informed by content, procedural knowledge and concepts, and the unit was built around it. Some enquiries were confined within a single session, whilst others spanned months.

In other words, enquiry wasn't something that was 'done' occasionally. The enquiry approach model (see Fig. 2.1, page 36) was on every geography classroom wall, and it was explicitly referred to in lessons.

Enquiry also allows us to slow down – to pause and consider different viewpoints. When it is an integral part of the curriculum, students become able to think and communicate like geographers. This will never be perfect, not least because of the gap between geography lessons and all the activity that happens in between, but enquiry used throughout a curriculum is an essential component to this.

Misconception 4: An enquiry must lead to new geographical knowledge

This is a common misconception from young people themselves. School geography is not about creating new geographical knowledge; it is about exploring a selected and carefully curated proportion of the current body of geographical knowledge. Whilst the topics are selected by the teaching team or dictated by an examination board, it is our responsibility to ensure that students understand that geography. Of course, the knowledge may be new to the young people – or at least, we would hope so!

What enquiry can provide is the lens through which to consider different viewpoints and explore how existing geographical knowledge applies to different places, spaces and times. The past few years have provided a wealth of issues that are geographical in nature but also demand that we test and question existing knowledge. Teachers need to use their professional judgement to decide upon what young people are taught and what they should be exposed to before they leave compulsory geography. One of the common mantras in my geography classroom is 'Prove it!', which demands the consideration of facts from different viewpoints.

The coronavirus pandemic rocked the world and changed the nature of space, whilst hammering home how interconnected and interdependent places and our lives are. Brexit has redefined what it means to be British and is one of the areas where 'fake news' and outright misinformation are commonplace. Geography's procedural knowledge, which can be honed though enquiry, is central to equipping young people 'with a general antidote to fake news, particularly when it is combined with [the] elements of geopolitics and statistical analysis' (Parkinson, 2020, p. 67). The world will constantly be changing, and soon some other event will again change the world.

Misconception 5: Enquiry is fieldwork

Scale is one of the fundamental geographical concepts. Enquiry also occurs at different scales. Enquiries can be very small in scale, as well as large. In the context of school geography, an enquiry can span a multitude of lessons, where students never leave the classroom. It does not only happen in fieldwork.

Yes, the collection of geographical measurements and observations are part of effective fieldwork. But enquiry needs measurements and observations that take place within the classroom. Exploring secondary data is an essential part of our subject's procedural knowledge. Indeed, any primary data collection should be informed by this knowledge.

Effective fieldwork demands that it be planned for in the classroom. Students then head out into the world, usually employing a range of techniques selected by teachers and restricted by what is available in terms of equipment and time. Students then return to critically evaluate and communicate that information.

Misconception 6: Enquiry explores hypothetical or fictional situations

Geography is the interaction between people and places. Geography therefore happens in real places. Whilst some of its concepts and ideas can seem abstract, they are intrinsically linked to a place or places.

Take the example of exploring a school's microclimate. Before exploring the school's grounds – or even the inside of a classroom or corridor – with meteorological equipment such as thermometers, students need knowledge of the difference between weather and climate, the individual components of weather and how they interact, how the components are measured and the factors that influence weather and climate. A common investigation is to suggest the site of a new vending machine or bench in an ideal location. However, unless this opportunity exists and the class genuinely has the opportunity to contribute to the process of siting such a resource, it really isn't a great enquiry.

Students could use measuring equipment to map differences in wind speed and direction and temperature. These can be used to create isoline maps, which can then be used in geographical writing where individuals describe the patterns found and suggest explanations for them. This allows students to recall and apply their geographical knowledge, rather than put forward fictional arguments to a fictional audience. If the audience is only ever the teacher, then students should write as if that is the case. Of course, there are often opportunities for young people to have a genuine input in decision-making or to present to senior leaders, in which case it would be appropriate to present those arguments.

Similarly, we should avoid developing and reinforcing stereotypes when presenting other viewpoints, without questioning the credibility of the source. Are these viewpoints from real people or a writer's representation of what they think would be said?

Misconception 7: Enquiry isn't compatible with educational research

Enquiry allows us to pause and get off the knowledge treadmill. It works alongside what we know about how learning works. I have already mentioned that enquiry allows individuals to think hard about topics. In addition, enquiry can also provide the opportunity for retrieval. Chapter 4 will expand on the misconception.

When sequencing the curriculum, this approach links the content studied in the classroom to the world outside the classroom. After all, one of the key advantages of our subject is that many of the processes form part of students' lived experiences.

The increasing body of knowledge around how children learn is vital to successful geography teaching when it is thought about and applied by expert teachers. I will explore how enquiry links to what we know about how children learn in the next chapter.

Reflection

Did you hold any of these misconceptions yourself? Are they held by your department, students or wider school colleagues?

Key takeaways

- Enquiry *is* geography. It isn't just a method, a fieldwork task or a skill to tick off. It's the signature pedagogy of our subject, shaping how students think, investigate and understand the world.
- Direct instruction matters; students won't be able to ask the big questions or analyse information effectively without a solid foundation of geographical knowledge. Enquiry doesn't replace teaching; it relies upon it.
- Enquiry is flexible and layered; the process is more important than a set of rigid rules and it must be contextualised to your setting.
- Your students bring a rucksack that carries a mix of experiences and prior knowledge. Enquiry builds upon that.
- Perspectives shape understanding: geography isn't neutral. How we frame questions, use language or present case studies affects what students notice, think about and therefore learn.
- Questions first, content second. A strong enquiry begins with a fertile question, and the curriculum should weave concepts together with procedural knowledge.
- Don't fall for the myths; enquiry works alongside evidence-based methods.

3 What is the point of enquiry?

In this chapter

In this chapter, I explore the current state of enquiry-based learning in secondary school geography, examining both the challenges and opportunities it presents. The case for embedding enquiry at the heart of the curriculum is made, showing how it can deepen student understanding, foster critical thinking and support anti-racist and decolonial approaches. Drawing on examples from classroom practice and curriculum leaders, a few lesson sequences are illustrated. Practical strategies are offered to navigate common obstacles, including time constraints, curriculum pressures and misconceptions about what enquiry entails. Throughout, I highlight the role of enquiry in connecting students to their local environment, building procedural knowledge and equipping them to engage thoughtfully and safely with complex or controversial issues.

As I have argued, enquiry is at the heart of geography. This chapter presents the 'why?', with a number of arguments for its inclusion within British school classrooms, with their focus on knowledge-rich curricula and pedagogical techniques, driven by the insights of cognitive science. Whilst a full discussion is beyond the scope of this book, we will delve further into each argument in later chapters, giving examples from classroom practice. They are offered here to provide a stimulus and provocation for you to think about your school curriculum and your classroom practice. The purpose of this chapter is to communicate why we need enquiry woven through our teaching, rather than what it looks like and how it works.

We begin with a brief review of the state of enquiry within schools and grapple with the time versus content conundrum. I then present eight arguments for enquiry being *at the heart* of our taught curriculum. They are crafted to assist geography specialists to communicate with non-specialist senior leaders.

The state of enquiry in schools

As a new curriculum leader for geography, I remember being invited to speak at an event at the Open University not long after the publication of a report from Ofsted (2011) on the state of geography. I remember sitting there and listening to how what was contained in the report could not possibly be the case. I stood up last and confirmed that it most certainly was the case and that, despite geographical enquiry being mandated explicitly in the current version of the National Curriculum, I agreed with Ofsted that there were insufficient opportunities for enquiry-based work. The point is that the landscape has not changed, and this is because of geography leadership in schools. Yes, there are other pressures, and these can be overcome, especially with compelling reasons to include enquiry within our subject.

Primarily, enquiry is the lens that allows students to think hard. It is not a bolt-on and can be used to structure the entire learning journey throughout a school geography adventure. As pointed out by the recent Ofsted (2023a) report into geography, enquiry works best when the curriculum is designed *around* questions, rather than them being added to the topic retrospectively. High-quality, contextualised geographical questions should underpin individual units. Most importantly, the unit should answer the question by the end of that unit.

The question that springs to mind is that if enquiry is so important and is identified as a 'good thing' by external bodies, then why is it still absent in many geography classrooms? My thought is that as enquiry *is* teaching geography, it actually is there, even if it is confined to once-in-a-key-stage fieldwork. It is just that we do not explicitly refer to enquiry and its component parts in each and every lesson.

The time versus content conundrum

I have often listened to the chorus that teachers simply do not have the time to teach enquiry *and* cover the content. This is false. By using enquiry in lessons, we make the knowledge that students already have and have been taught even more secure. One of the beauties of our subject is that so much content is connected to other subject matter. This is built-in retrieval practice!

Enquiry also provides a lens for students to look *beyond* the curriculum: to question why they are investigating what is in front of them; to question their teachers' viewpoints and perspectives, as well as challenge their own; to link what is being taught in that classroom to what they have experienced in their own lives. This is especially important when the knowledge being presented conflicts with what they observe in the world and their own views, or the views expressed by those with whom they interact outside of that geography lesson. There is undoubtedly a tension between teachers following their professional duty of enabling young people to achieve great results and their moral duty to teach the world as it is.

Let's consider this example to illustrate this point.

> ### Reflection
>
> Take the following extract from an AQA (n.d.) A level specification as a representative example of specifications as a whole:
>
> 'Population, resources and pollution model: positive and negative feedback. Contrasting perspectives on population growth and its implications; Malthusian, neo-Malthusian and alternatives such as associated with Boserup and Simon.'
>
> Pause for a moment and reflect upon this. Then answer the following questions:
>
> - Does this statement reflect the world that we see now or the world as it was?
> - How would you approach teaching this?
> - Should it be included in our teaching?
> - Why or why not?
> - What would the prior key stages need to include to tackle this topic?

> ### Activity
>
> Now take the exam specifications that you are teaching. Read through them and highlight any examples where the specified content does not match up with more recent development in geography, including different perspectives.

My argument is not against including such models and ways of thinking; after all, they are examples of geographical thinking in themselves. However, do we share the limitations and perspective of those geographers who created the theories, or do we present them as facts to learn?

I would imagine that great geography teachers will not be blindly teaching this type of content. However, the pressure of delivering external examination results, proving that young people are remembering more and the limited time afforded to foundation subjects all present a challenge. The answer? I believe that a well-crafted Key Stage 3 that allows students to critically think like geographers is the key to overcoming this.

When many countries around the world, from all parts of the economic spectrum, are experiencing population decline, with aging populations and declining fertility rates, the commonly accepted models, notions and explanations are no longer valid. Is it true that we are heading to disaster or that humans will innovate our way out of trouble? Who decides that increased population is trouble anyway?

Furthermore, complex models that aim to simulate and predict food security, and their interaction with climate change and population need to be considered. Some writers are predicting the end of rapid global population growth (Roser and Ritchie, 2023), and data visualisations go beyond the demographic transition model (for example, see the excellent resource from Ritchie et al., 2023). These sources show that global fertility has now halved. Worse, they can reinforce single stories and the ingrained prejudice of the UK curricula. Enquiry provides the antidote to this, in developing the procedural knowledge for young people to critically assess claims.

Of course, there is the ever-present challenge of staying up to date. Yes, we can rely upon the excellent resources of well-known geographers and the subject associations; however, they can also be influenced by their own individual perspectives. Enquiry is the tool to give us a way around this. This is the best that we know *now*. This situation is changing in terms of the content; however, our perspectives and way of approaching the moral dilemmas and issues around it may not. Simply by acknowledging to classes that geographical content changes, we can teach them about geographical futures and help to keep their minds open.

Reasons for enquiry to be at the heart of our taught curriculum

As well as being justified through the National Curriculum and exam specifications, here I present eight arguments for the inclusion of enquiry. It may be that you are evangelical about enquiry, in which case you can skip ahead! The arguments are presented here with the aim of assisting those that must justify their approach to non-specialist senior leaders, as well as our external accountability friends. When I was a curriculum leader of geography, I always believed in going in heavy with the arguments. Of course, we must also consider educational outcomes and the wider curriculum aims of the school. For that, I always linked my development plans to those of the headteacher or principal. A final point is that I am yet to find a credible argument *against* using an enquiry approach.

1. Enquiry allows the design of a curriculum and sequences of lessons

By using enquiry, we can revisit and go deeper into the key concepts of geography throughout the curriculum. I would advocate using individual locations and countries to explore multiple topics and case studies.

Consider the following sequence of lessons in Table 3.1, which I developed and taught to Year 7 students. The unit didn't have a timescale attached to it and was used to introduce many of the concepts within geography, whilst exploring selected locations around the globe. It would be updated each year to reflect new developments, but the locations were chosen because of their stability.

In this unit, enquiry questions are used as the lesson titles. The idea of 'lesson' is fluid, as whilst the unit was designed to be a pacy examination of Earth whilst introducing key concepts, the enquiry question could span more than one individual lesson. The important aspect is that the enquiry question is answered, even if it is with a degree of uncertainty.

The unit is an in-depth investigation into Portsmouth (where the school is located) and replaced two other units: 'What is geography?' and 'Atlas/map skills'. The intention was that those skills would be taught and practised in the context of real geographical issues and ideas.

Table 3.1: Year 7 lesson sequence: Amazing places

Enquiry question	Parts of enquiry taught	Learning objectives	Geographical concepts	Links to personal geographies	Place(s) encountered/notes
How do I ask geographical questions?	Ask geographical questions Communicate	Decide on suitable geographical questions. Locate countries on a world map. Describe the location of a country. Make links between a country's location and climate.	Space Environment Diversity	Locations that individuals know or have heard about. Using own experiences to ask about similarities and differences.	All those in the unit, as well as those experienced (whether in person or through media). The questions are framed so that they can be answered within the first two lessons.
Does new always mean better? How can geographers find out about places?	Critically evaluate information	Assess the use of traditional and neo-geographical sources of information. Select the most appropriate method of finding information.	Place Interpretation	What information sources do students already have awareness of?	A link here to the UNICEF Rights Respecting School Rights of the Child (1989), Article 17: access to information from mass media. This lesson builds upon the questions from the previous lesson.

Enquiry question	Parts of enquiry taught	Learning objectives	Geographical concepts	Links to personal geographies	Place(s) encountered/notes
Where on Earth is Iceland?	Gather information	Locate Iceland. Describe Iceland's physical and human features using secondary data.	Place Earth systems Environment Interpretation	Using lived experiences of Portsmouth to compare similarities and differences.	Iceland: chosen pragmatically because the department visited Iceland.
How does folklore connect Icelanders to Iceland?	Gather information Critically evaluate information	Know that a sense of place is location plus meaning. Know that a sense of place contributes to identity and belonging.	Place Environment Interconnection Time	Fairytales and other stories from childhood. Rumours and urban legends.	Exploring the idea of folklore and how it creates a national sense of identify and connection to places. This will later be explored in the context of the students' locale and the UK.
Does Iceland exist?	Gather information Critically evaluate information Critically evaluate the enquiry Communicate	Be able to identify reliable sources of information.	Space Place Interpretation	Builds upon previous lessons.	The purpose of this lesson is to question the teacher and what has been taught, allowing the explicit reaching of procedural knowledge in the form of enquiry skills (see Rogers, 2012). The solution is to find a range of information that confirms the existence of a place many would not have visited.

(*Continued*)

Table 3.1: Continued

Enquiry question	Parts of enquiry taught	Learning objectives	Geographical concepts	Links to personal geographies	Place(s) encountered/notes
How sustainable is Dubai?	Ask geographical questions	Describe ways in which people can affect the environment both positively and negatively. Know the features of a desert climate.	Place Environment Interconnection	It is highly likely that through social and mass media, young people have some idea of Dubai already.	Dubai This place holds a fascination for many and is a good example of where a country is trying to diversify from oil. This place is revisited often, looking at greenwashing.
How are Earth's natural wonders used by people?	Ask geographical questions Critically evaluate information	Appreciate that different people consider different places as a natural wonder. Know what the aurora borealis are and where they occur. Distinguish between human and physical geographical features. Create an annotated field sketch of a location in Iceland showing the impact of tourism.	Place Earth systems Environment Diversity Interconnection	It is likely that natural wonders have been studied at some stage. In addition, in the age of viral social media, it is likely that students have some idea of natural places elsewhere in the world.	Going back to Iceland. Also considering whether there is agreement about 'natural wonders.' Getting comfortable with an idea that is not concrete. Asking questions such as 'who decides on this list?'. Introduction of UNESCO World Heritage List (n.d).

Enquiry question	Parts of enquiry taught	Learning objectives	Geographical concepts	Links to personal geographies	Place(s) encountered/notes
Do we feel a connection to nature? If not, what can we do about it?	Ask geographical questions Critically evaluate information	Describe what is meant by a 'sense of place.' Locate and summarise local folklore examples. Explain how folklore helps create a sense of belonging to a landscape.	Place Interconnection	Exploring how connected to nature students feel and link to folklore of Iceland from previous lessons.	Local area The idea here is to link to the ideas explored during the Iceland folklore activity. Building on work by universities and amateurs alike, it allows students to question the origin of web-based information, which is curated and presented to the class. As enquiry is about understanding the world so that we can make it better, a homework activity is suggested from various books.
What's causing the hassle at Heathrow?	Gather information Critically evaluate information	Describe the location of Heathrow Airport and its links to this unit. Identify possible impacts of a third runway if it is built at Heathrow.	Environment Time Scale Interconnection	Many students will know about plane journeys, although care must be taken as many may not have had the opportunity.	This is a teacher-led enquiry.

What is the point of enquiry?

The first lesson of Year 7 was a baseline assessment, where students wrote about a place using a range of resources given to them. The resulting extended piece of writing provided valuable insight into the relative substantive and procedural knowledge that the young people already had. As a side note, I've never subscribed to blaming primary school colleagues for gaps in information. Given what we know about long-term memory, if knowledge isn't revisited, it is forgotten, and skills not practised lose their automaticity. In general, I believe that we still expect far too little of young people from lesson one of Year 7.

> **Reflection**
>
> Geography is constantly changing. Consider how relevant each of the locations and examples are in the Year 7 unit in Table 3.1. Are there better examples? Are these places that would be known to our students? Are there more relevant places to them that also illustrate the geography?

'What is the point of this unit?' I hear you ask. What is important is that it introduces young people to the potential and scope of geography. They are to be introduced, at an age- and stage-appropriate level, to the big concepts that thread throughout the curriculum. They find out what geographers study and care about and they can explore personal agency. What is the point of geography? It is so that geographers can make the world a better place.

Whilst this unit doesn't have a unifying enquiry question, it explores the process of enquiry and, I would argue, inspires a curiosity about the world. Students do not finish the unit as expert geographers, but they have a good understanding of the procedural knowledge and the fact that geography happens in places.

The next example unit, in Table 3.2, is taken from Year 8. It is another example of floating topicality, which will be explored in Chapter 6. Throughout my career, migration has been a hot topic. Young people cannot escape the messages that bombard them from social media. The enquiry approach allows us to examine conversational topics by considering the established facts through different lenses, rather than by emotive language. The final lesson of the unit is an opportunity to pause to answer the overarching enquiry question. I have included some explanatory notes for the reader that expand on the purpose of each enquiry question.

Table 3.2: Year 8: Moving stories: What is migration and does the world need it?

Enquiry question	Learning objectives	Links to personal geographies	Notes
What is migration and why do people move?	Describe push and pull factors. Know the terminology around migration. Appreciate that different groups of people have different perspectives on migration.	Concept mapping explores what students already know, as well as their personal experiences of migration. Exploring the terminology of migration and the common misconceptions that students have.	Using the personal geography of teachers, describing their personal migrations. With sensitivity and knowledge of the young people, asking students to reflect upon their own geographies. The class explores Lee's push and pull model, including work on what a model is and why geographers use them (Lee, 1966).
Why do people want to move away from Mexico? What barriers are there?	Locate Mexico and the USA. Describe relative development characteristics of the USA and Mexico. Describe the role of governments in controlling migration.	At the time of writing, but throughout my experience of teaching, young people have some knowledge of this issue. Linking back to what we have learned about the drawbacks of using secondary data. Evaluating the source of news.	This is a topic that is always in the news. We chose to look at the USA before returning to consider UK migration issues in Year 9. It is also an opportunity to start exploring fake news.

(Continued)

Table 3.2: Continued

Enquiry question	Learning objectives	Links to personal geographies	Notes
How does the USA defend its borders?	Be able to identify the impacts on the physical landscape of borders. Assess development data and create hypotheses.	At the time of writing, but throughout my experience of teaching, young people have some knowledge of this issue. Linking back to what we have learned about the drawbacks of using secondary data.	When examining the continent of Africa, the concept of borders and how they come about can be explored. There are also links to the Russian invasion of Ukraine, as well as the role of NATO and the UN.
Why might Mexican people choose to migrate north instead of south?	Be able to use secondary information to compare the development of Guatemala with the USA and Mexico.	Evaluating the source of news.	Using Gapminder and also exploring the impact of political policy. This can be linked to the current 'stop the boats' rhetoric in the UK.
What are the impacts of migration?	Describe the positive and negative impacts of migration. Explore UK migration statistics.	An opportunity to explore the perspective of individuals, e.g. do they automatically think about negative impacts on them and their locale? What about negative impacts of the source country?	An appreciation that impacts can be positive as well as negative on different groups of people.

Enquiry question	Learning objectives	Links to personal geographies	Notes
What evidence of diversity is there around our school?	Know how to make observations in the field. Be able to identify evidence of diversity in the local area and on the school site.	Tapping into the lived experience of young people and their journey to school. There is a wealth of ideas for turning everyday walks into opportunities to explore diversity.	This is an opportunity for on-site 'over the fence' fieldwork. It also connects young people and makes the abstract idea of migration tangible. It helps to stop migration being something that happens in other places and to other people.
Have British people created diversity in other countries?	Interpret migration statistics. Interpret media articles about the migration of British people.	This is an ideal opportunity to explore existing misconceptions around this highly contentious and sensitive topic.	In the post-Brexit era, this is an opportunity to look at the rights lost.
What is migration and does the world need it?	Understand that different people have different points of view. Know where to find reliable information on migration.	Linking back through the unit in order to answer the question.	Revisit the concept map. Students usually appreciate that they need more information and that it depends on one's own perspective.

> **Activity**
>
> Look at the Year 8 unit of work in Table 3.2 and, using the enquiry model in Chapter 2, identify the aspects of enquiry that could be developed.

As shown, enquiry questions provide a template that can be applied to any geographical content. There is always more to find out; there is always more to uncover. Deciding upon the overarching questions and units leads to lively debate amongst colleagues and provides a fantastic focus of departmental meetings.

One of the challenges we face is that geography isn't a subject where any content is in isolation; everything is interconnected. Therefore, everything can be evaluated from a particular point of view. For example, whilst the established facts of how sea defences work and the process of longshore drift are fixed, the relative value of the sea defences and their effectiveness will differ according to the perspective and connection that the relevant parties have to those defences.

Within the geography curriculum, there is tension between the time we spend on content and the depth that we go into. In addition, geography lessons can inadvertently create and strengthen misconceptions of the world, and that can result in single stories. This is a challenge that enquiry can solve.

If we accept that enquiry provides the conceptual framework that allows young people to understand geography's substantive and procedural knowledge, then using the enquiry process to organise sequences of lessons and medium-term plans makes sense. We shall look at some additional examples of this in Chapter 5.

2. Enquiry is central to creating an anti-racist, decolonial school geography

Enquiry provides a pedagogically sensitive way to explore how geographical knowledge has been created, enabling us to engage in humane dialogues with students about why they hold their views. It allows young people to think like geographers by asking critical questions about information from textbooks. Enquiry gives permission to teachers and students to pause, think hard and think differently. It helps to create a classroom where all questions and viewpoints are welcome.

School geography in UK schools is rooted in the white-dominated, colonial and racist viewpoints through which subject content has been created. At the time of writing, geography was one of the least diverse subjects amongst its cohorts at A level and university, with ethnic diversity declining at every stage of education (see, for example, GA, 2025).

Quite rightly, there has been increasing focus and discussion around this issue. It is easy to feel lost and inadequate in addressing these issues. I know that I have. Enquiry can provide the reassurance that we are doing everything possible to examine geographical issues from different perspectives. We do not have to hold all the answers, but we should be comfortable to acknowledge insightful queries from young people and model how to do so in an assertive yet thoughtful manner.

Example

I'll always remember being at the University of Exeter as a keen undergraduate geographer. The unit that still sticks in my head today is where we were exposed to theory and methods employed by those teaching us. Not only did I learn about the different paradigm shifts in our subject (meaning that I accepted that geographical knowledge is not fixed), but we were given the published articles of the team, together with their field notes. Whilst what was published wasn't false, it was a chosen version of the truth. I learned that this is often to satisfy funding arrangements, publication rules or a set of data that doesn't make sense. I thought to myself, if these are the very people creating geographical knowledge, how am I to trust anything I read?

Geographers seek to make sense of the world, sometimes through models that generalise and simplify. Coupled with the tension between covering content to pass examinations and delving deeper into subjects, there can be a polarised simplification of issues, particularly around development, that takes the vibrancy out of geography. For example, simple statistical comparisons can erase a country's rich and unique characteristics and history and silence Indigenous voices (Winter, 2023). Rather than presenting students with a list of facts, we can use enquiry so that they critically evaluate that information – even if just to acknowledge that different perspectives exist. In addition, by explicitly teaching students how geographical knowledge has been created, they understand that some of it is not fixed and reflects a certain perspective.

Often, we look at the geographies of difference and adopt a Eurocentric approach. James Esson, speaking on the GA's GeogPod (2024b), argues that we should also look for similarities. Enquiry allows us to start by asking, 'How is this place similar to what I know about here?'

Enquiry provides the framework within which to revisit places to use for multiple examples and case studies, so that we can explore similarities and move beyond simplistic, single-story ideas. There is no reason why we can't use the relative freedom of Key Stage 3 to explore the nature of places to be studied at later stages of education. There is no rule stating that every case study must be from a different location. Indeed, by doing so, we ignore the interconnection that people and places have around the world.

Enquiry also allows us to look at students' own everyday geographies (Parkinson, 2022) in a constructive way and to connect their everyday knowledge with more formal school knowledge. This requires geography teachers to acknowledge that young people exist beyond our classroom and school grounds. For me, this reminds me of what Peps Mccrea (2025) suggests is required for planning sequences of lessons that optimise student learning.

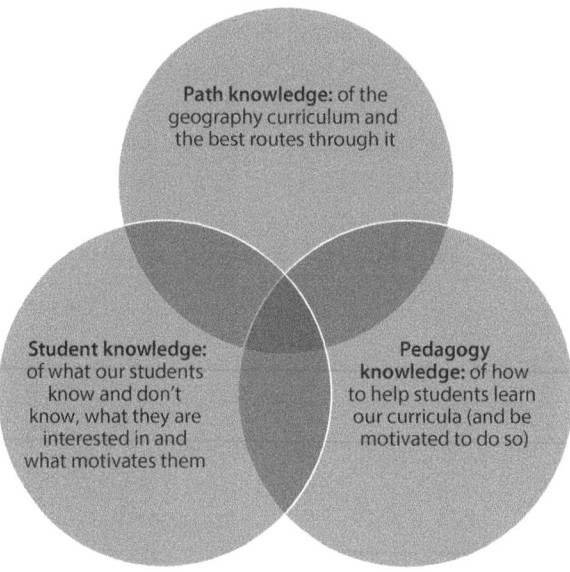

Figure 3.1: Planning expertise (adapted from Mccrea, 2025)

For effective learning to take place, one vital aspect is to know our students. This means not only utilising formative assessment but also understanding students' perspectives and what knowledge and misconceptions they bring to the classroom, both collectively and individually.

> **Example**
>
> A good example is the excellent 'Personal geographies' approach shared by Iram Sammar (2024). Iram starts with her own personal geography and allows students to explore the question 'Who am I?' whilst exploring the links between their geography and how they are connected through this to people and places around the world. Iram argues that this Key Stage 3 activity 'allows a direct engagement, or conversational opportunity, between teacher and students, bringing together the shared nature of personal geographies rather than just focusing on the value of young people's experiences in isolation' (p. 23). This type of activity, used *as part of a planned sequence of lessons*, provides us with additional student knowledge.

Finally, it is important to explore the role of geography when in its exploration phase, which spanned the early fifteenth century and lasted until the seventeenth century. A simple yet effective way of considering the impact of European colonisation is to point out that figures such as Columbus and Cook did not discover anything. They were simply the first Europeans to get there, apart from the Falkland Islands, which were uninhabited when discovered by Europeans. Why did colonial powers name desert areas with names such as the 'Empty Quarter'? Was it so that it was easy to own such spaces, as they didn't seem occupied when compared to the European sense of the word? How does this continue to impact the world today? Again, enquiry provides the toolkit to explore these questions.

3. Enquiry provides the opportunity for 'pause points' where knowledge can be consolidated and revisited

> **Example**
>
> Geography is, in its very nature, synoptic. Knowledge from different parts of its content is needed to successfully master the key concepts, such as place and interconnection.

Globalisation: As an example of the complex nature of geographical content, consider globalisation. What concrete content do students need to grasp before they fully understand this abstract concept? For example:

- interconnectedness, with countries becoming more dependent on each other
- economic interdependence, such as trade in goods, services and intellectual property
- cultural exchange of values, customs and ideas and the spread of popular culture and ideas around education, health and the environment
- technological advancement and how goods and ideas move with increasing speed around the world
- how governments, businesses and non-governmental organisations (NGOs) play crucial roles in globalisation
- the positive and negative economic, social, political and environmental impacts of globalisation
- how international trade, foreign investment, cultural exchange and migration are all examples of globalisation.

Reflection

Look at the features of globalisation in the example above. How could young people's geographical rucksacks help them begin to understand these? What concrete everyday lived experience might they have in relation to some of these abstract concepts?

At GCSE, decision-style papers provide a challenge for students to bring together other content not explicitly mentioned in the questions (unequal development and sustainability can often be linked to most situations). Similarly, at A level, top answers demand a level of synopticity, where students demonstrate how the different threads of geography link together to give an understanding of the whole.

Enquiry can provide an opportunity to introduce this, especially at Key Stage 3, but also, I would argue, at carefully selected points of GCSE. Enquiry, when used in this way, provides the opportunity for students to recall and apply past knowledge to a novel situation. Doing so demands that young people think hard about their geography. They have the opportunity not only to answer the question, but also to reach into their long-term memory for other relevant content, and they can also start to identify and appreciate gaps in their knowledge.

The curriculum also needs to provide both the time and place to answer the big enquiry questions; otherwise, they are merely attention-grabbing unit titles. The most recent Ofsted report on geography (2023a) stated that enquiry 'had the greatest positive impact when the topic had been designed around the question. It was much less successful when the question was added to the topic retrospectively.' Using geographical pause points allows students to communicate their knowledge, and when designing units of work, we should ensure that we are going to teach the knowledge required to answer the questions posed.

4. Enquiry allows us to connect young people to their local environment and therefore care about it

An enquiry approach allows teachers to connect young people with their local area and to search for the similarities and differences between it and other places. For young people, geography can be illusive and abstract, especially when exploring ideas such as a sense of place or nature connection. We often assume that students know about where they live; however, their knowledge of their local area is limited by their interests and lived experience. For example, those from low economic backgrounds may never have travelled to London for the day, nor may they value time at the beach in the same way as a more affluent peer. In short, young people are not interested in what we are and they also have underdeveloped tools of enquiry: they don't look at the world as geographers.

Enquiry allows students to think geographically about their locality by using geographical questions. They can also look for similarities between their experiences and places that are far-flung. This can be explored through fieldwork, whether in person or through freely available tools such as Google's Street View. In his book *Local* (2024), Alastair Humphreys spent the year exploring the Ordnance Survey map of the area around his home, one grid square at a time. This approach, adopted as part of a classroom enquiry, demonstrates the sense of scale.

I wonder what students would find by exploring their own grid square? What habitats are there? How diverse are its inhabitants? What services are available?

How do physical processes affect it? Information from the census and Office for National Statistics can be used in an enquiry to augment their observations and experiences. If young people can see how processes work and how changes can be made at a local level, and then draw similarities between this and far-flung places, perhaps they can begin to believe that they have agency to positively change and impact their places.

In a world that is facing huge challenges, enquiry can help young people explore their local area and show them how their actions could change it. This could even be at a classroom or school level. I wonder how many school councils are informed by robust information that is representative of the educational and community setting?

We should also consider using more examples with which students may be familiar, either from their local area or at least within the UK. For example, how many of you explore the characteristics and processes occurring in temperate rainforests in the UK before zooming over to the tropical rainforests?

Example

Another example is illustrated through Tom Moorhouse's book *Elegy for a River* (2021). Moorhouse uses the example of the invasive species the signal crayfish to illustrate what the general public is aware of and engaged in. His conclusion was that large sections of the public do not know about this issue. This awareness goes on to decide how active political organisations are and, ultimately, which projects get funded. Many are unaware of the threat and the loss of biodiversity that is occurring in Britain. In addition, by looking at the loss of biodiversity in places such as the Amazon Rainforest, enquiry allows us to ask the question: are there places I have personal experience of that have lost biodiversity?

The British landscape is almost entirely owned by private individuals. I wonder how much time we spend trying to understand the structure of British woodlands and the impact our geographical connections have had on their biodiversity and use? Do we consider how effective the 15 National Parks of the UK are at protecting our important landscapes? How have political systems, such as subsidies, grants and quotas, impacted on this? If students have experience of pheasants, are they aware that they aren't native?

5. Enquiry provides a framework for young people to become aware of their own perspectives

Geography has many controversial topics. That helps us make the subject relevant to young people and get them comfortable with the uncomfortable feeling that comes with the realisation that there is no 'correct' answer. Students come to us having lived life and been exposed to a multitude of opinions and information from fake news, false claims and social media, as well as their family and friends. Young people are often passive consumers of media in bite-sized chunks. Enquiry enables us to explore the knowledge that young people bring into the classroom and how their perspective changes when we carefully teach them the content needed. This fits well with what we know about how children learn. They are more likely to attend to what they are interested in, and they will map new knowledge taught to them to their existing knowledge.

Finally, as seen with Sammar's (2024) example on page 71, the personal geographies of teachers and students provide a useful way to move from concrete lived experience to the overarching, more nebulous geographical concepts. Enquiry helps us to explore students' individual geographical rucksacks, identify misconceptions and introduce different perspectives. Whilst this is not a book about behaviour management, our main responsibility as teachers is the safety and wellbeing of the students in our care. This includes creating a safe space where all contributions are welcome and unacceptable actions and language challenged, with education about why they are wrong. Geography classrooms must be safe spaces for contributions, although we must be aware that some may not want to share. Ultimately, although wide-ranging geographical discussions are important, students are assessed through what they write.

All people have lived experience. Students come to us with knowledge. Whilst this does not make them geographers – at least not until they have been given the procedural and substantive knowledge of abstract concepts – they have experienced geography. They will have informal knowledge of issues, and they are certainly likely to have well-established values and perspectives. They may also have developed many misconceptions, as well as have a different viewpoint to the one that you have as a teacher.

By providing prompts that encourage students to make contributions from their own geographical rucksacks, we can then anonymously include those views in future lessons. This in itself is valuable feedback to the individual (that their contribution matters) and the class (that there are different viewpoints).

In doing so, geography teachers must be supported by data and information and refrain from giving our own views of things.

It is important that, for more effective learning to occur, young people not only see themselves in the geography classroom, but also connect their lived experience with the abstract global forces in play. The mapping of new knowledge onto existing knowledge helps strong schemas to be built. Unfamiliar content should be related to what students already know (Ofsted, 2021).

Example

Early in Year 7, we asked students to write a list of ideas, experiences and thoughts about their home city of Portsmouth. We collated these and displayed them in the next lesson. This not only showed that the same place can be experienced in multiple ways, but it also helped to develop a sense of place. Over proceeding years, we built up a large dataset based upon these responses and used this to connect students to what we were studying.

A simple way of achieving this is to relate what is being studied to what students know. For example:

- comparing the width of the Amazon's mouth to the Solent and English Channel
- comparing the height of a hurricane's storm surge with the height of the classroom
- comparing daily population change to the size of the city we are in
- comparing the number of people affected to the school's size
- comparing the height of a waterfall to the school building.

In addition, there is no 'typical' student. Intersectionality means that all nine protected characteristics, as well as other factors such as income levels, will have shaped each individual's lived experience. As geographers, we need to value and make space to include contributions from all students. One way we tried to do this was to have student 'Curriculum Makers', who regularly reviewed and made suggestions to our schemes of work. They didn't create the curriculum, but their contributions were invaluable, and I am proud that our curriculum was co-created. The mechanism for doing so was driven by keeping our curriculum documents in the cloud software so changes and contributions could easily be tracked and viewed by the entire team. Student Curriculum Makers had training (including the constraints of the accountability system) as they got involved with the curriculum.

Another way we tried to get student voice into the curriculum was to hold regular surveys, again using digital software. Again, the funding of these was analysed by the geography team in curriculum meeting time and provided a wealth of information about what is relevant to the young people in our context.

Activity

Write the answers to the following questions:

- What is in your geographical rucksack?
- What perspectives do you have and why do you want to teach geography?
- How do abstract global forces, such as globalisation and sustainability, change these views?

6. Enquiry allows young people to 'disagree well'

It is likely that our knowledge of geomorphic processes will remain static and that limestone will always erode quicker than granite, but most of the discipline does not have a correct answer. We cannot so easily decide upon how to protect coastline communities, as political policies shift; the climate crisis becomes ever-more urgent and technology changes. This is especially the case when we make geographical decisions. These are laden with value judgements and linked to our previous understanding of the world and its geography.

For example, take planning, an area that will directly impact young people, wherever they live, and one about which they often have very strong views. Should we build within a National Park? Many would say no, because we need to protect the natural landscape. Does that mean that we should avoid the need for affordable housing? What about infrastructure such as hospitals and schools? As we know, the political viewpoint of the sitting government has a fundamental impact on spending, budgets and policy for green initiatives. This also sits within global agreements and frameworks, such as the United Nations Conference of the Parties and the agreements reached. The commitment to agreements such as those reached in Kyoto and Paris ebbs and flows. Take the USA's commitment, for example, which seems to reply upon who sits as president.

It is not our role as educators to give our viewpoint of the world, no matter how correct we think we are. The lens of enquiry allows us to examine different perspectives and facts, enabling young people to construct arguments that align with those. It shows that they can decide on different outcomes, and that is OK.

7. Enquiry encourages students to explore the interaction of physical and human geography

Geographical knowledge does not easily fit into the silos of human and physical. Whilst this distinction is a useful way for novice geographers to learn and remember the fundamental knowledge, the truth is that so much is interconnected and interdependent and that people influence the environment, just as the environment dictates what people do on the land.

Let us consider the concept of sustainability. I love teaching about sustainability because, like much content in geography, even the definition is contested and often misunderstood. The widely cited definition of sustainability for the geography classroom is:

> *'meeting the needs of the present generation without compromising the ability of future generations to meet their own needs'.*
>
> (WCED, 1987, p. 41)

However neat and acceptable an assessment answer this is, in order to reach a full understanding of the concept, students need to have knowledge of a wide range of content that spans both human and physical dimensions.

> **Activity**
>
> Think about the physical and human aspects of sustainability. Create a table and write them down. For example, population dynamics and development are human aspects, and climate change and weather systems are a physical dimension.

Each of these dimensions of sustainability may form individual units that deepen students' knowledge of sustainability each time. Often, urbanisation is taught separately to river flooding, but each is connected.

Enquiry allows us to plan sequences of lessons that ask questions that challenge students to think hard about how each aspect of sustainability is interconnected. For example, what impact does rapid urbanisation have on the surrounding ecosystems? How do farming systems in the UK impact on geomorphic processes and subsequent landforms?

8. Enquiry reveals the dynamic world as it is

Our subject is full of case studies and examples. It is a demanding task for teachers to update these. Enquiry provides a framework for students to interrogate our existing resources to see the link between the real world and what they learn in the classroom.

Geography is about the world, and the appeal of the subject is that what is studied in the classroom can be seen outside of it. This is sometimes measured in moments and helps us to show the appeal of our subject. It is also useful when extending learning opportunities. How much geography can be practised on the walk to school? How much can be seen on social media?

The GA's Chief Executive, Steve Brace (2024a), wrote how 'zombie resources' such as out-of-date Mount St Helens lessons stop young people from exploring eruptions that are happening now. This may well be driven by the need to satisfy exam specifications, and I would argue that seminal case studies can – and should – be incorporated into updated resources that consider more recent examples.

When considering the temporal element of geography, which is vital when trying to make the world a better place, we need to consider to which version of that place we wish to restore it. For example, Jay Owens (2023) explores in detail both the Aral Sea, in central Asia, and the Owens River basin in the USA. The Owens River changed in 1913, when the Los Angeles Aqueduct was built; the area transformed from the 'Switzerland of the West' to a dust bowl. Threaded throughout the story is the othering of the local Indigenous people, as well as the attempts to restore the area. A great question for geographers to consider is to which timescale should places like the Aral Sea and the Owens River basin be restored?

This question is still relevant to UK examples. The government has committed to protecting 30 per cent of the UK's land and sea by 2030 (DEFRA, 2024), as well as its legally binding biodiversity target to restore or create more than 500,000 hectares of wildlife-rich habitat by 2042 in England (DEFRA, 2025). Students can consider why the South Downs National Park (n.d.) has branded rewilding 'ReNature' and find out what counts as 'wildlife-rich' and to which version of nature we should be restoring.

These are great illustrations of how some case studies do not have a shelf life. Yes, the Eyjafjallajökull eruption occurred in 2010, when my son was one year old, but its impacts will inform civil aviation for years to come, and the management of it must be considered as part of a continuum that includes Heimaey in 1973 and the recent eruptions on the Reykjanes peninsula, ongoing since March 2021.

The inclusion of new events must be balanced with the time that we have, and a good solution is to return to case studies at a relevant point later in the learning journey, as well as creating the 'multi-purpose' case study, where one location is used to illustrate multiple topics.

Activity

Which of the eight reasons explored in this chapter is most relevant to your current context? It could be that you need to convince a senior colleague or a fellow geography teacher. Narrow down the top three arguments that would work in your context. Now check the references section and read a bit further around that particular aspect.

Key takeaways

- Enquiry is central to effective geography teaching, encouraging critical thinking and deeper understanding of both content and context.
- Well-designed enquiry enables students to question existing knowledge, challenge perspectives and engage meaningfully with complex issues.
- Embedding enquiry supports inclusivity, allowing for anti-racist and decolonial perspectives and connecting learning to students' personal geographies.
- Sequencing lessons around enquiry questions strengthens curriculum coherence, procedural knowledge and relevance to students' lived experience.
- Addressing practical barriers like time limitations and curricular pressures is possible through strategic curriculum design and collaborative approaches.
- Enquiry promotes the development of transferable skills, such as evaluating sources, synthesising information and communicating arguments effectively.
- Geographical enquiry helps to create classroom environments where diverse views are explored safely and constructively, preparing students for the complexities of the world.

4 How does enquiry link to educational research?

In this chapter

In this chapter, we shift away from the 'what' and 'why' of the enquiry approach to explore the 'how'. This chapter begins with defining what educational research is, before examining how it can inform geography teaching whilst acknowledging its limitations. The importance of teacher agency and professional judgement is highlighted if research-informed strategies are to be adapted effectively for the enquiry classroom. This chapter considers the role of schemas, cognitive conflict and elaboration in supporting deep learning, emphasising how enquiry encourages students to connect new knowledge to prior understanding. When reading, I encourage you to ask the following questions:

- Has this been tested in the *geography* classroom?
- How could this make learning in the *geography* classroom better?
- How can these insights be applied to the *geography* classroom?

Ultimately, this chapter argues that enquiry provides a coherent framework for applying research insights.

What is educational research?

There are many terms that have become ingrained into the UK classroom; straplines such as 'evidence informed' are plentiful. I remember in many meetings being asked to provide the evidence for claims. What most people think of with regard to educational research comes from the laboratory studies linked to psychology and cognitive science. Educational research is a very broad term and refers to the communication of findings based upon a study that has sought to answer clear questions about teaching (EEF, 2024). Evidence can come from research evidence published in peer-reviewed journals, be school-based or come from other sources.

> ### Activity
>
> In recent years, there has been an explosion of writing about educational research. Think about any that you have heard of.
> 1. Have you applied any findings to your own practice?
> 2. What practical implications did they have on the geography classroom?
> 3. Can you identify any gaps in the research?

Certainly, there are some agreed fundamentals of cognitive science that are applicable across different subject domains. However, when it feels as if cognitive science is being mandated, it is important to pause and think about how these insights can be translated into geography classroom practice. Researchers such as Perry (2022) have pointed out that there seems to be little discussion about what we don't know or may have gotten wrong and how our learning can be applied to the *geography* classroom. This seems to run counter to how geographers think. To think geographically and use an enquiry approach is to think about different perspectives and the origin and limitations of knowledge and to critically evaluate what is presented to us. I would argue that geography teachers have become adept at tackling the world of geographical content well and now need to apply this approach to the world of cognitive science.

Let's, for a moment, consider the use of geographical models (see definitions box), such as that of Burgess (1925), in teaching geography. This is distinct from teachers modelling and demonstrating in class. Geography

> ### Definition
>
> **Geographical model:** A simplified representation of real-world spatial patterns, processes, or relationships that helps geographers understand, explain, or predict how places and phenomena are organised and change over time. Models abstract the complexity of the real world, highlighting key features while ignoring less relevant details, so they are easier to study and analyse.

models are abstractions of reality and are used to describe and predict the world, creating a simplified version of it. Examples are Christaller's central place theory and the Burgess model, as well as physical models such as infiltration tables, hydraulic river flumes or sandboxes. As geography teachers, we should teach about such models critically, including their limitations as well as what they can tell us about the world. The same approach should be taken with educational research. I will explore the use of models in Chapter 8.

Let's move on to consider some of the limitations of our knowledge of research studies in cognitive science (Perry, 2022):

- Much of the evidence comes from laboratory research and uses undergraduates.
- A very small proportion of studies happen in realistic classroom conditions. Those that do tend to:
  - be small in scale, with fewer than 100 students involved
  - cover a limited number of subjects, mainly in maths and science, between Key Stages 2 and 4
  - be short, lasting a few weeks only
  - not control sufficiently for the impact of teachers, students and the curriculum content
  - have little effect when run at scale.

So how do we explain the gap between the high effect sizes of the laboratory tests and the disappointing results of large-scale classroom studies? Put simply, it is because of the multitude of variables that make teaching a craft that is learned and honed over many years. It is important that the basic cognitive science is not in question (Perry, 2022) – just that the multitude of variables are controlled for outside the laboratory science.

Teacher agency

I believe in the power of teacher agency. All we know and do is only as good as how it is implemented on a day-in-day-out basis by individual teachers in classroom settings. John Hattie (2003) identified that around 30 per cent of the variance in achievement can be attributed to teachers. It wasn't the largest factor, which was the students themselves, making up 50 per cent, whilst the home environment was responsible for around ten per cent.

Teachers, as the decision-makers and collective curriculum-makers, create shared resources that are then crafted. Scripted lessons remove the nuance and adaption that teachers, with their knowledge of the young people in front of them, can make. We may have to spend a bit longer on securing a particular concept or be able to move ahead quicker.

This means that what teachers do makes a difference. What we teach and how we teach it are important if young people are to leave with the qualifications and qualities that they need for the next stage of life.

How teachers think about the pedagogy that they employ is important. As geographers, this means thinking carefully about whole-school policies and ensuring that they apply to the geography classroom. We have the agency to do this. Whole-school approaches to teaching and learning – for example, with feedback – provide continuity and ensure that young people know what to expect when they are in lessons, so that they can focus on the learning. However, as already mentioned, mandatory approaches rarely apply to every subject, and I would argue that many do not fit what makes geography learning better.

So how do teachers make a difference? Over my career, there has been an increasing focus on cognitive science or the science of learning. Whilst I welcome this, it is not without its drawbacks, especially when applying what we know to the geography classroom.

Whilst I acknowledge that the workload of teachers is immense, if we work together, both as department teams and as a wider community of geography teachers, then we can move forward. And the information is out there. For example, the Education Endowment Foundation (EEF) publishes its methods and openly identifies the limitations. Indeed, as Roberts (2023) argues, 'the teacher's role is critical in enquiry-based learning in geography', (p. 43). She goes on to argue that this extends not only to deciding how much control we have over the content and establishing a respectful classroom, but also to how to best apply educational research.

Finally, we also must unravel the impact of national government policy and the regulatory framework. Whilst a controversial opinion refers to the relative curriculum stability since the changes ushered in by Gove at the beginning of the coalition government in 2010, the accountability framework has been tumultuous, as various Ofsted and inspection frameworks have changed.

Cognitive science and how it might be applied in the geography classroom

I will next consider the main areas of educational research, as identified by the EEF in its 2021 report. This report excludes 'lab studies'. I will briefly summarise the general principles, before suggesting how enquiry can be used to help the relevant area. What I would ask you to do is remember that general recommendations cannot assist the geography teacher in implementing them for your students in your classrooms – and that is where it gets complicated!

What follows is not an instruction manual to be devoured without thought. They are purely suggestions, stories and ideas that have worked for me. Geographical enquiry allows students to stop and think hard. Kate Jones (2024) argues that conversations drawn from the science of learning should be a regular component of classrooms, and I agree, especially because when routines and habits are formed, workload decreases and learning gets better. This is also an argument to share how geographical knowledge is created: through the enquiry process, with students. In addition, I argue that geography teachers should use the enquiry approach to question the educational research itself, and not just geographical content.

In other words, if *teachers* do not think hard and they take shortcuts, then less learning is likely to take place. This is encouraging from the point of view of valuing the professionalism of geography teachers.

More recognition for the role of expert geography teachers and their professional judgement is based upon their knowledge of the curriculum, pedagogy and the young people in front of them. Just as there are common weaknesses of educational research, some can be applied to the curriculum level, and some are concerned with individual pedagogic techniques. Like enquiry and the geography curriculum, the use of educational research needs to be contextualised to your setting.

1. Spaced learning

What is it?

Spaced learning refers to the spacing of content over time between intervals of *unrelated* content. This is an alternative to massed or clustered teaching, which follows a linear route (see Figure 4.1).

A massed, linear teaching approach would be this, with each shade representing an individual unit of work (perhaps migration or natural hazards). The width of the diagram represents one academic year:

Spaced learning could look like this:

Figure 4.1: A visual representation of spaced learning vs. massed learning

Spaced learning increases the likelihood of young people retaining knowledge in their long-term memory, as the teacher asks students to regularly revisit key concepts, ideas and skills.

How could it work in the enquiry classroom?

As with any teaching strategy or tool, this is best used when embedded within a curriculum, rather than in an ad hoc way. Spaced learning requires frequent reviews and opportunities to practise procedural knowledge. The nature of geography and enquiry link to spaced learning well. As already mentioned, enquiry provides the opportunity for students to pause and think hard. Threading enquiry throughout the curriculum also allows students to commit to long-term memory the key concepts, such as place, and key skills, such as interpreting maps.

Enquiry enables teachers to mix new and old information within lessons. Take the Year 7 unit in Chapter 3 (pages 60–63), which introduces many of the key concepts and skills that will be revised throughout the geography learning journey.

2. Interleaving

What is it?

Whilst the evidence of the effect of interleaving is limited to maths in the 8–14-years age group, it is worth considering in the context of geography. Interleaving is like spaced learning, with the difference being that interleaving spaces slightly different material, with some likeness or commonality, whereas spaced learning uses unrelated content. In other words, interleaving works when the information being learned is related.

Interleaving allows the comparison between similar and related items, which describes most of the substantive knowledge in geography. For example, in teaching about biomes, we may also teach about climate zones and the atmospheric circulation model at the same time. Interleaving also helps to develop strong schemas as students layer new content onto related, already learned content.

How could it work in the enquiry classroom?

Interleaving requires a longer-term view of geography and should be developed into the curriculum. Geography is synoptic in its nature and lends itself to interleaving well through enquiry. When thinking about learning new content, it is probably best illustrated at Key Stage 3. When viewed in this way, it is clear when students will revisit similar content. For example, consider the sequence of learning in Table 4.1, selected from across a three-year Key Stage 3.

Table 4.1: Key Stage 3 learning sequence

Content	Description
Our place	Exploring the local area; development of 'sense of place'.
Weather	What impact does the school have on its microclimate? What are the components of weather and how is it measured?
Climate	Earth's climate zones distribution; factors affecting climate.
Climate change over geological time	The evidence of climate change and the impacts; personal carbon footprints; consumption.
Ecosystems	The distribution of ecosystems; a look into temperate and tropical rainforests.
Paradise lost? Tourism	Tourism unit linked to rainforest locations.

The question becomes when to revisit this related content. As geographical enquiry demands that we teach content in the context of real places, the concept of place will thread through each aspect. In addition, we can add in development statistics for each place studied.

Throughout the units in Table 4.1, students will also come into contact with global governance, as well as many of the key and organising concepts in geography. If interleaving is threading related content through the curriculum, then enquiry is the thread that assists geography teachers in helping young people to retain the information. I will say that it is not a simple case of saying that everything is related to everything in geography – more a case of explicitly planning links.

Multi-use case studies can also be used to interleave related content. This is where the same region or place is used to layer students' knowledge. By using a familiar place and adding in related content, students may build strong schemas.

Interleaving can be visualised as part of a longer-term spiral curriculum, like a dartboard (Atterton and Dixson, 2009), and whilst that approach was developed for an earlier curriculum change, this type of visualisation is best used for having an overview of the curriculum and how different parts of it relate, rather than considering the detail.

In practice, interleaving sometimes works because of the pragmatic decisions made by the head of curriculum. Several times throughout my career, classes have been split between two colleagues. This always leaves us in a dilemma, although it works very well at A level, when learners are further along their journey in becoming geography experts and able to make a greater degree of decisions independently. The solution that I always took was for each teacher to take a different but *related* topic, as in Table 4.2.

Table 4.2: Example of planning for shared classes

Key stage	Teacher 1	Teacher 2
3	Ecosystems	Climate patterns and geological timescale climate change
GCSE*	Changing climate	Sustaining ecosystems
	Dynamic development	Resource reliance
A level**	The changing economic world	The challenge of resource management
	Physical landscapes in the UK	The challenge of natural hazards

* Based upon OCR B: Geography for enquiring minds
** Based upon AQA A level specification, www.aqa.org.uk/subjects/geography/gcse/geography-8035/specification/specification-at-a-glance

The challenge of this approach is that it requires careful communication. It is not always the case that the content and skills planned are fully covered. Sometimes, a particular group may have more misconceptions or, perhaps through off-timetable days, have missed crucial content. An additional issue is that physical and human geography, whilst presented and organised in neat silos, are interdependent and interrelated. However, tactically, taking this approach allows young people to prepare for examinations well.

3. Retrieval practice

What is it?

Retrieval practice is getting students to recall information with minimal prompting. It is considered better than teacher-led recapping of content and works because the more often knowledge is studied and recalled, the more memory 'strength' increases. By retrieving information repeatedly, it becomes more accessible for the learner and is more securely retained in the long-term memory.

Recalling previously taught knowledge means that students may become aware of their own gaps in knowledge and strengthen their memory of key ideas and concepts.

How could it work in the enquiry classroom?

When training to be a teacher, I was always taught to start with what is known and to retrieve relevant information to the forthcoming lesson at the start of the lesson. This can be extended to recalling information that isn't needed straight away and covers all the content previously taught. The most common form of retrieval practice is low-stakes quizzes, but whilst these are useful, there have been criticisms, as they avoid engaging higher-order thinking and don't to provide the opportunity for students to think hard, as they cover simple material (Coe, 2019).

This is where enquiry can work well. For example, we could provide a photograph at the start of a lesson and ask students to use their geographical knowledge to analyse that information. We could also give them a few complex graphs and diagrams and ask them to summarise each one, retrieving procedural knowledge and developing their analytical skills.

4. Managing cognitive load

What is it?

For content and procedural knowledge to be learned, it must move into the long-term memory. The working memory is the gateway to our long-term memory. Cognitive load theory relates to the limited nature of our working memory: it can only hold a certain amount of information at once. In addition, the working memory can become overloaded quickly, especially when covering new content or skills. Cognitive overload is a situation where one is given too much information at once or there are too many simultaneous tasks.

This means that our working memory is overloaded, causing information to be lost rather than stored in the long-term memory.

Teachers must avoid cognitive overload if we are to allow learners to successfully transfer new information to their long-term memory.

Figure 4.2 is a simple visual model of the learning process:

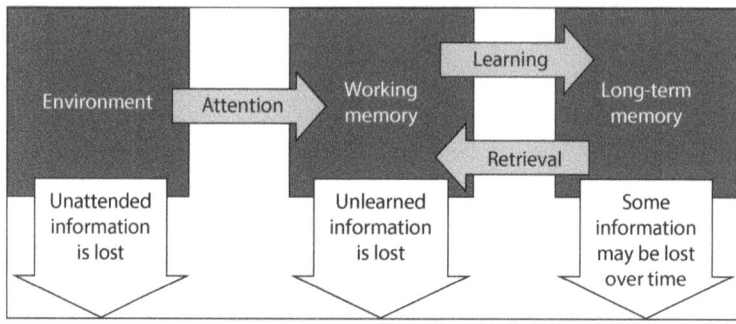

Figure 4.2: The learning process

How could it work in the enquiry classroom?

It's important to note that there are no examples outside of maths and science. Although there is certainly an overlap in content (for example, using statistical techniques and looking at the chemistry of weathering), like most cognitive science-based approaches, they need to be used with caution. Some strategies consider the presentation of material and redundancy of classroom displays.

I am often reminded of the curse of knowledge, which is the cognitive bias and assumption that novice learners will share my expertise as a teacher of geography. Whilst there are several ways to reduce extraneous load, such as worked examples, those most applicable to enquiry are the careful sequences of lessons that build knowledge in a chunked manner and use enquiry to develop strong procedural knowledge, so that tasks, such as evaluating graphs and maps or thinking about different perspectives, become automatic.

Enquiry also encourages us to start from simple questions and move on to more complex ones, naturally chunking complex information. Through a sequence of learning that slowly introduces new material, and then using an overarching enquiry question, students will be less likely to encounter extraneous load.

Progression through enquiry also allows teachers to slowly reduce the need for scaffolding. Whilst scaffolding and worked examples can help reduce extraneous load to begin with, there is evidence that as students become more familiar with material, the effect is removed. The enquiry process and its component parts become second nature to young people, allowing their working memory to focus on the new content being learned.

5. Working with schemas

What is it?

We have already identified that young people come to the geography classroom having already developed some conceptions about the subject through their lived experiences. Schemas, or mental models, are structures that organise knowledge in the mind. When new content is learned, the mind connects it to pre-existing content, skills and concepts, therefore developing existing schemas.

As any geography teacher will know, every individual student will have different preconceptions, misconceptions and conceptions (see Dove, 1999). This makes working with schemas a challenge for geography teachers. This is further complicated because schemas are not fixed, and we are unlikely to know how an individual student's schema is organised.

That said, there are some 'good-bet approaches' to working with schemas. This means that, from what we know, these approaches are likely to lead to better learning, as stronger connections are made in learners' schemas.

How could it work in the enquiry classroom?

The enquiry approach, by asking questions, aims to link new content to students' pre-existing knowledge. There are several strategies that help to build schemas.

Roberts (2023) writes about the importance of concept maps in supporting geographical enquiry. They are very useful when pausing to allow students to think hard. Students can use concept maps to connect their existing knowledge and experience to the question being considered. For enquiry, using concept maps for students to summarise their own existing knowledge can be very useful, especially in organising their thoughts before communicating their findings.

The EEF (2021) looked at concept maps and knowledge organisers, noting that knowledge organisers shared with students at the start of units can prove useful, as the content is pitched beyond the students' existing knowledge; however, they point out that there is little evidence that makes it clear about the type of task for which concept maps are useful. This illustrates some of the problems around educational research: different publications and researchers draw different conclusions. Whilst the EEF does not present conclusive recommendations, there is enough evidence that concept maps work well in enquiry to help learning.

Creating cognitive conflict is also a strategy for developing schemas. Enquiry aims to develop young people's ability to think geographically. Cognitive conflict is where students are made to think hard about problems that create tension between existing beliefs or understanding and the new content being presented. I remember when I first started teaching and the work of Leat (2001) and *Thinking Through Geography* was widely used. The book presented a wide range of ideas, and the importance of *debriefing* was paramount. Debriefing provided an explicit opportunity for students to think about their thinking. Whilst there was a proliferation of fictional exercises, the original ideas stressed the importance of basing thinking activities around *existing knowledge*. In addition, the activities allowed teachers to debrief on metacognition. I would argue that thinking through geography activities still has a place in the enquiry classroom, especially when teachers have a better understanding of the underlying research theory.

A final strategy for developing schemas is to get students to elaborate. By doing so, they question concepts and ideas and therefore strengthen their learning. Enquiry is at the heart of elaboration. Not only does enquiry expect young people to question what they are being given, but over time they will be furnished with the questions that make them think deeply. Elaboration is a key feature in the communication phase of enquiry, and two simple prompts can be used to encourage elaboration:

- So what? This means that a great point has been made but more elaboration is needed – for example, a link to another geographical concept.
- Prove it! This means that a great point has been made but some evidence is needed to support the assertion.

6. Multimedia learning (including dual coding)

What is it?

Our working memory has two components: one that processes visual and spatial information and another that deals with auditory information. Our auditory working memory is engaged when we read. Dual coding is the theory that by presenting information in different formats, both systems are engaged. This means that cognitive overload is reduced and learning strength is higher.

Dual coding sits within the broader cognitive theory of multimedia learning (CTML), which links the ideas of dual coding, cognitive load and generative learning. Fiorella (2023) defines generative learning as 'making sense' of the provided material by actively organising and integrating it with one's existing knowledge. The key point is that it is unlikely that students will perform this process on their own, especially if they are relative novices. In summary, the theory can be considered a sense-making framework and involves three main assumptions:

1. There are two separate channels in our working memory (dual coding theory).
2. Each channel has a finite capacity.
3. Learning is the active process of working with this information.

How could it work in the enquiry classroom?

Enquiry is rich in multimedia and dual coding is not something new, although the explicit implications of the theory are more recently understood. Geographical enquiry demands the use of multimedia, such as:

- visual representations and illustrations
- diagrams
- spatial visualisations
- graphic organisers.

When I first read the EEF report (2021), I assumed that the diagram used to illustrate this area of educational research was from a geography classroom. On closer inspection, the example is from a US fourth-grade science classroom (Coleman et al., 2018, cited in EEF, 2021). Having said that, there is evidence of a positive impact on learning of using an accurate process diagram that combines images, arrows and text.

Otherwise, the report points out that often dual coding leads to teachers using diagrams 'for the sake of it' (EEF, 2021, p. 39) and that there is little evidence that visualisation can assist learning.

What is clear is that good geography teaching using an enquiry approach is compatible with this area of educational research.

7. Embodied learning

What is it?

There is a much wider range of factors affecting learning outside of cognitive science and psychology. Any teacher that has taught a class straight after lunch will know that nutrition can have an impact, as do the quality of sleep, the level of physical activity and even the emotions of young people, such as anxiety.

Embodied learning describes the multisensory approach to tasks and activities, suggesting that by adopting such approaches, information is made more memorable. In other words, embodied learning is an approach that emphasises the engagement of the whole body in the learning process (Jusslin et al., 2022). Activities include play, gesturing, physical movement and tracing.

Embodied learning does not see cognition as separate from the rest of the body, although there are several definitions and some disagreement.

How could it work in the enquiry classroom?

Many of the ideas contained in embodied learning apply to whole-school approaches, and the evidence is too limited to be able to make a judgement on the applicability of geographical enquiry to this area of research.

Rosenshine's principles of instruction and enquiry

In any review of the research, it is important to include Rosenshine's principles of instruction (2012). Rosenshine's principles have been widely quoted and are compatible with an enquiry approach to geography teaching. The principles are based upon three areas of information:

1. Research in cognitive science.
2. Research on the classroom practice of master teachers.
3. Research on cognitive supports to help students learn complex tasks.

In the second area of research, master teachers were identified as those who had excellent outcomes in achievement tests. As a curriculum leader for geography, our GCSE outcomes were higher than for other subjects in the school and showed fantastic progress for each individual student. This was achieved by employing an enquiry approach, and therefore the team would have fallen into the 'master teacher' definition. As Rosenshine's research was undertaken in US schools, it is unlikely that geography was included, as it is subsumed within social studies.

Rosenshine's principles apply to the behaviour of teachers, so the link to the enquiry approach needs to be made explicit. For example, we want to expose students to high-quality geographical questions and model how we critically evaluate information. We can do this through questioning. The ten principles are detailed in Table 4.3.

Table 4.3: Principles of instruction within geographical enquiry (based upon Rosenshine, 2012 and Enser, n.d.)

	Principle	Links to cognitive science and psychology	Links to enquiry
1	Begin a lesson with a short review of previous learning.	Retrieval practice, spaced learning, interleaving.	Ask geographical questions; link to students' geographical rucksack; gather information.
2	Present new information in small steps, with student practice after each step.	Cognitive load, chunking the curriculum.	Gather information, led by the teacher, and practise communicating using this information in teacher-led tasks.
3	Ask a large number of questions and check the responses of all students.	Working with schemas, cognitive load.	Ask geographical questions (see Wood, 2006); critically evaluate information.
4	Provide models.	Working with schemas, cognitive load, multimedia learning.	Teachers can model any stage of the enquiry process, but particularly when presenting new information (gathering information); critically evaluating information and communicating.
5	Guide student practice.	Working with schemas to avoid misconceptions.	Teacher-led enquiry to open enquiry; providing scaffolds to guide communication.
6	Check for student understanding.	Working with schemas to avoid misconceptions.	Building model answers to a question and asking geographical questions.

(Continued)

Table 4.3: Continued

Principle	Links to cognitive science and psychology	Links to enquiry
7 Obtain a high success rate.	Working with schemas to avoid misconceptions, ensuring that threshold concepts are fully understood before independent work.	Moving from closed, teacher-led enquiry to framed and guided enquiry once concepts have been successfully learned.
8 Provide scaffolds for different tasks.	Working with schemas, multimedia learning.	For example, when selecting information to gather to support communication, we could provide structure strips or other scaffolding; sharing success criteria and enabling students to critically evaluate their enquiry.
9 Require and monitor independent practice.	Working with schemas, multimedia learning.	Providing pause points, where students tackle extended writing and collaborate to challenge thinking.
10 Engage students in weekly and monthly review.	Working with schemas, interleaving, spaced practice, retrieval practice.	Providing that pause point, where students tackle an enquiry question that spans a number of units already studied; a concept map could be used to organise thoughts before extended writing.

These principles are compatible with the enquiry approach, especially if we consider that enquiry can be led by teachers. Just because we use enquiry, it does not mean that we give all decision-making to the student.

What other factors impact on learning?

There are a huge range of factors that impact learning in modern geography classrooms. Hattie (2003) lists 252 influences on student achievement split into six areas: the student, the home, the school, the curriculum, the teacher, and the teaching and learning approaches employed. This chapter has only considered one or two of these areas. Table 4.4 summarises the factors that influence secondary students' outcomes.

Table 4.4: Factors influencing secondary students' outcomes (based on DfE, 2024)

Young people's individual characteristics	SEND/ACE*	Home environment	School
Cognitive capabilities and priory attainment	SEND	Family socio-economic circumstances	Transition periods
Non-cognitive capabilities	Children in care	Parental attitudes and behaviours	School characteristics, systems and structures
Physical health and risk behaviours	ACE	Family structure	Culture and leadership
Wellbeing and mental health issues		Resources and enrichment activities	Teaching and pedagogy
			Student attitudes and relationships
			Curricular and extra-curricular activities
			Attendance and absence

* SEND = special educational needs and disabilities; ACE = adverse childhood experiences

This is a wide-ranging list, and doesn't even take into account the impact of a wasp entering your classroom or the heating, lighting, layout or whether you teach after PE on the last period of a Friday. The point? Enquiry is compatible with geography teaching, and geography teachers are experts in imparting knowledge. Not only that, but the very nature of geographical knowledge tackles some of these issues head on. I never forgot that, for some young people, the geography classroom could have been one of the few places where they felt a sense of belonging and success.

The evidence base for geography is limited. Indeed, even within the heavily tested areas of maths and science, applied classroom studies are not abundant. It is therefore difficult to find secure geography-specific examples at scale. The wonderful examples contained in geography-specific journals, such as *Teaching Geography*, do give insight, and there are many examples of individual geography teachers who have used and adapted the principles of educational research. Whilst these present a useful starting point, they should be treated with caution, as the schools in which they are based are not always representative and they are often small-scale, case-study-style reports.

There is no doubt that educational research provides the key fundamentals that are useful. The problem comes in the application of these principles to the messy world of real geography classrooms. Indeed, the very nature of our subject (and other subjects) is that the content and skills with which we work are constructed in a geographical way. Geography has its own distinctive pedagogy that is not compatible with other domains. Take the idea of the line of best fit, for example: having line-managed science, maths and geography departments, each discipline takes a slightly different approach to teaching it and a slightly different definition applies.

Geography, whilst having components of science, history, maths and English, is its own subject. We have our own approach. Before throwing out older teaching techniques, I would urge looking carefully into their underpinning theory and finding out whether they are underpinned in research. Most of the time, they are.

Much educational research gives useful prompts for curriculum-making. Many of them need to be embedded in the curriculum rather than used as bolt-ons. In this aspect, enquiry provides a coherent model upon which to base effective sequences of lessons informed by educational research. Teachers can enquire about educational research and have rich discussions in department meetings about curriculum structure, as well as the geographical misconceptions that may develop in young people. Mainly, this looks at a curriculum and sequence-of-learning approach, which enquiry learning enables and encourages.

Key takeaways

- The enquiry approach and educational research are compatible; geography teachers can apply evidence-based principles within an enquiry framework.
- Much educational research is lab-based, limited in scope or not directly tested in geography classrooms, so careful adaptation is required.
- Teacher agency is crucial: teachers' decisions, their knowledge of their students and their professional judgement and collegiate approach drive effective learning.

- Cognitive load, schemas and multimedia learning highlight the importance of structured, scaffolded sequences in lessons.
- Embodied learning and attention to students' wellbeing contribute to deeper engagement but require context-specific adaptation.
- Rosenshine's principles of instruction can support enquiry by structuring lessons, scaffolding understanding and promoting higher-order thinking.
- Teachers should continually question both the content of geography and the applicability of educational research.

5 What does progression in enquiry look like?

> **In this chapter**
>
> This chapter explores how enquiry can be systematically developed and sequenced to ensure clear progression in students' knowledge, skills and thinking. It examines what it means for students to 'think like a geographer', linking together both substantive and procedural knowledge. The role of the teacher is highlighted at every stage. A model of progression is presented that moves from simple closed enquiries to open enquiries with little teacher input. The importance of scaffolding, cognitive load management and context-specific adaptation of teaching is highlighted. I will connect enquiry to external exam specifications and show how well-planned progression ensures that students consolidate learning, make meaningful connections and develop the independence needed for advanced study and real-world geographical reasoning.

So far, we have considered what enquiry is and why it should be included in or used to organise the geography curriculum. We have also found out that educational research provides the permission for us to use enquiry. The next stage is to ensure that we have a systematic and well-sequenced approach to enquiry that provides a clear progression route. In simple terms, how do we know that students are getting better at enquiry?

As mentioned previously, a lofty aim for geography teachers is that young people can independently identify suitable enquiry questions and have very little input from teachers into the enquiry process. They do this to investigate *existing* geographical knowledge, not to create new content. At the time of writing, NEA at A level can be considered an example of the end-point of enquiry if students study our subject until the age of 18. But what if they stop at the age of 14 or 16? What must be clear is that the teacher is in control of the content and skills learned and that choice is slowly introduced, when students are ready for that step.

By now, the reader will be familiar with the refrain that enquiry and geography must be contextualised to your setting. Similarly, progression in enquiry will depend on the aims of your individual school curriculum and how it is enacted at your institution. One end-point of enquiry could be that students think, act and write like geographers, and this chapter will consider how that can be measured and accounted for.

This chapter will consider what we want enquiry to achieve at the end of education, defining what is meant by 'thinking like a geographer'. I will review what external sources like exam specifications expect from young people in terms of their enquiry skills, before presenting some models of progression in enquiry.

The simple model of progression in enquiry

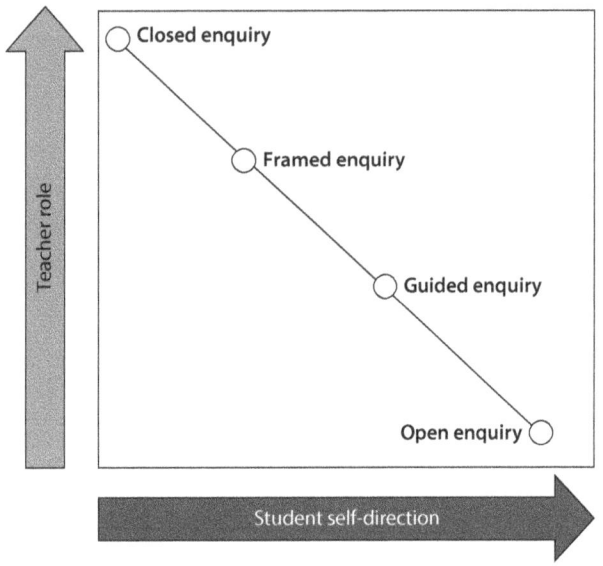

Figure 5.1: Progression in enquiry

The visual framework in Figure 5.1 shows the four levels of enquiry that I have adapted from Al-Momani (2019), incorporating ideas from Roberts (2023). At all stages, there should be teacher direction. Indeed, even at the pinnacle of A level – which is the NEA, an independent investigation – there will still be some teacher guidance. Not only that, but open enquiry is where students use their existing geographical knowledge to hypothesise and apply it to a new situation, rather than discovering new geography, whether for themselves or for the wider discipline.

The framework can be considered a progression of enquiry, where learners move from the top left to the bottom right over time. Self-direction and decision-making from students increase as we move into the bottom right of the framework. However, progress can also be non-linear. For example, planning in an open enquiry towards the end of Year 9 is a good way of maintaining engagement in lessons (particularly for those who have not chosen geography) and revisiting the knowledge taught during the entire key stage.

Table 5.1 on the next page describes each type of enquiry and gives an example. Progression moves from the top to the bottom.

Closed enquiries mean that the teacher is in control and learning outcomes are thus predictable. This approach is essential to ensure strong schema development and avoid the development of misconceptions. It also helps student motivation, which requires success in learning; too much struggle early on can demotivate young people.

When there is some secure learning in place, relinquishing control within defined content and boundaries helps young people to connect what they have learned to their own experiences. Open enquiries are – and should be – a rare event in the geography classroom. If a free choice is given, misconceptions can easily develop. As mentioned, even at the NEA level – and, indeed, even at undergraduate level – there is always some steer or restriction placed upon the choice by exam specifications and the expert guidance of a teacher.

What is the curriculum for?

Before expanding upon this model of progression, it is useful to pause to consider what the geography curriculum is aiming to achieve and, to an extent, what geography is. Many of the phrases prevalent now, whilst appealing, are not hugely useful when trying to establish the specifics of what should be taught and when – for example, Ofsted's (2019) mantra that students 'need to know more, remember more and be able to do more' or, for that matter, the aim for students to think, speak and act like geographers, which is often talked about by geography teachers.

The task of agreeing upon a progression model is also complicated by the fact that geographical knowledge (of which enquiry forms part of the discipline's procedural knowledge) is not arranged hierarchically but by its organising concepts, such as place and scale. This means that students come

Table 5.1: Descriptions and examples of each type of enquiry

Type of enquiry	Description	Examples
Closed enquiry	The teacher is in control of the enquiry, setting the question, providing material and deciding upon the content and skills. It leads to predictable outcomes and is great for tackling new content and ideas.	Students investigate land use in cities, using a range of resources selected by the teacher. Fieldwork investigations where students all complete the same tasks and reach a closed conclusion, such as 'Is there evidence of coastal processes at … ?'
Framed enquiry	The teacher remains in control of the question, content and material but may introduce a wider range of resources or evaluation techniques from which students have to choose. It leads to a wider range of student conclusions, depending on the choices made, although the same content is learned, just interpreted in different ways. There are a limited number of ways 'through' the enquiry.	The location factors of human activity – for example, asking students to evaluate the choice of location. The location factors remain the same, but their evaluation of its success will vary. A fieldwork question is set and students may choose which primary techniques they are going to employ. A pause point where students are asked to consider an overarching question, linking to the content of other units. A decision-making exercise in a GCSE exam paper.
Guided enquiry	This is like framed enquiry, but with greater student autonomy. The questions, resources and evaluation have choices but set within a curriculum area. The number of resources increases. Teachers provide feedback and point to prior learning to help students retrieve and apply knowledge to a new situation. Students may create their own questions before receiving feedback to hone them.	Students investigate microclimate by using thermometers located at different aspects of a building. After learning that aspect affects temperature, they can be challenged to create their own way of measuring weather variables around the school site. The NEA is a good example of a guided enquiry.
Open enquiry	Students choose the focus of the enquiry and make their own decisions about gathering and evaluating information and communicating their conclusions.	At the end of Year 9, students were given a free choice of enquiry, generating their question, finding their own information through homework and communicating this.

back to key concepts and content and practise their procedural knowledge when revisiting topics. In this way, the school geography curriculum can be thought of as a helix, rather than a map, with many interconnected facets.

Secondly, as the geography curriculum, including its content and procedural knowledge, does have some overarching fundamental ideas, it must also be contextualised to the school's location and young people. I'm an advocate of sitting down as a team and having rich conversations around the nature of geographical progression in *your* school. This is even more important when we consider the contested nature of geographical concepts.

Crucially, although I believe that enquiry is an essential part of every sequence of lessons at every key stage, it does need to fit into the external pressures, such as examination specifications. It must also align to what we know about how children learn, as previously discussed.

Start with the end in mind: Qualifications and qualities

I've always found it useful to start with the end in mind. When leading geography, we sat as a team to consider two things: with what qualifications *and* qualities do we want young people to leave at each stage of their education? We accepted that young people may leave geography education at the end of Key Stage 3 or go on to study at university. We accepted that the core purpose of geography was to prepare young people for the next stage of their education, and this meant gaining qualifications in external examinations.

Therefore, in terms of enquiry, we were aware that students would need to undertake their own independent enquiry at A level and that we had the responsibility to prepare them for that. In addition, we spent time considering what enquiry looked like at each stage of the learning journey. Not only is linking to the NEA important when preparing young people for their future education, but enquiring about the world and understanding it using existing knowledge is what geographers do.

We also considered the qualities and wider educational aims. These include developing a love for learning, providing meaningful experience, such as learning outside the classroom, developing an idea of personal agency and civic responsibility, and giving a sense of purpose and meaning. Remember, geographers enquire about the world so that we can make it better.

> **Reflection**
>
> Consider the following question: What qualifications and qualities do we want students who pass through our geography department to have by the end of each stage of their education?'
>
> Are your thoughts limited to external examination results or are they much wider?

What does 'thinking like a geographer' mean?

A student who *thinks like* a geographer is one that is curious about the world. Geographers want to understand the world. But what does that actually look like in the classroom, where the teacher's role is to cover content and knowledge whilst safeguarding against the development of misconceptions? This is where the academic world and the classroom environment diverge: we often do not have the time to debate the nature of what geography is. Whilst this is a shame in terms of workload, it is welcome. There is nothing wrong with taking documents that already exist and building our progression model around them.

There have been a few attempts to define what thinking like a geographer means. When considering them, it is important to note that learners in the classroom do not have the knowledge to be expert geographers.

> **Definition**
>
> **Thinking geographically:** Morgan (2013) concludes that 'thinking geographically' cannot be pinned down, and there have been many attempts to define what this term – widely used in geography classrooms and resources – means. It is a contested term. Here are some examples:
>
> - Bonnett (2008)
>   - Geography is what geographers do.
>   - Geographers attempt to find and impose order on a seemingly chaotic world.

> - Matthews and Herbert (2008)
>   - Geographers are the bridge between the human and natural sciences.
> - Jackson (2006)
>   - Geographers take everyday life and link to wider, abstract global features.
> - Gardner et al. (2024)
>   - Geographers build an understanding of how key concepts are interconnected.

This leaves work for teachers to do, using our professional knowledge of pedagogy, the curriculum and our students. As such, it is not for me – or any author – to present *the* definitive answer. Expanding upon Jackson's idea and work by geographers such as Alan Parkinson is how I have developed the pragmatic approach: geographers seek to understand their world so that they can make it better. They do so by making links between concepts and ideas.

For example, on the cover of Parkinson's 2020 book *Why Study Geography?*, there sits a simple pile of beans. The author points out that a geographer will see much more than this. They will wonder where the beans were produced and understand that their purchase opens up conversations around food miles, food security and links to global trade.

If we tie this back to enquiry, we want students to get better at asking questions, making their own observations, critically evaluating information and, in communicating geography through their writing, making conclusions and links between concepts. Starting with the students' lived experience, including the wide range of perspectives and backgrounds, we can then zoom out, layering the abstract onto this experience. This means that we help students to remember more as they build reliable schemas.

Activity

Take a moment to think and try not to look ahead! Define what a young person needs to do to 'think like a geographer'.

Table 5.2 was created by a former colleague, Jo Coles, and went through many iterations. It used the external exam specifications and created a graphic that could be used in all year groups. At first glance, it is clear that being a geographer requires a huge range of knowledge and skills, which is why planned progression is important: a Year 7 geography student will be unable to do many of these things well and will lack the detailed substantive knowledge required to reach informed conclusions.

Table 5.2: Think, apply, know and study like a geographer (with thanks to Jo Coles)

Apply like a geographer	Know like a geographer
Apply knowledge	Location and place
Apply procedural knowledge	Environments and resources
Fieldwork	Processes
Secondary research	Scale: local, national, global
Present coherent arguments	Context: social, environmental, economic, political
Link knowledge together	Geography of the UK
Justify and support views with evidence	Compare similarities and differences of places
Critically evaluate evidence	Human and physical characteristics
Consider different viewpoints and perspectives	
Study like a geographer	**Think like a geographer**
Maps skills and GIS	Link to sustainability
Research and data collection	Explain similarities and differences
Graphicacy	Evaluate and make recommendations
Data analysis	Make decisions
Enquiry and curiosity	How factors are interrelated
Independence	How people and their environment interact
Collaboration	How what is being studied changes over time and space
Literacy	How the environment and resources are managed

Looking at Table 5.2, thinking like a geographer means enquiry. The detail in this table applied to all key stages at our secondary school. It also served as an evaluation tool used by teachers and students. The language used created a common language that was used in department meetings and with students.

But how did we come up with this list? It was quite simple in the end. We looked at the GCSE specification and drew out the explicit reference to what young people had to do. Whilst this may not be the best source of information, it did relate to our context and our young people. We also couldn't find too much to argue about within it.

I argue that we should aim for our learners to think, speak and write like geographers; however, whilst everyone has experiences of geographical phenomena, the process of schooling turns young people into geographers, and this is a process that takes time.

Activity

Use Table 5.2, ideally when meeting other geographers in your school or local area. Which other aspects of being a geographer does enquiry link to? Which do you agree with? Are there any missing? Which would you not include?

Geographical concepts

We have already established that finding agreement on what geographical concepts and knowledge should be taught in schools is difficult. Personally, I would cover fewer topics in favour of developing a deeper understanding of the organising concepts of the subject.

What is critical is that there is a link between the abstract concepts (identified by the GA) of place, scale, the lived experience of young people and the enquiry questions that allow teachers to develop the knowledge and understanding needed. Brooks (2013) uses Taylor's approach here, and it is a useful way to illustrate how enquiry questions can provide a framework for young people to develop their understanding of geographical concepts.

The top hierarchical concepts, such as place, space and interconnectedness, can be explored though organisational concepts. For example, change can be used to generate enquiry questions. If we are finding out about a place, students can ask how it was different in the past or how it is viewed from different scales, from local to global. If we use the organisational concepts of perception and representation, students can ask how different people experience that place or how they communicate about it.

There is no universal agreement and this aspect of geography is contested. In this case, it would make sense to use the concepts in the GCSE or A level specification that you have chosen to identify the key concepts needed.

> **Reflection**
>
> Review your exam specifications. Do they explicitly mention their hierarchical and organising concepts? How do these translate into your Key Stage 3? What are the concepts that underpin geographical knowledge in your department?

What do the examination specifications say?

Whilst I would stress that examination specifications are not the curriculum, they are a very useful starting point when considering progression. This is because, in a secondary setting, our job is to ensure that every individual leaves with the very best GCSE in geography that we can. When looking at specifications, some of the following skills are often cited as an outcome. For example, successful GCSE students will be able to:

- infer human activity from map evidence
- link different geographical topics synoptically
- apply relevant geographical knowledge to unseen contexts
- interpret and draw evidenced conclusions from a range of different types of data
- write evidenced and informed conclusions about geographical questions and issues
- identify a successful sequence of enquiry.

From looking at examination specifications, in order to be successful at GCSE, students need to master the enquiry approach. In other words, they must think and communicate *like* geographers. To become fluent at these aspects of enquiry, it is vital that students are exposed to high-quality and challenging work from lesson one of Year 7, exposing them to the enquiry approach. Indeed, we used to challenge Year 9 geographers with tackling their own independent enquiry. Whilst not as sophisticated as a GCSE project, it was an opportunity for them to test their knowledge and skills

Finally, enquiry gives us a chance to pause and allow young people to not only consolidate and revisit their existing knowledge but also practise their fluency in key procedural knowledge. It is why, when I was a head of geography, enquiry was an integral part of every sequence of lessons. We can teach through enquiry as well as teach how to complete an enquiry. We can have teacher-led lessons that use enquiry as the lens and ensure that young people are taught the content they need. I would argue that to develop the synoptic knowledge demanded for success at GCSE and A level, enquiry must be used so that students can pause and think hard about some overarching geographical questions.

Progression maps

It is difficult to offer a complete progression map for enquiry, as much of it depends on the knowledge and skills of individual students and the context of your institution. Not only that, but enquiry can also be seen as a continuum, as teachers will move between closed, framed and open enquiry, matching the approach to what is most appropriate for the content being learned. Similarly, students will move from concrete teacher-led examples to more abstract knowledge, where the teacher will guide and monitor students so that misconceptions are not developed.

Having said this, once we have the end-points that we wish to reach, we can use them to plan for progression. Essentially, students should be able to carry out their own independent enquiry at some point. In addition, remember that students are not creating new knowledge. They are learning knowledge new to them and making connections between that knowledge and knowledge that they already have. In the later stages of their school journey, they will need to recall this knowledge and apply it to new situations. This could be an unseen scenario or an event in the news that is being considered in a lesson.

I agree with Margaret Roberts and her assertion that the role of the teacher is crucial in developing both enquiry and geographical knowledge. Geography teachers are the experts and professionals employed to teach geographical knowledge. It is our job to ensure that we do not introduce open-ended enquiries too soon. This would place too much extraneous load on students and has been shown not to allow students to experience success.

Table 5.3: An enquiry progression map (based on Roberts, 2023 and Kirschner and Hendrick, 2020)

Progression →

Type of enquiry	Closed	Framed/guided	Open
Role of the teacher	More teacher explanation and guidance		Less teacher guidance and explanation
Role of the student	Learning new content and knowledge through lessons		Applying existing knowledge to novel situations
Perspective	Decided upon by the teacher, curriculum or specification but clearly communicated	Some choice of perspective	Students use their own lived experience and perspectives to frame the enquiry
Ask geographical questions	Focus of enquiry and questions decided by the teacher/curriculum	Students use scaffolding to create their own geographical questions within the topic studied	Students decide upon the questions and focus of the enquiry
Gather information	Information is selected and presented by the teacher/curriculum; teachers explain why geographers find the information useful	The teacher provides a range of information sources and students gather their own secondary and primary information, with guidance from the teacher	Students plan their own data collection from primary and secondary sources

Type of enquiry	Closed	Framed/guided	Open
Critically evaluate information	Sequences of lessons and guided activities set by the teacher are tackled by students; the teacher explicitly explains and models the procedural knowledge needed to evaluate the information	Students independently evaluate information following step-by-step guides and help from the teacher	Students independently select the best way to evaluate the information gathered.
Communicate	There are predictable outcomes using a limited range of perspectives and viewpoints; students answer exam-style questions	Using writing models, students present a written alternative viewpoint to their own	Students reach their own conclusions and use a range of perspectives and viewpoints to inform their justified conclusions
Critically evaluate the enquiry	Students are taught about the limitations of the enquiry	Students identify limitations of their work	Students self-reflect and identify the limitations of their work and the impact of them upon their conclusions and future study
Cognitive science	Worked examples and modelling	Students follow the sequence of steps to a new task or complete assignments that are partially complete	Students solve a problem without any support
Summary	The teacher ensures that geographical content is learned without misconceptions being developed	Students apply their knowledge to a novel situation that the teacher has chosen	Students apply their existing knowledge to a novel situation that they have chosen

The next chapter considers what a curriculum that supports enquiry could look like. The spoiler is that it is very likely to be the curriculum that you have already crafted and sequenced with care. What we need to do is ensure that there are opportunities to bump into enquiry at every stage and in every lesson. Therefore, students will become more fluent, more confident and more successful, both in external examinations and when navigating through their own personal geographies.

Key takeaways

- Enquiry must be sequenced to show clear progression in both substantive and procedural knowledge.
- Students gradually move from closed, teacher-led enquiries to guided and open enquiries, with autonomy increasing over time.
- Teacher guidance and explicit instruction remain essential throughout, to prevent misconceptions developing and to manage cognitive load.
- 'Thinking like a geographer' involves curiosity, linking concepts, applying knowledge and making informed conclusions.
- Enquiry integrates substantive knowledge with procedural knowledge.
- Progression must be contextualised to the school, curriculum and student needs.

6 What are the features of an enquiry curriculum?

> **In this chapter**
>
> So far, we have learned that psychology and cognitive science provide us with the permission to pursue an enquiry curriculum, informed by some of the fundamental principles of educational research. This chapter will demonstrate how this could look at the curriculum scale, zooming out before we zoom into sequences of lessons and individual activities. This chapter highlights how enquiry acts as the golden thread that runs through the geography curriculum, shaping not only what is taught but also how students learn to think, question and connect knowledge. It emphasises the importance of a curriculum built and owned by expert teachers that is contextualised to local needs and responds to the dynamic nature of the subject. Rather than a static product, the curriculum is presented as a living framework that evolves.

Thinking about the curriculum

I remember, as a new and eager head of geography, wishing that I could find a curriculum somewhere. Of course, this was an impossible task and also undesirable, as a curriculum should be contextualised to the institution and learners. Whilst this may seem like an unnecessary workload burden, I became a secondary geography teacher because I love thinking about the curriculum. The collegiate approach to curriculum-making was one of the highlights of the job, whether through departmental meetings, local network groups or national and international networks facilitated through social media. I would not have been satisfied to be a simple deliverer of a curriculum handed to me.

To be effective, the curriculum must be developed by the local team of geography teachers and contextualised to its location. I realised early on that geographical enquiry is what makes geography geographical. I wanted to use enquiry as the main lever to drive and improve the non-existent curriculum that I had inherited. I wanted students to leave not only with a great GCSE grade but having had the opportunity to work like a geographer and think like a geographer, as well as getting involved in trying to change their world at a school scale. This wasn't always successful, but did allow students to understand how the world works!

The GA has produced an excellent framework for starting to think about the geography curriculum; however, it is likely, given Ofsted's focus upon the curriculum, that yours needs review rather than complete overhaul.

Whilst I do believe that, as expert geographers, we do not do anything purely for Ofsted or SLT, this does not reflect the current reality of school classrooms. We are in an accountability culture, where external and internal forces outside of the geography team shape the decisions and learning experiences in the classroom.

I would urge you to be brave, though. Use what we have discussed thus far and argue well. Here, I do not set out to present a completed geography curriculum nor a step-by-step guide to how to integrate enquiry into your existing curriculum. To do so would be to assume that what you have now isn't up to the job. What I would say is that if you are able to weave these features into your existing curriculum, it will be even better. Students will leave ready for the next stage of their academic and non-academic lives, with the qualifications and qualities needed.

Of course, I recognise that undertaking a curriculum change is a huge piece of work. It is also one that never ends – and nor should it! Indeed, the Priory School geography curriculum was never a finished product and, even with a blank slate, it took a continued programme of development year on year. Consider Figure 6.1. The first model is the ideal model, which many assume to be school geography. However, our beautiful subject is dynamic if it is to reflect the world outside. Seemingly simple changes, such as a pandemic, or India eclipsing China as the most populous country, have seismic ripples that reverberate throughout our subject. In other words, it doesn't stay still. A small change or new knowledge in one area impacts on many, due to the interrelated nature of the concepts that we teach.

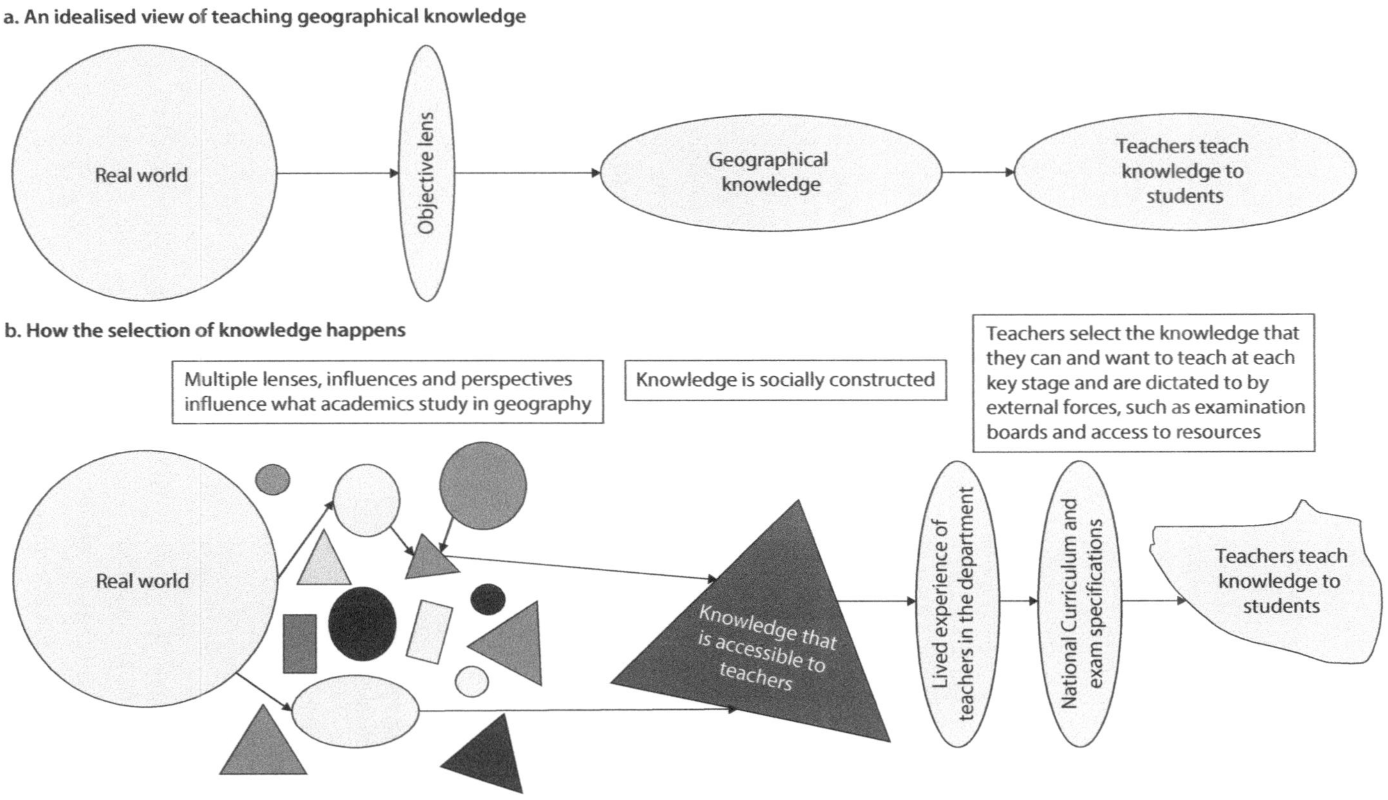

a. An idealised view of teaching geographical knowledge

Real world → Objective lens → Geographical knowledge → Teachers teach knowledge to students

b. How the selection of knowledge happens

Multiple lenses, influences and perspectives influence what academics study in geography

Knowledge is socially constructed

Teachers select the knowledge that they can and want to teach at each key stage and are dictated to by external forces, such as examination boards and access to resources

Real world → Knowledge that is accessible to teachers → Lived experience of teachers in the department → National Curriculum and exam specifications → Teachers teach knowledge to students

Figure 6.1: Idealised teaching versus how knowledge really happens

What are the features of an enquiry curriculum?

What the curriculum isn't

No school geography curriculum is ever going to cover the entire body of geographical knowledge. In Early Years to Key Stage 3 in particular, we should aim to cover less in more depth, giving space to develop and practise geographical enquiry and develop an understanding of the key concepts at the heart of the subject, taking time to pause to be able to develop students' synoptic knowledge.

In addition, expert teams of geography teachers need to be aware of not only their own perspectives, shaped by their lived experiences and unconscious bias, but also those of the knowledge that they select to include in the curriculum. We need to be able to justify its inclusion in our own school curricula. We simply cannot cover it all. School geography, quite simply, is not and cannot be 'everything'.

Similarly, a GCSE specification is not a curriculum. Think about how it fits into the entire learning journey. For example, as a head of geography, I always used to teach economic development as the first unit at GCSE, as it underpins everything that follows. But it wasn't the first time young people had encountered the ideas and content required, as we pulled this into Key Stage 3. We decided to teach procedural knowledge within a geographical context, so out went the maps unit, for example, to be replaced with a tour of the main organising concepts of geography though a wide variety of examples. From the outset, this allowed students to develop enquiry but also hammered home the synoptic nature of the subject.

> **Example**
>
> Chapter 3 (pages 60–63) contained the first sequence of lessons for Year 7 when arriving. The enquiry questions were:
>
> 1. How do I ask geographical questions?
> 2. Does new technology always mean better? How can geographers find out about places?
> 3. Where on Earth is Iceland?
> 4. How does folklore connect Icelanders to Iceland?
> 5. Does Iceland exist?

> 6. How sustainable is Iceland?
> 7. How sustainable is Dubai?
> 8. How are Earth's natural wonders used by people?
> 9. Do we feel connected to nature? If not, what can we do about it?
> 10. What's causing the hassle at Heathrow?
>
> Note that there was no 'What is geography?' lesson. We simply got on with *doing* geography.

During such units, teachers can pause to consider the nature of the subject. This can be done by starting an explanation with 'as geographers, we approach this in this way, because…'. We don't need to divide the subject into physical and human when we could introduce the key organising concepts in an age-appropriate way straight away.

Enquiry provides the golden thread that weaves its way through the curriculum. Whilst the content may change and be selected, the enquiry approach provides the procedural knowledge and tools to teach the geography that we select.

Features of an enquiry curriculum

As mentioned, enquiry is the cornerstone of geography. Presented here is a series of features that a successful enquiry curriculum will have. By successful, I mean that students leave ready for the next stage of their education and with great qualifications. It is not expected that it will lead to an overhaul of your existing curriculum, but it is a tool for auditing what you have and making tweaks.

1. The curriculum should be challenging, inspiring and driven by expert teachers

This may seem obvious, but geography teachers are subject experts and bring different perspectives, knowledge and experiences. Geography teachers should drive the curriculum, not non-specialist SLT or those without knowledge of your context. It is essential that subject meeting time is used to focus on continued curriculum development and our own subject knowledge.

> **Reflection**
>
> Consider your own curriculum:
>
> - Does every teacher in your institution know what they are teaching and why?
> - Have case studies and examples been contextualised or selected because of the ease and accessibility of resources?
> - Do you have a clear plan of curriculum evaluation and development?
> - Is your curriculum dynamic or fixed?

2. The curriculum should be one unified curriculum

I see the geography curriculum as being one unified journey throughout your institution. Yes, at certain stages students may opt out, but compartmentalising Key Stage 4 from 3 doesn't allow the coherent development of enquiry. Your curriculum may be one that starts in the Early Years and finishes at GCSE. It may be an 11–16 one. It should certainly consider the stages before and after the stage of learning with which you directly come into contact.

Whilst the learning pathways published on many school websites often show this overview, they fail to communicate the interconnected nature of the geography curriculum, especially when it comes to procedural knowledge and enquiry. In this way, a carefully sequenced geography curriculum will always be revisiting past concepts and examples.

If your school teaches to A level, then it makes sense to use the specification's key concepts to organise the entire curriculum, from the first moment at which students come into contact with the subject in your school.

3. The curriculum should be diverse and representative

The geography curriculum must represent your school's cohort and its community. It must also look outwards to faraway places and contrasting places. Schools are not detached from their local area. It is useful, when considering the selection of case studies, enquiry foci and examples, to start from different places. Is the climate crisis seen the same in Mali as it is in the United Kingdom? Whilst geography can be '*wonderfully* vast' (Freeman, 2024, p. 6), that doesn't mean that we have to teach it all. Young people need to feel a sense of belonging in your classroom if they are to become successful geographers.

Enquiry and the features of most geography teachers lend themselves well to challenging established or presented viewpoints. We can simply ask the questions and encourage students to ask them:

- What other viewpoints are there?
- Who created this geographical knowledge?
- Is this model of the world appropriate to what we know now?

> **Example**
>
> There has been great work in the area of challenging Rostow's (1959) model of development, and changes are starting to be reflected in published materials and specifications. Hannah Steel (2023) has used enquiry questions so that students can challenge this contentious model:
>
> - 'To what extent does Rostow's model not account for the impact of development on marginalised groups in Ethiopia?
> - How does Rostow's model ignore the impacts of social and environmental well-being in LIDCs [low income developing countries]?'
>
> This approach allows us to develop students' critical skills and understand how our current understanding of development has been reached.

4. The curriculum should incorporate 'floating topicality'

As a young geography teacher, I was lucky to encounter Jeff Stanfield. As the Hampshire geography inspector, I remember vividly when he came to observe a lesson during my second year of teaching. I had been moved into an English classroom because of building work and I was then told that the inspector would be along to observe my lesson. It went well and Jeff ignited a passion in me, nudging me from someone who was there to do a job and enjoy the holidays to a geography advocate. Jeff has had a significant impact on my approach to teaching geography, and one of his key ideas is 'floating topicality'.

Floating topicality is sequencing the curriculum in such a way that it is more likely that events will happen 'in the real world' as they are being studied in the classroom. Although we cannot predict earthquakes, coups and a wide range of other phenomena, for others we have a fairly good idea of when they may occur. For example, teaching about the sequence of a depression as it travels across the UK is infinitely easier when tackled in the autumn or spring terms, when a sequence of depressions is more likely to be in effect. Similarly, UK flooding is more likely at certain times of the year and tropical storms are more likely to coincide with others.

Floating topicality also gives permission to pause the curriculum for students to consider the impacts of a significant event. This must be done with considerable thought and sensitivity. For example, leaping to teach the latest disaster whilst the rescue operation is occurring is not a good idea. However, in our geography classrooms we used geography in the news with all year groups as both a retrieval activity and a chance to consider how our existing knowledge is connected to it.

Floating topicality allows us to show that geography is a concrete subject that is alive and happening outside the classroom every day, rather than a fossilised, vague subject that happens in the past. I give some examples of floating topicality in Chapter 9.

5. The curriculum should be driven by key questions that span sequences of lessons

Much has been written about the use of 'fertile' questions to frame units of work. The main workhorse of a geography curriculum is the scheme of work. As the Ofsted report (2023a) identifies, enquiries that are fully embedded within the curriculum rather than added on are more successful. In other words, students know more, remember more and are able to do more linked to that particular content. This means that enquiry must weave its way through the curriculum, rather than being consigned to small chunks of time or fieldwork activities.

For me, sometimes it is useful to have one single question that spans a sequence of lessons. At Key Stage 3 in particular, there is no need to be shackled by a half-term-long unit. Yes, there are assessment points where data needs to be fed into whole-school systems, but they don't necessarily need to be at the end of a unit. Nor do they have to be confined to the content taught in that unit.

At other times, a question may span a single lesson. For example, 'Does Iceland exist?' is a lesson based upon the phenomena of phantom islands appearing in Google Maps (see Map Men, 2024). This Year 7 lesson examples the reliability of information and demonstrates that geographers need multiple sources of information. Students use computers to triangulate information. After all, if Google Maps can be wrong, what can we trust? Whilst this may seem a random lesson after a lesson on Iceland, it also introduces students to being able to question the teacher. After all, geographers should be able to disagree well and challenge everyone's assumptions. Is this knowledge true just because my teacher told me? What other perspectives are there?

6. The curriculum should aim to eliminate single stories by clustering examples and case studies that are informed by your context

In a time-pressured curriculum, we can be in danger of rushing through content and not really thinking carefully about its selection. For example, back in 2010, during the eruption of Eyjafjallajökull, you would be forgiven for thinking that the entirety of Iceland was destroyed by the apocalypse, as the 24-hour news services led with startling, attention-grabbing images and headlines. This found its way into geography classrooms without the wider context being considered. Iceland as a whole was barely affected by the eruption, despite it causing widespread disruption to other places. If we only ever use faraway places, like Iceland, to look at the contrasts a place has with the United Kingdom, or look at the spectacle of an eruption, students are in danger of developing misconceptions about those places. In this case, students will remember Iceland for this single eruption rather than its well-thought-out and practised response or most of the country's population being unaffected. As James Esson argues in an episode of GeogPod (GA, 2024b), geographers should start with the similarities and some wider context about a place before considering the case study material.

There is a tension between the demands of GCSE specifications, particularly around the topic of global development, where oversimplification, stereotyping and misrepresentation of the colonial past that develops an 'us and them' narrative (Winter, 2023) can be countered by including these places at Key Stage 3. Enquiry provides the vehicle to explore places fully, helping to tackle the tension between ensuring that young people pass examinations and students' own lived experiences out of school. Whilst we wait for a reform of the exam specifications that encourages anti-racist geographies, this seems like a way forward. It would also be refreshing to see research in this area outside of global development.

7. The curriculum should be living and flexible

Our subject is constantly changing and the curriculum needs to reflect that. Early in my career, there were many fossilised parts of the curriculum. They were detached from both the lived experience of students and also university geography. Whilst there have been great strides in this, especially at Key Stages 3 and 5, our subject is constantly shifting. It is the role of geography teachers to teach great geographical enquiry and content despite the limitations of GCSE. This is a professional challenge that should be relished, and enquiry provides the vehicle and lens to enable this.

Enquiry allows teachers to reduce workload, as its toolbox of activities and approaches (examples of which are covered in Part 2 of this book) can be tweaked and applied to this new knowledge. '"Living Geography" is geography that is alive and relevant. It supports and encourages curiosity about the wider world through an enquiry approach and develops pupils' ability to give creative and critical responses to everyday issues.' (GA, 2008)

Simply by including the question 'is this the most up-to-date information?', we provide a road map into keeping the curriculum relevant. Of course, no discussion around relevance is complete without considering how old case studies should be. As mentioned, geography *should* aim to reflect the real world outside of the classroom. However, how far back we go is important.

> ### Example
>
> The Aral Sea was included as part of a unit on crime and asked students the enquiry question: 'Is what has happened to the Aral Sea a crime?'. This was answered after a sequence of lessons that introduced the area and its historical context, linked with the USSR and the causes of the shrinking of the Aral Sea and its effects on the local population and landscape. We also asked: 'How do we restore the Aral Sea?'.
>
> An even more pertinent question is: 'Which version of the Aral Sea should we be aiming to restore?' The answers to these questions all depend on how far back we go.

8. The curriculum should recognise that geographical knowledge is messy and contested

If we sit several geographers in a room, they are likely to arrive at a slightly different set of core concepts that should be used to organise the curriculum. Similarly, geographical knowledge is often not universal. There is a difference between a different viewpoint and a misconception. Geography should be real and contextualised, which means that we must also include voices with which we would disagree.

Lambert and Morgan (2010) observe that geographical concepts have 'multiple meanings that cannot be reduced to a single straightforward definition'. In addition, geographical concepts change and are created in response to changes in the natural and human worlds. For example, take the pandemic or the change to the position of the United Kingdom in the world after Brexit. Finally, ways of looking at the world, such as regional geography, fall out of favour only to re-emerge later.

Similarly, as geographers, we must treat grand claims and models, such as 'the world is shrinking', with caution. Whilst travel time has reduced dramatically over the years and globalisation has meant that the same stuff can be found all over the world, both are unequally accessed. It still matters where you are. The rise of social media and the easy access to a wealth of information means that the media can 'misrepresent some of the changes that are happening to suit their own agenda' (Parkinson, 2020, p. 7). As teachers, we need to be aware of this.

We only need to look at Trump's first 100 days in office in 2025 to see how quickly things change, and in the age of the algorithm, geographical enquiry has a key role.

9. The curriculum should include moral and ethical aspects

When training to teach at the University of Durham, I was introduced to the idea of moral dilemmas. It is true that most decisions we face are not a simple choice between good and bad. They are almost always different shades of bad. Take the example of international tourism. We could use the enquiry question 'Is tourism good or bad?', but this would not look at contextual information and really probe a real location. Certainly, students need to be furnished with the potential benefits and costs of tourism, perhaps using Butler's (1980) tourism area life cycle model (including its limitations) to look at how geographers have described tourism.

Students could map where they live to Butler's model – for example, my son always wonders why tourists bother to visit Worthing or Brighton. Students can also consider a range of overseas and UK locations. Why, for example, is Margate so keen to attract tourists? What if we took away tourism from some areas? Students often feel uncomfortable within geography because there are often no 'correct' answers to some of the questions. Introducing and practising this early on is vital in order to counter it.

> ### Definition
>
> **Butler's model:** Butler's tourism area life cycle model describes how tourist destinations change over time. It begins with *discovery*, where few intrepid tourists visit, followed by *growth and development*, where investment and tourist numbers increase. *Success* follows, leading to even more tourists and development, which then leads to a *problem*, such as a lack of sufficient sanitation services to cope with the tourist numbers. This is followed by *stagnation* and then *decline*, where visitor numbers drop.

This is an example of where students communicate their findings by arriving at different conclusions. In this example, the information can support a range of conclusions. Students can communicate these whilst learning to disagree well. Indeed, their opinion will almost certainly shift through time as more information comes to light. Such units of work may be better placed when students have a good understanding of the underlying content and impacts, helping to prepare them for the 'to what extent do you agree?'-style questions at GCSE.

10. The curriculum should combine physical and human geography

Whilst the separate substantive knowledge is useful to consider in isolation, enquiry can provide the pause points where the human and physical worlds combine. After all, geography is about the interaction between people and their environment and, at least in the UK, there are no 'natural' spaces that are untouched or influenced by people. For example, the geomorphic features of a river such as the Arun or Adur cannot be understood in isolation from the surrounding land use and effort to protect land from the annual flooding that occurs. Decisions to allow coastal erosion to take place or to 'hold the line' need to be understood in the context of the political divisions of the landscape, as well as the economic value of the land. Take, for example, Highcliffe and Barton on Sea – two very different approaches within a few steps of each other, resulting in different landscapes.

11. The curriculum should demand that students think hard

If learning is the residue of thought, then enquiry allows us to create a curriculum that asks young people to pause and think hard. Pauses can be given in the curriculum, not only to consider opportunities presented by floating topicality, but also to combine several geographical units to a new situation. This allows students to retrieve and apply their existing knowledge in the pursuit of answering a question.

Such skills and knowledge are needed for students to successfully tackle decision-making-style papers. To adequately prepare for these, opportunities for decision-making and for applying existing knowledge to new situations must be provided for throughout the curriculum.

12. The curriculum should include shared resources

If a curriculum is to be living, it must be easily adaptable. However, a constantly changing subject can lead to increased workload issues. I can certainly remember sticking with the existing content rather than spending a few hours updating it.

A successful enquiry curriculum should have shared teaching resources; this ensures that there is an entitlement between different teaching groups, but also saves time. In addition, using a service such as Google Docs, together with Google Drive means that changes can easily be added and changed by anyone. Tweaking a lesson with a new resource is much easier when everyone can access that resource.

13. The curriculum should include opportunities to put action into real spaces (advocacy)

Great geographers understand the world so that they can change it. I am sure that you can think of several issues that students would like to make better in your own institution. This doesn't have to be large in scale and it shouldn't take up a lot of space in the curriculum.

> **Example**
>
> **How representative is our school's physical space of its community?**
>
> This enquiry question was tackled each year by Year 9 students at Priory School. Students were given several data-collection techniques, as well as the secondary data built up over time. This included analysing anonymised datasets, including protected characteristics of the student and staff body. Students then mapped the school's physical environment, making a note of signage and making qualitative judgements around how they felt about locations. This led to individual students writing up their investigation and conclusions, including some recommendations. For example, signage was only in English when there were 39 languages spoken by students and staff at home.
>
> Students also timed how long it took to get around the school, linked to different disabilities, such as being partially sighted or in a wheelchair. Their conclusion was that access to education was not equal for all young people. This went against the published aims of the school.
>
> Students were then selected to present their findings to SLT and lobby for changes. The reality? Changes were slow, but that reflects real life and allows conversation around how real change happens. What was clear was that the geography classrooms did change, ensuring that all our community saw their place in the curriculum.

This example shows how students can be engaged with change in their setting and use enquiry to provide well-researched and -argued ideas. After all, great geographers understand their world so that they can change it for the better. The procedural knowledge used was bumped into in subsequent units.

14. The curriculum should tackle big datasets

Finally, a curriculum that develops geographical enquiry should tackle large real-world datasets. There is a wealth of freely available data, such as that from the 2021 census. Combine this with programmes like Esri's Digimap (free to schools) or even Excel, and it is possible to interrogate and understand data quickly. Why take an interpretation of migration statistics when we can go to the source? It also allows us to explore the best way to present such data, as well as its limitations.

For example, when looking at the ability to speak Welsh in the 2021 census (ONS, 2023), one is presented with the information that the census was undertaken during a period of rapid change, and therefore users should take care when using the data.

This immediately sparks curiosity and enquiry questions. What were the causes of the rapid change in 2021? What impact will that have on the reliability of the data presented? Why are they only estimates? These are limitations that are not usually included in sensational headlines or the soundbites of politicians.

When we delve into the information, we find all sorts of patterns, which in themselves spark questions. For example, why does there appear to be a Welsh-speaking community in Darlington?

An example of a curriculum

As we have established, sitting down as a department and deciding what an enquiry curriculum looks like in your context is vital. In Table 6.1, I share an example from Kate Stockings. This curriculum, from the outset, defines what enquiry is and, more importantly, what it isn't. Fundamentally, the curriculum set out to enable young people to be able to answer the enquiry – or fertile – question by the end of the unit. It is an excellent example of where geography can thrive with its own distinctive pedagogy, whilst retaining what we know about how young people learn.

Table 6.1: 2022–23 Hampstead School geography curriculum rationale (with thanks to Kate Stockings)

Our enquiry approach is not…	Aiming to teach students generic skills through geography; geographical knowledge lies at the heart of our enquiry questions.
	Simply finding answers to questions. A culture of learning and geographical thinking is built: students are required to reason and think critically.
	Problem-based learning; it is not student-led and it is not open-ended. Our enquiry questions are strongly teacher-guided, disseminating knowledge from the subject specialist to our students.
Our enquiry approach is an approach to teaching geography that…	**How is this achieved?**
Covers a range of approaches used in the classroom to ensure that students are actively engaged in investigating questions, problems and issues.	Students are aware of the key questions that frame units of work; these questions act as a 'hook' in students' minds and are referred to at the end of each lesson.

These questions suggest that what is being studied is something to be investigated, rather than something simply to be transmitted. |
Aims to establish a classroom culture in which there is a 'need to know' and so constant questioning is valued.	
Is question-driven. Schemes of work are focused on investigating interesting and challenging geographical questions – none of the questions can be answered with a simple 'yes' or 'no'.	
Allows students to extend their geographical knowledge and understanding at the same time as they learn skills – skills that are specific to geography and generic skills used in other subjects and contexts.	
Enables students to connect their prior knowledge and experience with what they are investigating. They make connections between what they already know and new information.	Explicit links and connections are made in the topic overview documents and in the lessons; 'link' boxes are used in lesson presentations.

Shows students that enquiry should be supported by evidence. Sources help students make sense of what they are studying, support their arguments and justify their conclusions.	Students study multiple sources of geographical information. Examples include reading book chapters or articles, studying data or collecting their own data.
Allows students to reflect and be critical. Students become critical of what has been learned, the criteria used to make judgements and how the enquiry could be developed further.	Students are given a task at the end of each unit to reflect on the extent to which they have answered or explored the questions posed at the outset. As part of this task, they reflect on the extent to which the evidence was sufficient, on whether the techniques they have used to analyse or interpret were appropriate and whether the conclusions and judgements they reached were sufficiently supported by the evidence.

If we look at one unit as an example, in Table 6.2 we see that the sequence of learning is structured around enabling young people to be able to answer the question at the end, whilst defining the key knowledge that needs to be taught.

Table 6.2: Example of enquiry through a unit of learning

Topic: Tectonics

Fertile question: Why are some volcanoes and earthquakes more deadly than others?

Lesson	Core knowledge	Links forward/back
L1 Introduction	• Japan is more developed than Haiti. • The 2010 Haiti earthquake killed more people than the Japanese earthquake of 2011. • Evidence from development indicators suggests that the Haiti earthquake would be more deadly and have a greater impact.	• BACK: To consideration of development in Year 8 'Development' and Year 7 'Almighty dollar'

(Continued)

Table 6.2: Continued

Lesson	Core knowledge	Links forward/back
L2 Plate tectonics	• The earth's crust is divided into tectonic plates. • Convergent boundaries result in the strongest earthquakes and most explosive volcanoes. • Divergent boundaries result in more gentle volcanoes and earthquakes. • Conservative boundaries result in strong earthquakes. • The Japan earthquake happened on a convergent boundary, whereas Haiti was on a conservative boundary.	• FORWARD: GCSE 'Tectonics' • FORWARD: L6 and types of volcanoes
L3 Magnitude vs. location	• The magnitude of an earthquake tells us how powerful it is. • Earthquakes are measured on the Richter scale. • The stronger the earthquake on the Richter scale, the more likely there is to be severe damage. • The shallower the focus, the more likely there is to be severe damage. • The closer the epicentre to a major population centre, the more people are likely to be affected.	
L4 Haiti earthquake	• The Haiti earthquake of 2010 caused severe primary and secondary impacts. • Haiti is still recovering from the earthquake, despite lots of international aid.	• BACK: To consideration of development in Year 8 'Development' and Year 7 'Almighty dollar'
L5 Haiti's vulnerability	• Haiti is vulnerable to natural disasters because of the location, the deforestation of the island and the legacy of colonialism.	• FORWARD: GCSE 'Development' and the factors that cause inequality
L6 Impacts on Japan	• The main impacts of the Japan earthquake of 2011 were infrastructure damage. • Because it is so developed, Japan is able to make its buildings hazard-resistant.	• BACK: To consideration of development in Year 8 'Development' and Year 7 'Almighty dollar' • BACK: To consideration of the importance of infrastructure in Year 7 'Almighty dollar'

L7 Tsunami	• A tsunami is caused by an underwater earthquake. • The wave forms because of the displacement of the ocean. • The tsunami in the 2011 earthquake caused most of the deaths.	
L8 Types of volcano	• There are two types of volcano: shield and composite. • Shield volcanoes are found on divergent plate boundaries and are gentler and less explosive. • Composite volcanoes are found on convergent plate boundaries and are more explosive.	• FORWARD: GCSE 'Tectonics'
L9 Pompeii	• Mount Vesuvius is a composite volcano that erupted in 79 AD. • This eruption killed thousands of people and destroyed the town of Pompeii, mainly due to the pyroclastic flow.	• BACK: L6 and types of volcanoes
Assessment	Why are some volcanoes and earthquakes more deadly than others? Essay plus 20-marks knowledge quiz.	
Locational knowledge	Location of Haiti and Japan throughout.	

Balancing key knowledge with flexibility

I do not subscribe to the view that teachers should be passive deliverers of a curriculum. Scripted lessons and a homogenous approach do not reflect the diverse nature of geography. Having said that, it is vital that there is a clear entitlement of all students to encounter the same knowledge; this is a moral imperative, as well as being vital to pass external examinations.

The following extract from a scheme of work in Table 6.3, driven by key questions, provides the key knowledge and activities, whilst also suggesting optional ideas. The document was 'living' on a cloud platform; colleagues added in extra ideas and resources, in turn making the curriculum living.

The Power of Geographical Enquiry

Table 6.3: Example extract from a scheme of work

Key question number	Key question we are learning	Common knowledge and activities	Suggested activities/ opportunities for further development	Resources
1.	What is migration and why do people move?	<ul><li>Definitions of key terms.</li><li>Different perspectives of why people move – starting in different places.</li><li>Using development data from different 'source' and 'destination' countries.</li><li>Models of migration, including Lee's push–pull model and how useful it is.</li><li>Lived experience of migration – teacher and class.</li><li>How do we know that migration statistics are accurate? Limitations.</li></ul>	Examination of current news stories. Do textbooks hold the truth? Impact of UK migration to places such as Spain. Migration in popular culture.	*Westside Story* and lyrics. Definition matching. Link to PowerPoint.

Activity

Take the numbered headings from this chapter and audit your existing curriculum. This is best done in a departmental meeting through conversation. You should also consider the context of your curriculum, including the educational outcomes as they are now.

The curriculum should:

- be challenging, inspiring and driven by expert teachers
- be one unified curriculum
- be diverse and representative
- incorporate 'floating topicality'
- be driven by questions that span sequences of lessons
- aim to eliminate single stories by clustering examples and case studies that are informed by your context
- be living and flexible
- recognise that geographical knowledge is messy and contested
- include moral and ethical aspects
- combine physical and human geography
- demand that students think hard
- include shared resources
- include opportunities to put real action into spaces (advocacy)
- tackle big datasets.

Key takeaways

- Enquiry provides the unifying thread that links knowledge, skills and concepts across the geography curriculum.
- Geography curricula must be adapted by teachers so that they are contextualised and responsive to change.
- The geography curriculum is dynamic and should evolve in relation to new events, new geographical knowledge and the changing experiences of learners.
- Diversity, representation and tackling single stories are central to a meaningful geography enquiry curriculum.
- A strong enquiry curriculum prepares students for success in qualifications and for developing the qualities to think like geographers.

PART 2

What does enquiry look like in the secondary classroom?

We have learned that enquiry must be defined and contextualised by expert teachers working in their individual contexts. It requires teacher-led activities, and new content and skills are encountered and can provide pause points, where the synoptic nature of our subject can be fully grasped.

Educational research does not provide any evidence that enquiry does not work, and there are powerful reasons for including enquiry in our classrooms. This means that we need to work together in teams to create a curriculum driven by enquiry.

This section aims to present a range of practical ideas for developing enquiry across sequences of lessons. Each chapter will examine one stage of the enquiry model presented in Chapter 2 (page 36), beginning with a more detailed version of the boxes presented in the model to exemplify what is included. The chapters will then delve deeper into each stage, giving a range of practical examples. Remember that although the mode of enquiry presented in this book is a cycle, each part can be taught independently.

7 How do we ask geographical questions?

In this chapter

This chapter explores the central role of questioning in the enquiry approach showing how high-quality geographical questions spark curiosity, frame learning and connect classroom geography with students' own experiences of the world. We consider what makes a question distinctly geographical, how complexity develops over time and why teacher guidance is essential in shaping progression, from simple factual enquiries to complex ones that answer huge, overarching fertile questions. Practical strategies are shared to allow students to formulate, refine and evaluate questions. The chapter emphasises how questioning is not just the starting point of an enquiry but a thread that runs throughout, enabling students to think geographically, engage critically with different perspectives and deepen their understanding of the interaction between human and physical geography.

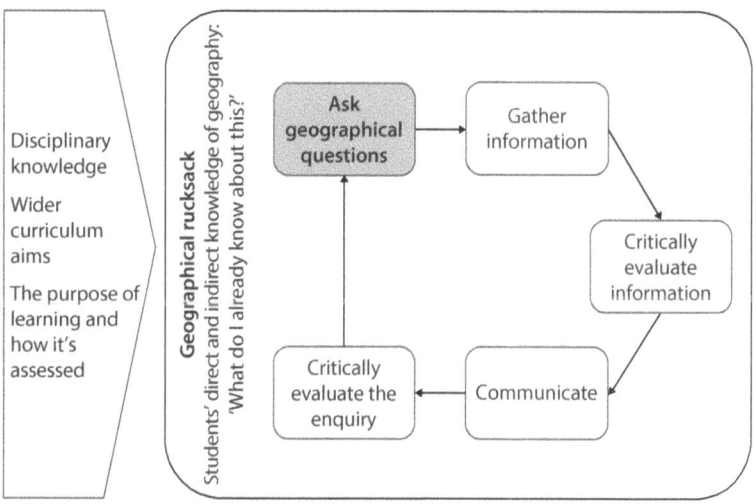

Figure 7.1: The simplified enquiry approach model: Ask geographical questions

The first stage of the enquiry approach model is to formulate high-quality geographical questions. The box below xxx expands on the model presented in Chapter 2 (see Figure 7.1) by using a list of considerations. These are explored within the rest of this chapter.

> ### Ask geographical questions
>
> - Who? Where? When? Why? What? How? (Contextualise the question within a place or places.)
> - What timescale? (Questions can be a single lesson or span whole units.)
> - Why do students need to know this?
> - What is the purpose of the enquiry? (Transmit knowledge, explore disciplinary knowledge, pass examinations or make a change.)

What does this stage of the enquiry approach model mean?

What is a geographical question?

Asking geographical questions allows teachers to connect the world represented in school lessons to their own experience of the world. Students have their own thoughts and perspectives that impact on the questions they wish to investigate. Asking good geographical questions is difficult to develop, as it needs existing knowledge and understanding to be present. For example, a novice geographer will not be able to ask complex analytical questions that link to a few different geographical topics; they will develop the ability to do so over time.

A geographical question is one that focuses on an aspect of Earth and the interaction between it and people. Geographical questions will have a locational and spatial element, as well as focusing on how different elements interact and influence each other.

Geographical questions spark curiosity and tell students why they need to learn the knowledge contained in the lesson. Well-crafted enquiry questions can provide the hook required to drive interest in the subject.

> **Activity**
>
> Think of your current curriculum. Write down some enquiry questions that are contained within it. These could span a single lesson or a sequence of lessons.

Developing geographical questions

Developing quality geographical questions is very difficult, and it needs to be taught carefully to young people if they are to move from simple questioning ('Where is this?' 'What is happening?') to questioning that is more complex. As Roberts (2013) points out, students should be aware of the geographical questions being asked and the type of questions that geographers ask and learn to formulate geographical questions.

Whilst enquiry contains a myriad of procedural knowledge, asking questions is at the heart of it. Asking geographical questions is a key component at every stage of the enquiry approach model seen on page 36. It is therefore worth spending time to develop questioning. At the beginning of Year 7, the overarching enquiry questions will be set by the teacher. As learners learn more geographical content, they will start to choose between geographical questions, perhaps selecting the best out of a selection. During the NEA, this process culminates with students choosing their own geographical question, guided by their teacher, to form the basis of their NEA.

From the start, we should be explicit and share the enquiry questions that we are exploring, even when the lessons are tightly structured and students reach a known destination, which is the case in many lessons until later in the progression journey.

It is important that questions are contextualised within your place and that they focus on concrete examples before moving to more abstract theories. This enables students to develop the knowledge required to understand more abstract concepts, as well as lining their own experiences (either directly, through their own lived experience, or indirectly, through media).

Questions should also link to the big picture. Why do they need to know this? What big concepts and ideas is this building towards? What will they be able to understand better and how does this help them answer the overarching fertile question?

This also allows us to introduce, from the outset, different perspectives and ideas. We can do this by teaching how geographers use this knowledge. For example, why is there a public meeting and consultation about a local bingo hall? Will everyone's voices be welcome? What steps are being taken to ensure that every voice is included? Why is this subject of interest to geographers and how does it make the world better? An example would be understanding how inequality changes the severity of impact of geographical processes.

Of course, we should not shy away from explaining that some knowledge is required purely to pass the examination or that it builds towards wider knowledge.

Activity

Asking good questions is difficult. Consider the following questions. For each, list the substantive knowledge to which it links, as well as the concepts. Then can you contextualise each question so that it fits to your school, community and curriculum?

- Should the retirement age be raised to 80?
- Is immigration vital to the UK?
- Does the 'UK' exist?
- Is it better to support local or low income developing country (LIDC) economies?
- How do European colonial views and actions influence the 'Middle East' today?
- Is our understanding of the world wrong?

Progression in questions

Each stage of the enquiry model can also have its individual progression journey. Students need to start with simple questions before tackling more complex ones. Teachers need to decide upon what questions to use when teaching new content so that misconceptions do not develop. Geographical questions should be shared with students and, even more importantly, allow students time to answer them. Table 7.1 is my own understanding of the progression in the types of questions that can be asked by the teacher or, at the appropriate part of the journey, by students. Questions get more complex towards the bottom of the table.

Table 7.1: Progression in questions

Classification	Purpose	Scale	Examples
Foundation enquiry questions	Ensuring that students learn geographical content and avoid misconceptions; these could span individual lessons or there could be multiple questions in one lesson. Checking for understanding and transmitting knowledge; can also form the scaffolding for supporting learning. They should: • be closed • be small enough to answer within a short time period • pose a question that can be investigated rather than a statement • relate to a geographical issue • have a clear link to small chunk of geography.	Spanning individual lessons or many questions within one lesson. Supplementary questions to a fertile question.	What are the geomorphological processes that occur at the coastline? What are the human and physical features of Worthing? How does international trade work? What is ocean acidification? How does land use change along a transect from rural to urban Inverness? What are the sustainable features of tourism in the Lake District?

(*Continued*)

The Power of Geographical Enquiry

Table 7.1: Continued

Classification	Purpose	Scale	Examples
Complex questions or fertile questions	Overarching big questions that encourage a deeper understanding of content. Give a reason why students are learning what they are. Linked to a key concept(s). They should: • be open, with multiple answers and opinions • challenge misconceptions • enable different perspectives to be explored • be connected to different parts of geography • be provocative • have information available to students so that they can explore and answer.	Whole units of work	How do colonial boundaries and place names continue to shape and influence India? Is the UK ready for a rise in sea level? Why might attitudes to migration in the UK change in the future? Does the UK exist? Will Lagos be able to meet the challenges created by rural–urban migration? Why is South Sudan considered the poorest country in the world? Do National Parks work?

Classification	Purpose	Scale	Examples
Application of geographical content and concepts to other, unknown problems	Decision-making exercises. Link a range of geographical content together – for example, urban regeneration and climate change. More focused to individual issues. They should: - have a real-world relevance to real decisions being made - include conflict between different groups of people, such as environmental campaigners, local residents and energy companies - involve a wide range of geographical resources available to students - have synoptic links between geographical content - usually be linked to sustainability.	Individual activities	Should a new wind farm be built in Worthing? What should happen to the old Shoreham cement works? Should Happisburgh receive further investment in sea defences? Should Heathrow be expanded? Should new housing developments be allowed on greenbelt land around Manchester? Does the Belfast brand reflect its place?

(Continued)

The Power of Geographical Enquiry

Table 7.1: Continued

Classification	Purpose	Scale	Examples
Reflection questions	Meta-cognition that can be demonstrated by a teacher 'thinking out loud'. Consider different perspectives and identify weaknesses and strengths in their work. They should: • ask students to make a judgement about their work • focus on the entire enquiry process • explore limitations and improvements • encourage reflection on how enquiry questions have deepened knowledge of geographical concepts • link to evidence • consider different perspectives and ethical considerations.	Continuous Part of the self-evaluation of work	Is this knowledge contested? What perspective have I used? What perspective is missing? Have I avoided a single story? How reliable is my conclusion? How representative is my analysis?

Geography teachers ask lots of questions to students to check understanding as part of formative assessment. These can also be geographical questions. The complexity of geographical questions is that as students increase their geographical knowledge, even simple questions lead to complex discussions. For example, the question 'how does international trade work?' has changed beyond recognition since I started teaching, with different technology and successive political changes impacting on the availability and price of goods. As students journey through their geography career, they will begin to change their view of processes as their knowledge deepens.

Some parts of geography remain relatively static. For example, our understanding of geomorphic processes changes little, although how they impact upon people and how we should respond change over time.

Sequences of questions

Questions can be one-off 'guerilla geography' lessons or span an entire unit. Ofsted (2023a) found that where overarching questions linked a sequence of lessons together, students were taught the stages of geographical enquiry, as well as the key geographical content and skills, and learning was more effective.

There is a key concept at the heart of the big enquiry questions that span units, and the subsidiary questions that follow allow students to develop not only their understanding about this concept, but also how it connects to others. The core concept is the environment, although place is also developed. The unit has opportunities to develop interconnection, diversity and interaction. These overarching enquiry questions take conversation in departments and some deep thought. As Taylor (2021) points out, such enquiry questions should have both 'pith and rigour' (p. 4). This means that they should engage young people and get them to *want* to find out more, and allow high-quality geography to be taught.

A whole-unit example

Consider the example unit In Table 7.2 (overleaf). This is a Year 8 unit of work, structured around making a difficult decision surrounding the benefits and costs of tourism on a specific place. This is a key skill required at higher levels and in decision-making exercises. Young people need to develop their understanding of both sides of the argument.

Table 7.2: Example Year 8 unit of work

		Enquiry question	Notes
Sequence of lessons – each may span an individual lesson or longer, depending on the progress of the class	**Overarching geographical question:**	*Is tourism a blessing or a curse for Thailand?*	
	Subsidiary enquiry questions	What is tourism and why do tourists go to the tropical rainforest?	This is a link to the previous unit: ecosystems. They looked at Thailand in this unit, as it has rainforests.
		Where do Earth's people go on holiday?	Grappling with datasets and describing spatial patterns.
		How has tourism impacted on Iceland?	This links to a Year 7 unit on Iceland. Compares population with tourist numbers, revisits fragile tundra/Arctic environment. Briefly considers economic, environmental and social impacts. Focus on positive and negative.
		Is Benidorm really just the UK?	Looking at recent backlash against tourism in Spain. Quick look at social, economic and environmental impacts.
		Where on Earth is Thailand? What is it like and how are we connected?	Location, classification, perspectives. Looking for connections through travel and trade. Why do people travel to Thailand? Classification of tourists. Travel guides, adverts, films and novels.
		Who works in the Thailand tourist industry and what do they do?	Economic impact. Size of tourist economy. Big datasets. Classification of employment. Positive and negative impacts.
		How has Ko Phi Phi changed and what is its future?	Environmental impact. Evaluating sources of information. Perspectives. Voices. Include considering the validity of the Butler model with what we know so far.
		What are the social impacts of tourism in Thailand?	Social impact and geography in the news – what perspectives do we have in the UK of tourism there?
		Will climate change cause more flooding in Thailand?	Links to monsoons, deforestation and wider issues. Links to how people travel.
	Pause to tackle the overarching question.	Is tourism a blessing or a curse for Thailand?	A detailed extended writing response to the overarching enquiry question.

A small-scale 'guerilla geography' example

Dan Raven-Ellison (2012) sees guerrilla geography as 'daring people to challenge preconceptions about places; engage in social and environmental justice; and form deeper, more active community connections'. It's about thinking differently – thinking geographically. It's about finding out about our world to make it better.

This idea was taken to develop a mini unit that explored the concept of place, especially 'sense of place'. In addition, it develops the idea of 'geographical imaginations' (Massey, 2006) that recognises how places, people and environment are interconnected across different scales and how our own lives link to global processes. This unit also explores how people can influence others within the rigid systems of schools.

Whilst some may feel that such units should not be used, I personally feel that they are an essential element to a young person's geographical education. This enquiry allows the application of knowledge and the development of fieldwork skills, such as sampling. It also allows students to explore different geographical rucksacks and perspectives within the content that they all 'know'. Personally, I think that exposing students to prominent geographers such as Massey and Raven-Ellison is a good thing! It will inspire them and communicate that different people experience the same places in different ways!

The important element is that students are told a very clear set of expectations when conducting on-site fieldwork. Table 7.3 (overleaf) is also a good example of a framed enquiry, where there is a great deal of choice for students.

Students can also develop their own questions and work to sequence them. For example, during a unit on tectonic hazards, students started by being asked the following overarching question. In addition to the question, they were given a basic fact-file on the impacts of tectonic activities in Nepal and Iceland.

What roles do remoteness and wealth play in the impact that tectonic events have on the communities in Iceland and Nepal?

Students created questions that formed the subsequent sequence of lessons. Whilst sometimes an unexpected question would occur, planning and workload were reduced, as the types of questions asked by students were usually concentrated on similar themes, and this can be guided by the teacher.

Table 7.3: Guerilla geography unit

	Enquiry question	Notes
Overarching geographical question:	How does this school make us feel?	
Subsidiary enquiry questions	What are the 'hidden' features of the school, and have you noticed them?	On-site fieldwork using photographs of distinctive features around the school. Students locate using coordinates. These are from different perspectives.
	How do the places in this school affect our emotions?	On-site fieldwork, building on previous lesson to map 'happy' and 'unhappy' places around the school, capturing features of each place that may explain why.
	Does everyone feel the same about this school?	On-site fieldwork using LEGO® figures representing different people. Students explore the school thinking like 'that' person, e.g. recent unaccompanied refugee, hearing-impaired, parent, Year 4 sibling, headteacher.
	What annoys us about this school and how can we communicate this?	On-site fieldwork looking at places that students don't like and using 'Little Notices' (Smith, 2007) to highlight these. Mapping. Dotmocracy (https://dotmocracy.org) to decide on a single class focus.
	How can we influence decision-makers in the school?	A written piece to the governors, headteacher or SLT about what they feel.

Practical examples

Here are a number of practical examples for supporting students to ask geographical questions in the geography classroom.

1. Engaging young people with the emotion of place

If we are to avoid the single story, geography teachers should examine the wider context of the places studied, especially those that are unknown. One of the challenges – and delights – of teaching geography is that we have to cover parts of the world with which we have no direct experience. For these, it is even more important that we ask questions to avoid developing a stereotypical view of that place.

A simple way to do this is to ask, 'What similarities does this place have with our place?' We can also teach students what place names mean, as well as including authentic voices from different parts of the world.

Another way to engage in the emotion of place is to show a series of geographical items from a place. This can be enhanced by using teachers' personal experiences, if comfortable to do so. For example, consider the following items:

- a map in a different language
- mountaineering boots
- crampons
- a thick mountaineering jacket
- an ice axe.

Students can list the questions that they would ask the person, as well as describe what environment those items would be used in.

Activity

Think about a place that is studied in your curriculum. Write down a list of objects that could be used to inspire classes to ask geographical questions.

We can ask the following questions when asking students to write about their own places, and then apply them to the other places that they study:

- What do you see?
- What do you hear?
- What are your emotions?
- What can you smell?
- What is around you?
- How are you feeling?
- Will everyone feel the same about this place?

This link to how places make us feel underpins the interaction between human and physical geography. For example, when displaying a photograph of a happy teacher on a mountain, the question posed was, 'Why is Mr Rogers so happy?' This was a retrieval question, posed in the midst of a weather unit. The culture of the classroom meant that students knew that they were expected to come in and engage in the 'Do now' activity without instruction. They also knew that an extended answer was required, with justification.

The answer was that anti-cyclonic conditions meant that the view was spectacular. This may seem trivial, but it is the start of diving deeper. Of course, there are a multitude of answers. Indeed, those questions that do not have a 'correct' answer often cause anxiety amongst young people, and this example shows how this can be embraced.

2. Questioning the world around us

Students make multiple journeys. For example, as they journey to and from school, there are opportunities to assess the world around them as a geographer. Similarly, I used to enjoy walking and cycling around the local area, taking photographs to use in lessons. The example in Table 7.4, shared by Kate Stockings, is a great example of how to use everyday geographies and experience to develop enquiry.

Table 7.4: Using everyday experience to develop enquiry
(from Stockings, 2023)

'Lime': A new transportation network company (TNC)	A photograph of an abandoned Lime bike blocking a pavement was displayed here to act as a prompt for the class. As the school was located in London, students there were familiar with the bikes and seeing them in their locale.
• Where is this TNC based? • How is it an example of globalisation? • Where are the bikes made and what are the impacts of this?	
A blocked pavement	
• Who is affected if the pavement is blocked? • What are the disadvantages of this new travel infrastructure? • What needs to happen to ensure that these bikes are safe and useable for all?	
A sustainable transport source	**What else may a geographer see?**
• How sustainable are these bikes? • What will happen to their batteries once they can no longer be used? • Why are electric bikes more sustainable than electric cars? • Should we be encouraging more electric bikes or more use of public transport?	

This example could be adapted as a retrieval opportunity, adding in a novel situation for students to pause and consider how what they already know links to the questions. Importantly, the questions don't necessarily need to be answered, but such stimuli do encourage a culture of curiosity and question-asking. Such images can be collected and curated by teachers and added to the relevant unit, or they can also be used as retrieval activities, where students are challenged to ask a number of geographical questions about the image, linked to their knowledge at that stage in their education.

3. Making the leap

We can present a geographical question and suggest a number of steps for students to reach the answer. Table 7.5 can be displayed on a slide as students enter the room, and they are expected to silently write their ideas on mini-whiteboards before sharing.

Table 7.5: Example of 'Do now' task

Do now: How can using washing machines make a country more developed?

Start here ⟶	Using a washing machine means . . .	
Therefore, GDP per capita increases over time. This makes the country more developed as it has a higher standard of living (wealth).	**An image can be displayed here**	

One of the aspects of development that is often overlooked is the link between income and taxation. It is easy to allow the misconception that countries become rich quickly. Using the 'Do now' activity in Table 7.5, students are challenged to predict the two steps. This is based upon the story of Hans Rosling (2010; 2021, Chapter 1), and the key is that his mother's time was freed up so that she could read to him. That meant that a generation went on to gain qualifications and earn more income through different types of jobs. The taxation of this income meant that the state received more income, which could be spent upon providing services. An example of a completed grid may look like Table 7.6.

Table 7.6: Example of completed task

Start here ⟶	Using a washing machine means . . .	⟶ ↓
Therefore, GDP per capita increases over time. This makes the country more developed as it has a higher standard of living (wealth).	**An image can be displayed here**	*This means that women have more time. They can spend this on activities such as reading to their children, educating themselves or getting involved in economic activity.*
↑	*Over time, this increases the number of people in the country's workforce. In turn, this increases the amount of income tax that is collected by the government. Over generations, a more educated population is more likely to work in higher-paying jobs, increasing the amount of taxation again.*	↓ ←

This example in itself can be used as a story to explore across a whole sequence of lessons. For example, the role of women in the economy can be explored, as can the time taken for the country to rise in the gross domestic product (GDP) ranks, reinforcing that not all processes are fast. Of course, this doesn't mean that this can be taken and applied to any country worldwide. This represents a model: a simplified version of one person's story. It can, however, start the enquiry process for exploring other places.

4. Questioning grid

Another way of developing the questioning ability of students was shared by John Sayers (2013). An image or text extract can be placed in the centre of the grid in Table 7.7, with students encouraged to ask questions using the surrounding prompts. This activity could be at the start of an enquiry or used to compare student-generated questions with those of the teacher. Students first choose a word from the left-hand side of the grid, before adding a second from the top. They are asked to write at least three geographical questions. For added refinement, give some banned words that students can not use, such as 'people', 'things', 'stuff' and 'pollution'.

Table 7.7: Example question grid

		Chose a word from these second					
	Question grid	Is (Present)	Did (Past)	Can (Possibility)	Would/ could (Probability)	Will (Prediction)	Might (Imagination)
Choose one of these questions first	What? (Event)						
	Where? (Place)						
	When? (Time)			Place an image or text extract here			
	Which? (Choice)						
	Who? (Person)						
	Why? (Reason)						
	How? (Meaning)						

This could also be used to generate a list of questions that are revisited throughout a topic. Which have been answered? Which remain? These questions do not have to dictate the unit that follows but can be used to help young people generate high-quality geography questions. This grid incorporates a progression in questions. More difficult questions to answer appear at the bottom of the first list and on the right of the second list.

5. The use of AI to generate questions

Consider the following list of questions. Some have been suggested by AI and others were developed by A level students in the early stages of their NEA.

1   What are the major landforms in a specific region and how were they formed?
2   How does climate change impact local ecosystems and communities?
3   To what extent can Harbour Park be considered 'placeless'?
4   What is the role of geography in understanding the distribution of natural resources?
5   To what extent has the 'Brighton effect' driven gentrification along the train line in Worthing, Littlehampton and Lancing?

6   How much agency do the people of Littlehampton have in controlling coastal flooding?

7   What are the primary factors that influence population distribution in a particular country or region?

8   How do natural disasters, like earthquakes or hurricanes, shape the geography of an area?

9   How does cultural geography influence the way people interact with their environment?

10 To what extent is Littlehampton a product of its locale, rather than globalisation?

> **Activity**
>
> Examine the list of questions and, without reading on, identify those that are written purely by AI. How did you differentiate those that you have identified from the others?

Questions 3, 5, 6 and 10 are past NEA investigation questions and developed by students without the use of AI. The others are the product of a ChatGPT query. Whilst the NEA questions are clearly defined and located in named places, the others could easily form the basis of enquiries. These questions could be given to students to change and adapt so that they are specific, high-quality enquiry questions.

Many teachers avoid the use of AI, but there are brilliant geographical questions based around it, such as the location of data centres (see https://datacenters.google/locations) and carbon emissions (e.g. Tomlinson et al., 2024) attached to them. By avoiding the use of AI, we miss the opportunity to model how it can be a powerful aid to asking geographical questions. As a starting point, such questions can spark curiosity and then students can adapt and hone them.

6. Beat the teacher

This is a good way to start a lesson. Some geographical information is presented to students. This can be an image, fact, graph or, indeed, anything! Let's take the examples of the number 2.6 or an image of a ghost town in the USA. Students must first think about the relevance of the resource and write their own response. The teacher then invites questions from the class. These must be well-thought-out geographical questions. The class typically has ten questions that the teacher will answer. The idea is to listen to and build upon the previous questions so that an answer is reached. In this example, the number 2.6 reflects the average number of people added to the world's population each second (at the time of writing) and the ghost town represents migration in the USA.

7. Image of the week

I used to display a large image each week on the classroom wall. Students were encouraged to ask questions about it. I used to source the image from the middle of the *Guardian* newspaper, but any thought-provoking image will do.

8. Understanding questions

This is an opportunity to really think about questions and it is a skill that should be developed from lesson one of Year 7.

> **Activity**
>
> Students were asked to use a range of information and data provided, which included graphs, maps and written content, to consider the following geographical questions taken from Cambridge OCR's GCSE Geography B (Geography for Enquiring Minds) J384:
>
> - Evaluate the contemporary challenges caused by **inequality** within Mexico City.
> - Suggest how rapid urban growth can cause **consequences** in LIDCs such as Bangladesh.
> - Assess the extent to which climate change is a **natural** process.
>
> How would you teach students to understand them?

Examination-style questions were used when I taught in most lessons. By this, I do not mean teaching to the test in an exam-factory style, but getting students comfortable with being asked questions that test their geographical knowledge. This meant that responding became automatic and habitual. Like many other colleagues, I taught young people to:

- identify the command words
- underline any specific requirements, such as reference to resources, and key terms in the question
- plan out an answer.

However, we can also get students engaged in critically evaluating the enquiry questions themselves. Let's consider an earlier example in Table 7.8.

Table 7.8: Example of evaluating enquiry questions

What are the impacts of this status?	How is this measured?	How do the UK and South Sudan differ?	Where does the information come from?	What will happen in the future?
Who says that South Sudan is the poorest?	**Why is South Sudan considered the poorest country in the world?**			What is everyday life like in Sudan?
Is the information contained in this question correct?	Where is South Sudan?	What was South Sudan like in the past?	What is the colonial history of South Sudan?	What do the UK and South Sudan have in common?

This approach can be modelled by the teacher. By using a closed or framed enquiry approach, the teacher can talk through the process of questioning the question. When students get older and their geographical knowledge increases, they can suggest questions themselves.

Key takeaways

- High-quality geographical questions frame enquiry and drive curiosity.
- A geographical question must always be contextualised and connect real people, real places and real environments.
- Progression in questioning moves from closed factual questions to complex open enquiries.
- Teacher modelling and scaffolding is vital in developing questioning skills.
- Fertile questions that can drive whole sequences of lessons link knowledge, concepts and perspectives together.
- Questioning underpins the whole enquiry process and is not just a beginning.

8 How do we gather information?

In this chapter

In this chapter, we will explore the many ways in which information can be gathered to enrich geographical enquiry. By delving into both the practicalities and philosophies that underpin resource selection, we will consider not only what is available to us, but also how each curriculum artefact – textbook, digital tool, fieldwork activity or personal story – shapes the geographical lens through which students learn. Progression is presented as the journey from teacher-curated resources to student-led investigation, highlighting the evolving sophistication of procedural knowledge. At every stage, critical reflection and an awareness of multiple perspectives remain central to creating a classroom environment where curiosity and rigour go hand in hand. This chapter will keep in mind what is realistic within the time-poor and accountability-rich UK classroom.

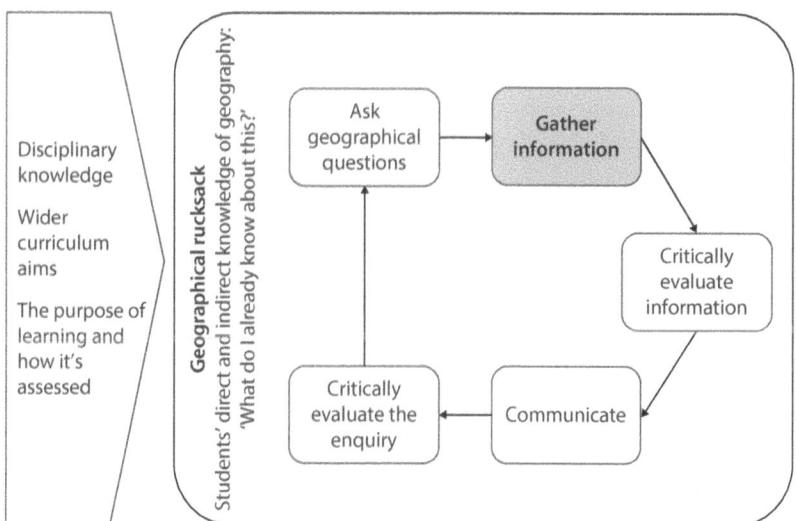

Figure 8.1: The simplified enquiry approach model: Gather information

The second stage of the enquiry approach model is to use the questions asked during the previous stage, in order to gather the information needed to answer the question. Whilst, in reality, most information is selected by the teacher and not the student, it is still important to teach this stage to students. The box below expands on the model presented in Chapter 2 (see Figure 8.1) by using a list of considerations. These are explored within the rest of this chapter.

Gather information

- What will be the curriculum artefacts?
- What do students already know about this?
- What gaps and misconceptions do students have?
- How do I know that the information I use in lessons is reliable, accurate and representative?
- What procedural knowledge is needed to explore this information?
- Should I seek out qualitative or quantitative information?
- Should the information be from primary or secondary sources?

Eyes were invented before maps

When training to be a mountain leader, one mantra that was indelibly written on my soul was that eyes were invented before maps. This meant, in the context of the mountains, that we need to take a moment and look carefully around. A positive off-shoot of this was a connection to nature. Linked to the classroom and the information that we collect, this means that we need to take a moment to think and look around at what there is. Do we take the single textbook example in front of us or look around for more? Do we take a moment to consider whether the resource we have selected (or listed in the scheme of work) reflects the world as it is?

Geography is a subject that demands a huge range of information. Students are expected not only to link to other topics synoptically, but also to be able to assess a wide range of data sources. Enquiry allows us to develop this area of procedural knowledge well. Of course, much of the information given will be secondary in nature and curated by the teacher through curriculum artefacts, such as textbooks, articles and information sources from the internet. Fieldwork can also provide information through the observation of geographical phenomena and collection of qualitative and quantitative data.

In the pragmatic, functional and practical world of classroom teaching, this usually involves teachers selecting and curating the information examined. This can include information from textbooks and various internet sources. This chapter will keep in mind what is realistic within the time-poor and accountability-rich UK classroom.

Chapter 9 will examine the critical analysis of such information; however, what we choose to put in front of young people needs careful consideration. What teachers select will influence the content and skills learned by our classes, including any bias.

This area is often restricted to the collection of primary data during fieldwork, but it is fundamental to consider all sorts of information if we are taking an enquiry approach, as only equating gathering information to the data-collection phase of fieldwork is very limiting.

Progression

As young people move towards being able to conduct their own open enquiries, the following progression will occur:

- Students start with a single artefact, selected and presented by their teacher, that focuses on one area of geographical content.
- Students will use an increasingly wide range of different artefacts, still selected by the teacher, which focus on one aspect of geographical content.
- These artefacts, whilst still chosen by the teacher, will then start to link to other parts of geography and include conflicting viewpoints and perspectives.
- Eventually, students will be able to find and select their own information.

Throughout this progression, students will develop their procedural knowledge as it becomes more sophisticated. From an educational research standpoint, it is important that students encounter and practise their skills of interpreting different sources of information as often as possible. In this way, those skills become automatic so that students can free up their working memory to focus on the question under investigation, rather than being distracted by the task of understanding the data. For this purpose, different types of artefact should be a part of every lesson.

For the avoidance of doubt, most sequences of lesson will involve students using materials gathered and presented by teachers. As students learn more geography and become more competent at reading different sources of information, we can slowly introduce more choice.

Curriculum artefacts

Definition

Curriculum artefact: This is a teaching and learning resource with special *geographical* significance, helping young people to learn geographical content and skills. The excellent GeoCapabilities resources available through the Geographical Association provide further reading on curriculum artefacts and their role in curriculum-making.

The curriculum artefacts that teachers choose to use have significant importance, so it is vital that teachers use their professional judgement to carefully select such information and explicitly share the source and the viewpoints and perspectives from which it was created. This is not to say that we can't use information that has limitations – just that we need to be open about it.

For me, the key distinction is that we, as teachers, actively decide to engage with and use these resources in the classroom, in order to underpin effective learning of geography. In this way, it is not really what we use and include but how we do so.

Activity

List all the types of curriculum artefact used in your classroom during your last teaching day.

Types of curriculum artefact

Any list of artefacts can be extensive but not exhaustive. Geographers think geographically and, because of this, almost everything can be considered a curriculum artefact. As mentioned earlier, the key feature is that they have a geographical dimension and help to develop geographic learning. As the enquiry model presented here includes the geographical rucksack of those we teach, a rich source of artefacts comes from young people themselves, including the stuff that they have and the journeys that they take.

Table 8.1 lists some examples of curriculum artefacts, classified into physical and digital resources. Physical resources are items that can be held by students, such as textbooks and paper maps, whilst digital resources are available online and can be used from the front of the classroom through a digital projector. Most resources are shared via screens these days, although it is still much better to give physical resources that can be manipulated by students, where budget and time allows.

Table 8.1: Examples of curriculum artefacts

Source	Examples
Physical resources	
Maps	Maps show spatial relationships as well as location data. Ordnance Survey is used widely, but there are many other map creators. As spatial relationships are key in geography, they remain a cornerstone resource.
Atlases	These compilations of maps also contain easily accessible data, such as population statistics and industrial location.
Graphs, diagrams, infographics	From the simple to the complex, every geography teacher will be familiar with the vast range of ways to visualise data.
Globes	Globes can display political or physical characteristics of Earth.
Books	A wide range of books can be used, from fictional novels set in real places to books written by journalists, such as *The Almighty Dollar* (David, 2018). Academic books are also useful, as are audio books.
Magazines and newspapers	Less common in classrooms these days, useful information can come from *National Geographic* and national, regional and local newspapers.

(Continued)

Table 8.1: Continued

Source	Examples
Journals	These include journals aimed at students, such as *Wide World* and *Geography Review*, plus academic journals and those from the Geographical Association. *Teaching Geography* and *Primary Geography* are of particular interest, as they often contain a mixture of articles written by academics and also teachers who have applied ideas to the classroom. Whilst one must take care in using these ideas from a different context, they are useful.
Textbooks	Whilst much has been written about the disadvantages of textbooks, their curated and selected information is still a useful resource for geography classrooms.
Worksheets	Created by teachers, found on the internet or part of a textbook series, worksheets can contain a huge amount of information via graphs, facts, song lyrics or diagrams.
Rocks, soil	Physical rocks, soils and sands from various locations in the world can be used. Seeing and feeling the difference between chalk, limestone and granite, or sandy and clay soils is powerful, as is handling volcanic ash and pumice.
Fieldwork, fieldwork equipment	Fieldwork is getting out of the classroom to observe and measure geographical phenomena. The school site itself is a rich resource. Fieldwork equipment can be used both inside and outside the classroom.
Experiments	Whilst fieldwork is the observation and collection of data outside the classroom, geography teachers can also use equipment to demonstrate phenomena inside or outside the classroom. Examples include: • water cycle in a bottle • wave tank • sundial • infiltration rates.
Geographical models	Whilst these can be both physical and digital, geographical models are representations of the world that aim to understand and explain spatial patterns and relationships. They can be physical, conceptual or mathematical. Examples include: • continental drift and plate tectonics • the water cycle

Source	Examples
	- Boserup's theory
	- urban land use models
	- climate models
	- Park response model
	- wave tanks
	- model oceans.
Digital resources	
Social media	Let's face it, most of our students embody themselves on social media platforms and use them to (re)craft their identities (Halliwell, 2020). If engaged with, these platforms enable young people to think critically about the world. Whilst we must be careful of its use in the classroom, and ensure that we stick to policies, social media – YouTube, WhatsApp, Strava, TikTok, etc. – *is* the internet to many.
The internet	Although vast, this is the place where most geography teachers turn to find curriculum artefacts, from the early days of the SLN Geography Forum to other social media platforms. The modelling of how to access and use the internet is vital. Teacher sites include geographyalltheway.com and geographypods.com, as well as classic resources such as the BBC (including BBC Bitesize). Websites such as Ground News provide tools to examine the bias of reporting. Living Geography contains a wealth of curriculum artefacts and information for geography teachers to access and keep up with subject knowledge. In addition, the Geographical Association, the Royal Geographical Society (with IBG) and many NGOs contain a wealth of curated curriculum artefacts ready for use. It is also possible to view company information.
Images	Images are very powerful in geography. Photographs are framed and therefore show a selected version of the world, but they can create curiosity, stimulate questions and provide a snapshot of a moment in time. For example, imagine the local high street shown as a sequence of photographs over the years.
'Big data' and data visualisations	I believe that all students need to experience handling raw 'big data' sets, including finding out and selecting the correct scale and area. Sites include the census, Ordnance Survey Open Data downloads and Our World in Data. Data visualisation provided by Gapminder (as well as its Dollar Street and other resources) is excellent.

(Continued)

Table 8.1: Continued

Source	Examples
GIS	First introduced into the National Curriculum in 1991, and often explicitly mentioned in exam board specifications, there are now some excellent tools through Esri's ArcGIS, which include the ability to collect and display information collected by students on mobile devices (e.g. West, 2021). There are also tools such as StoryMaps. Many local authorities and public bodies, including National Parks, also have open-access GIS platforms covering a wide range of information, from tourism and waste to brownfield registers.
Map visualisations	These are tools such as Google Earth and Google Maps. The ability to switch to satellite view, as well as using Street View, can be very useful.
Remote sensing	This is another example of artefacts that are underused explicitly, included here separately from map visualisation. For example, USGS EarthExplorer and NASA's Worldview provide a wide range of visual resources, making it possible to track the impact of El Nino and flooding.
Virtual fieldtrips	Whilst there may be no substitute to getting outside the classroom, sometimes we need to bring the outside inside. Indeed, that describes the role of a geography teacher! Virtual fieldwork, when done effectively, can support the enquiry process, especially with the increasing availability of virtual reality resources (e.g. Ying Chua et al., 2021). Essentially, an effective virtual fieldtrip will contain a wealth of resources from this list and beyond.
Online textbooks	Most textbooks now come with the option of a virtual option, curated by authors and often containing activities.
AI	As geography teachers, we ignore the potential of AI at our peril. Chatbots such as ChatGPT and Gemini provide an opportunity to ignite students' curiosity. AI can also provide succinct summaries of articles (see Allaway, 2024).
Audio	Audio is still an underused resource, from song lyrics to news reports and audio bulletins from the National Hurricane Center (NOAA). Radio can also be powerful.
Podcasts	These are useful for updating your own knowledge, including the GA's GeogPod, RGS's Ask the Geographer and *The Economist*. They are also useful for reading lists at GCSE and A level or for setting for homework to listen and summarise.
Film	Used carefully, film can be a powerful way to explore a sense of place, as well as a range of geography content.

Source	Examples
TV and documentaries	Documentaries include those from the BBC's Natural History Unit, whilst sitcoms and soap operas can provide a rich source of curriculum artefacts. Also, see the excellent Time for Geography. Of course, YouTube is also a rich source of information, including simple animations and visualisations of often physical resources. We also have the TV news.
Video conferencing	Several organisations provide video conferencing opportunities where classes can connect with researchers around the world. A good source of information on these is the Living Geography blog by Alan Parkinson.
Other resources	
People	As people who live and interact out in the world, we have a rich geographical rucksack of our own to use in the classroom. There is also a range of information available through blogs and vlogs (usually on YouTube or Vimeo).
	Let's not forget our own 'stuff', especially as we may travel around the globe. One vital skill for geography teachers is the ability to draw diagrams with students. Creating an artefact together is a good way to increase understanding, rather than presenting students with the finished textbook or a projected example.

Questions to ask when selecting and curating artefacts

> ## Reflection
>
> As mentioned in the opening of this chapter, it is vital to pause and think about the resources that we present to young people. As well as asking how this artefact will help students to learn the geographical content you have planned, you may want to reflect on the following list of questions:
>
> - How will this assist my classes in learning about geography?
> - What is the geographical content that students will learn about?
> - Am I focusing on teaching the geographical content, the procedural knowledge or both?

- Is it a concrete example or an abstract concept?
- Are there any misconceptions that could be reinforced or introduced?
- Who created this resource? What is their perspective and motivation?
- Who published this artefact? How did I find it?
- Was this resource created by geographers? Who and why?
- Is this resource authentic or does it represent 'made-up' knowledge, situation or place?
- For information about places overseas, does it represent authentic Indigenous views and knowledge?
- Does this artefact represent contested knowledge?
- What sampling strategies are used?
- Is this primary or secondary information?
- Is it representative of the real world and its diversity?
- Can this artefact be reused or will it date? Is it already out of date?
- What skills are required to access it?
- What is the reading age of the resource?
- What scaffolding and support do I need to give for all students to access this resource?

We must critically evaluate any curriculum artefact that we use in the classroom, sharing explicitly its provenance and how it was created. We need to explain why we are using it.

Geography teachers also need to audit sequences of lessons to ensure that young people are exposed to as many different types of information as possible, rather than relying on one type of artefact. In addition, we need to keep track of the different perspectives that we use. This can be done through a simple audit of what we use in the classroom; it is a technique I carried with me throughout my career, after being introduced to it at PGCE.

Let's take maps as an example. The following list is taken from Cambridge OCR's GCSE Geography A (Geographical Themes) J383 specification with respect to cartographic skills (2018, p. 13):

1 'select, adapt and construct maps, using appropriate scales and annotations, to present information

2 interpret cross-sections and transects

3 use and understand coordinates, scale and distance
4 extract, interpret, analyse and evaluate information
5 use and understand gradient, contour and spot height (on OS and other isoline maps)
6 describe, interpret and analyse geo-spatial data presented in a GIS framework.'

OCR states that the types of maps should include:

- 'atlas maps
- OS maps (1:50 000 and 1:25 000 scales)
- base maps
- choropleth maps
- isoline maps
- flow line maps
- desire line maps
- sphere of influence maps
- thematic maps
- route maps
- sketch maps.'

This is some list, but it provides a checklist. How many of these are encountered at Key Stage 3? Whilst it would be fantastic to get students to create their own maps, graphs and data, with limited curriculum time, I would argue that it is more important that they are exposed to as many different types of map and graph as possible, and are able to interpret them before creating them, perhaps after their own secondary and primary data collection.

Activity

Look at the GCSE or A level specification that your students study. What skills are listed? Audit your curriculum against these. Are there opportunities to get more exposure to these?

Practical examples

Whilst Chapter 9 will examine the critical analysis of these sources of information, here I include some examples to illustrate the range of curriculum artefacts we can employ. What is crucial is that we use a wide range of different resources throughout sequences of lessons, without an overreliance on one type.

Whilst there are undoubtedly issues with using some types of resource, I would argue that these can be addressed through teaching and learning strategies. An enquiry approach allows us to really *think* about what we are using in our classrooms. Most importantly, no resource should be used 'off the shelf'. It is for geography teachers to contextualise them and connect them to the curriculum in your institution for your young people.

'Never off duty'

I always felt like I was never off duty when teaching geography, because what happens in the real world is taught at some point in the curriculum. Whether running along the South Downs, ascending a ridge in Yr Eryri or even walking along the high street and spotting some graffiti, the whole world is a source of curriculum artefacts! Using these is important to inspire curiosity in those that we teach and to demonstrate that what is learned inside a geography classroom can be seen happening outside.

One example is when I was walking down Brick Lane in London. Famous for its street art, I was taken by an example containing a very familiar quote together with a QR code. The code, once scanned with my smartphone, took me to a retail website that was ready to sell me some very nice – if expensive – outdoor gear. This was a great example of a local custom being subverted for commercial use, so I incorporated it into a lesson that followed.

A more recent example was walking into the local grocery store at the end of my street to a notice declaring that the store (and chain) was having availability issues. The shelves were bare. This conjured up memories of the lack of food and toilet rolls during the early lockdowns. I snapped a quick picture that could easily be used in a starter activity. At the start of a lesson, the image could be shown with the open question: 'What has led to this?' The picture could also be used to drop into the relevant existing scheme of work or even as a retrieval exercise for students who have already studied food security.

The impact was actually from a cyber-attack. Taking this further, we could then link to the effects on food security and global transport of the 2010 eruption of

Eyjafjallajökull, making a comparison with the Fagradlsfjall eruptions between 2021 and 2025. This could be combined with the examples of Brexit, Ukraine, Trump tariffs and the *Ever Given*. This is a good example of weaving together a multitude of different resources to tell a layered and textured narrative of a key geographical concept: food security.

In summary, we can link together different aspects of geography and quickly update curriculum artefacts to tell a richer story. It doesn't mean discarding past events – just that there is always a major shift going on in geography!

I am not arguing that we should always be working, but that it is one of the charms of being a geography teacher that we think geographically. We are curious. We enquire. We make connections. By sharing stories of what we see and making them well-thought-out curriculum artefacts, we show young people that geography is all around us.

Textbooks: Everyone's guilty pleasure

Textbooks are a specific type of book designed to support teaching and learning, to be used by students. They are often closely aligned to a National Curriculum or exam specification. In the frantic world of teaching classes, plus form groups, assemblies, meetings and marking, it is little wonder that textbooks are used, even if only as a planning tool.

Like *any* resource, they must be used carefully and are not without their criticism. The lag in the authoring and publishing process, together with the expense of buying class sets, can lead to them being quickly outdated – a particular issue with the climate crisis (e.g. Teach the Future, 2024). Textbooks have also been criticised for providing an outdated, Eurocentric view of the world, reinforcing the problems of the 'Third World' and colonial viewpoints by othering places (e.g. Winter, 2018).

As someone who has been involved in authoring and editing textbooks, I can see grounds for this criticism. However, I used them throughout my own teaching and would advocate using them. Amongst other advantages, they save time, provide resources that young people can hold in their hands and ease workload. However, using a textbook as the taught curriculum without teacher input and thought is not good practice. As geography teachers, we need to treat textbooks like any other curriculum artefact and use them with careful thought.

For example, the guidance to schools requires them by law to promote British values. One of these values is a 'mutual respect and tolerance of those with different faiths and beliefs' (DfE, 2014, p. 5). In turn, this comes from the 2011 Prevent strategy, and the guidance has found its way into many school textbooks. I do not think this goes anywhere near far enough. Through geography, we can ensure that there is understanding, embracing and acceptance that go far beyond tolerance. This is a good example of where going back to the source material is important, rather than taking what is in a textbook at face value.

Teachers are presented with a choice. We can be explicit with students about the shortcomings of textbooks, choose not to use them if they reinforce misconceptions about the world or use them to illustrate one point of view, introducing other resources to expand the perspectives offered.

Even though new textbooks are published often, older stock is often still relied upon in cash-strapped departments. For example, one textbook series (*Geography at Work*) has an image of US border police trying to stop Mexicans crossing into the USA. The image shows two men with rifles, with no insignia visible. Using this resource with a class, I challenge students to ask questions about the image. Examples of what they asked include:

- How do we know that they are the US Border Patrol?
- Where did this photo come from?
- Who are these people?
- Why are they armed?
- Are all Mexican migrants armed and dangerous?

As teachers of geography, we need to accept that access to resources is difficult. With the many competing priorities in school life, we can forgive ourselves if we are unable to access truly representative resources. What we can do though, is ensure that we – and our classes – are exposed to the limitation of the resources that we use.

There are also a wide range of online textbooks. Whilst these can be simple ebooks, there are also websites that include structured units of work with resources, such as Oak Academy. Whilst I would not recommend using them as an off-the-shelf replacement for your own contextualised curriculum, such websites do provide time-saving resources and tend to be quickly updated. Like any tool, it is for us to take it and adapt it to our context.

Another online textbook resource, containing a range of resourcing linked to an upside-down world map, is the OpenLearn 'Learning from the Global South' resource (Pryke, 2024). This resource presents six videos that bring different voices in response to the climate crisis.

Books

Books are a broad term for any written or printed work. Here, I include any printed resource that isn't designed for use directly with students to support teaching and learning. I am a great fan of using different books as curriculum artefacts and here suggest a few examples. Geographical enquiry provides the opportunity to include descriptions of places from a range of novels and non-fiction books. I should add a note of warning here, that I am a geography teacher, not an English teacher, and I have an interest in history but no qualifications. It is important, then, to stick to what I know!

When examining geomorphology and landscapes, it's useful to define what a landscape is, the components and landforms that comprise that landscape, how people use them and how they make people feel. I use some quotes from Edward Abbey (1968, p. 7), together with some images from Arches National Park in southern Utah.

> 'The desert says nothing. Completely passive, acted upon but never acting, the desert lies there like the bare skeleton of Being, spare, sparse, austere, utterly worthless, inviting not love but contemplation.'

Although looking at landscapes and geomorphology, there are also links to tourism, more eloquently put than I could ever hope to achieve!

Another example would be from the folktale about Gelert, a faithful dog.

> 'Beddgelert is a beautiful place set among the mountain of Snowdonia. The two rivers that flow through the village foam and dance over rocky river-beds. The slopes rise steeply.'
>
> (ap Dafydd, translated by Lewis, 2005, p. 7)

This quotation was used when examining the post-glacial landscape of Yr Eryri. With the help of maps and photographs, students can identify human and physical features. As this is a Welsh folktale, it can also be used to illustrate the power of folktales in connecting people to their place. We can also link to the idea of rewilding, with the government pledge to protect at least 30 per cent of land and sea for nature by 2030 and rewilding projects becoming prominent in the news. Could wolves return to Wales, as elk could return to England, or should we stick to beavers?

There are also non-fiction books, some of which have gone on to spawn whole schemes of work. I have included some of my favourites in the further reading section (page 278). Whilst these books can provide an excellent insight into processes such as globalisation, rivers and folklore, we must always remember that students in geography classrooms are not the intended audience. The facts will date quickly but we must also be aware that many are written by journalists with a natural flair for telling a captivating story. Whilst others are written by scientists and naturalists, we must use them carefully and critically. In other words, we must never rely upon a single book to drive enquiry; we must also share the perspectives and background of the author.

Books can also be used to keep our own knowledge fresh and give different perspectives. For example, I never saw the point in trespassing. I simply wanted to get the young people I had in front of me interested in the national park that could be seen from the urban classroom window. However, after reading *The Lie of the Land* (Shrubsole, 2024), I had a new perspective, where trespassers had discovered illegal activity.

Books can provide teachers and students with access to different perspectives. If thinking about places, books such as *I Belong Here* (Sethi, 2021) and *Black Sheep* (Pace-Humphreys, 2022) provide the perspectives of women and ethnic minorities, comparing their stories to the white narratives of *A Pennine Journey* (Wainwright, 1986), *Coasting* (Downing, 2021) and *In Search of Kazakhstan* (Robbins, 2007), personal stories of how landscapes are experienced and travelled through by people with different backgrounds and perspectives. Similarly, books such as *Red Dust* (Jian, 2001) have introduced a different perspective. It isn't that any perspective is inherently bad; it is just that it is a perspective: a story, a narrative from a single viewpoint.

A final example is through reading non-fiction books written by artists and those who engage with nature, such as *Under the Stars* (Gaw, 2020), *Fifty Words for Snow* (Campbell, 2020) and an *Elegy for a River* (Moorhouse, 2021), which have convinced me to include the night sky and enquiries about invasive species in the curriculum.

It is impossible to include all the books that have influenced and been included in my teaching as curriculum artefacts here, but I hope that it has provoked some thought. I have also used travel guides and guidebooks in lessons when appropriate. Books can provide insight into and commentary of geographical processes but they can also be used to provide descriptions of place and to show that different people have different experiences of the same places. I may not use all these books in their entirety –if at all – but they shape my understanding of the world and, when used carefully, provide excellent curriculum artefacts. We can read books with a geographical enquiry lens.

> **Activity**
>
> Review the books you currently use in your curriculum. From whose viewpoint are they written? Are there any units that rely solely upon one book? What other artefacts do you use in conjunction with these to provide a richer curriculum from multiple perspectives?

AI

AI is everywhere. As a runner, it now sums up my attempts at running, telling me just how unfit I am! This may be controversial, but although I believe we have a responsibility to teach students with resources with which they are not familiar, we should also meet them where they are. AI is an example where students think they know what they are doing but could benefit from having its use in geography modelled to them.

I thought I'd ask an AI chatbot about the benefits and pitfalls of using it. I have summarised the response in Table 8.2.

Table 8.2: Pros and cons of using AI in geography teaching (courtesy of AI!)

Prompt	Response
If I am writing advice to UK geography teachers about whether they should use AI in the classroom, what would you say to them? Give pros and cons in 100 words.	**Pros:** • personalises learning • helps students grasp complex geographic concepts at their own pace • offers instant feedback • generates engaging resources (e.g. quizzes, maps) • saves teachers planning time • AI tools support creative tasks and enquiry-based learning.

(*Continued*)

Table 8.2: Continued

Prompt	Response
	Cons: • may reinforce biases • provides inaccurate content without teacher oversight • over-reliance on AI risks weakening students' critical thinking and research skills • some schools lack the infrastructure or training for effective AI use. The advice given was to use AI thoughtfully, as a supplement to other resources. Teachers need to pair it with strong pedagogy and check outputs for accuracy and curriculum relevance.

AI can provide a starting point. Whilst being aware of the irony of how this will quickly date, the point of most AI chatbots is that it is a generative process, with follow-up questions needed.

Whilst not perfect, AI does provide a good opportunity to model with classes how to find reliable information. AI cannot replace a geography teacher's knowledge of the curriculum or their students. In addition, those with geographical knowledge and enquiry skills will be able to utilise AI better than those without it. AI should be integrated into our toolbox as an additional tool; it is not a replacement (Hickman and Ghosh, 2024).

> **Activity**
>
> Spend some time with an AI chatbot.
>
> - Ask it to summarise a real-world case study that you already use.
> - Input a graph or chart, such as a climate graph, and ask the chatbot to analyse it.
> - Input some exam questions and ask for some model answers.
>
> Consider the outputs.
>
> - Is the output accurate, relevant and appropriate to the age group?
> - Are there a range of perspectives given?

- Does the AI interpret the data accurately?
- Does the AI provide a high-quality answer and could students critically judge the strengths and weaknesses of it?

Photos

A great way to use photos is to provide images as part of a lesson introducing other information. I used to stand at the doorway and welcome each student to the class. When they sat down and got their equipment out, there was always something to do – a 'Do now' task or a starter. The key is that it was an opportunity to hook students into the topic, as well as retrieve any relevant information from past units. Sometimes I handed out some questions. As the class got to grips with the activity, I wandered the classroom to check compliance and pick up on some good answers to use as feedback.

The first example, which demonstrates contextualisation, is a photograph of a blue plaque I spotted whilst wandering around Worthing. The plaque was displayed as part of a sequence of lessons on tourism. It read:

> Donated by Roffey Homes limited
> On this site in 1899
> George Warne
> 1864–1916
> Founded his hotel in part of York Terrace
> WARNES
> Was Worthing's premier hotel
> Famous visitors included
> King Edward VII and King George V
> Emperor Haile Selassie and his family
> Winston Churchill
> General Montgomery
> General Eisenhower
> John Philip Sousa
> WARNES closed in1985
> Burned down 1987
> The Worthing Society 2006

Students were asked to answer three questions, using their knowledge of tourism developed through the unit:

1. Why would these people have come to Worthing?
2. Why would tourists come here today?
3. What else do you notice about the plaque?

Another example uses images shared on social media. For example, the incredible achievement in 2024 of Briton Jasmin Paris, the first women to complete the gruelling Barkley Marathons, an infamous ultramarathon held each year in Frozen Head State Park, Tennessee is fantastic. The event covers around 100 miles, with around 18,000 metres of ascent and a time limit of 60 hours. In the running world, Jasmin is a well-known advocate of sustainability and had used the same pair of running shoes for several years by repairing them. Her message was that by taking simple steps, we can make a difference. Following this astonishing achievement, a photo of her running shoes, with the caption 'Be more Jasmin! Four years old and repaired!', was shared with the class, alongside the question: Does keeping your running shoes going for four years offset four transatlantic flights?

I have also combined images of Instagram influencers camping high up on mountain ridges with information about increasing parking violations and a rise in mountain rescue call-outs; students consider the impact of social media on influencing others, perhaps using the questioning grid from the previous chapter (see Table 7.7, page 157). I challenge classes to decide whether influencer culture is causing parking trouble, more tourists to visit these areas and/or more rescue call-outs. Classes quickly realise that the information may not exist or, where it does, reflects one point of view, which relies upon opinion rather than facts. This is a great issue to examine, as there are also clear benefits of more tourist numbers.

Thunks

Thunks originated from Independent Thinking and Ian Gilbert (2007). They are short pithy questions designed to make students' brains hurt through thinking. The idea is that, in the safe environment of a classroom, a thunk makes students really think hard about an everyday object. I include them here as a curriculum artefact rather than questions, as I combined them with images, with the thunk being a question about which I wanted the class to write a response. For example:

- How can you prove what a place is like if you have never been there?
- How do you know an island exists if you have not been there?
- How do safe shopping streets lead to a better standard of living?
- Is aid always good for a country?
- Why don't all countries have four seasons?

Audio

As mentioned, this is still one of the most underused resources for curriculum artefacts. It can enable us to bring in authentic voices. A good homework activity is to give students an image of a place and ask them to select a music track that they think links to it. The key here is not the track selection but the writing that follows this activity, asking students to justify their choice. The activity can sit well on online platforms.

This can be taken further when in the field or on a school visit. Keeping to your institution's policy on mobile devices, give students time to observe and listen to their surroundings, before trying to find a track that matches what they see and feel.

> ### Activity
>
> Take a selection of images that are used in your curriculum. Find a good track that matches what you see. Why did you choose that track? Do colleagues make the same, similar or contrasting choices?

Another example is found in a unit that explores tropical storms, sequenced to coincide with the North Atlantic hurricane season. The National Hurricane Center provides audio briefings that are available for four hours after their publication, which can be downloaded to use at a different time. Get students to listen and note the main points covered in the briefing. Provide some prompts, such as wind speed, storm surge, rainfall and any places mentioned.

Several podcasts aim to highlight authentic Indigenous voices. Examples include Holding the Fire (www.resilience.org/holding-the-fire-podcast) and, although actually video, the Indigenous Voice project from Survival International (www.survivalinternational.org/indigenous-voices). Some of these podcasts provide alterative viewpoints that can be used in the classroom.

Map visualisation tools

I am fascinated by the impact that human activity has on the landscape. Borders are of particular interest, and visualisation tools such as Google Maps can be used to present information in an enquiry.

One example looks at the impact of borders on the landscape. Students are presented with an image showing the border between the USA and Canada, but with the labels removed. They predict where the border is, purely by using information shown to them. Are there roads or rivers? Are there subtle changes in the field patterns? Can infrastructure be seen?

Students are then given an image showing the USA/Mexico border. They predict the border location with ease in this one. This prompts wider questions, and a sequence of information can be shown, such as a map with the number of countries north and south of the USA, information about their economic development and documentaries about the borders. Even news headlines about tourists accidently crossing the USA/Canada border are used to delve deeper.

Two other locations are then looked at, one showing the area around Niagara Falls and the other deep in the desert. This prompts students to ask why I chose to present them with the information that I did.

It strikes me that when I started teaching this, I used Michael Palin's *Full Circle*, a 1997 BBC travel documentary charting the 50,000-mile clockwise trip around the Pacific Rim, to illustrate the border. Stephen Fry did something similar in 2008 and, more recently, Simon Reeve in 2019 and Sue Perkins in 2022. Simon Reeve has also visited and produced similar documentaries about the border areas. Looking at and comparing this information about the same topic, rather than relying upon the latest visit, presents an ideal opportunity to consider how things have changed over time. Have attitudes changed? How many migrants are there? Is it really the biggest issue that the USA faces? The theme continuing to be a focus in mainstream documentaries also illustrates that it is a current issue of interest, which geographers should understand.

The colonial impact of enforcing borders on the continent of Africa and the Middle East can also be introduced by using GIS software from the front of the classroom. A GIS can overlay additional information, such as ethnic groups, historical political maps, dates of independence, ethnolinguistic groups' trade routes, transport infrastructure and resource distribution. By comparing the historical borders with the various layers, students can start to identify the potential issues and problems before looking in detail.

Documentaries

Documentaries take students to those far-off places that they are unlikely to have visited. Indeed, I often had not been to the places covered by the curriculum I had to teach – for example, when teaching about the flora, fauna and how Indigenous people use the tropical rainforest.

Although Sir David Attenborough did teach a geography lesson in 2020 (Newsround, 2020) and does appear in *Teaching Geography* (Attenborough, 2008, p. 86), he is not a geographer but a broadcaster and biologist. The BBC Natural History Unit programmes, such as *Blue Planet* and *Planet Earth*, are very useful in showing students what it may be like in a place, but these programmes are aimed at the armchair botanist and not a specialist geography audience. The frames used in the visuals show us a selected view of the place, often not in the primary rainforest, and the anthropomorphic stories of animals and having to wait a long time to capture can give a false sense of place. That is not to say that they are not useful.

Similarly, I have always found it difficult to find authentic Indigenous voices and resources when teaching some topics. Bruce Parry's *Tribe* provided some engaging context and an awareness of diversity and the challenges being faced by these groups. However, the series gives limited Indigenous agency and is often an over-simplified outsider perspective, with the narrative shaped by Parry. There is also a danger of commodifying Indigenous cultures rather than providing a deep, respectful analysis.

There is some value in using such resources, and an enquiry lens allows us to also seek out complementary resources; we should never rely upon one artefact. I will explore how we can include authentic Indigenous voice and decolonise geography in Chapter 9, but for now it is important to note that resources are available that provide a counterpoint to the white Eurocentric view. For example, the Windrush Foundation (n.d.) has a range of resources and there are research projects trying to provide such resources. However, there are challenges in getting authentic, quality resources, and there is no central, government-backed strategy to decolonise the curriculum.

If you have relied upon such resources, such as I did, it can leave you feeling like we have failed to provide a wide viewpoint. This is where enquiry comes in. Milner (2020) offers a few strategies to use:

- Expand single case studies into a multifaceted approach; we should not use any single resource, as this will result in misconceptions about places.
- Use critical enquiry by getting students to critically analyse the resources being used.
- Draw upon the experiences of students and teach them so that they have agency.
- Be open with classes about how geographical knowledge has been created and its habit in UK classrooms of prioritising white and Western viewpoints.

I hope that the availability of quality resources providing an authentic Indigenous viewpoint, including data-collection techniques and view of the world, will improve. There is certainly a role here for the subject associations and government, especially as there is currently a Curriculum and Assessment Review underway. There is no mention of decolonisation in the interim report (DfE, 2025), although there is note that the curriculum does not meet the needs of all and that societal change must be considered.

Personal stories as information (migration)

It is far too easy to fall into the trap of 'othering' people and places. One way in which I have tried to tackle this, albeit from a white male perspective, is to share some of my own stories. These are carefully curated. For example, I tell the story of my migrations, both within the UK and to the USA and Australia, and for a variety of reasons. Given as a narrative, students note down push and pull factors, as well as marking the places on a world map. They start with the definition that migration is moving to another place to live or work.

Once the story is told, we can look at how much agency I had in each situation. For example, before the age of 18, I had no choice in where I lived. I also explain that, when in Australia, I had to work for a short while without having the correct working visa. This made me an illegal immigrant. Is this what students would expect? Does it change their viewpoint?

Sharing personal stories can be powerful but should be used with caution, as they only give one perspective and, understandably, we should not share our entire lives with classes.

The news – secondary comments

Local news is a fantastic source of information. Not only are local issues raised, but authentic comments are linked to the stories. Consider the following headline, taken from a newspaper and displayed to students. They were asked to predict the topic.

Headline: *Astounding new figures show record numbers of migrants are crossing the world in search of better lifestyles.*

Sub-headlines:

- *Should they be welcomed?*
- *Are they parasites?*
- *Or should they all go back to where they came from?*

The subject of the article was actually the impact of UK nationals who had migrated to southern Spain. This approach allows preconceptions and viewpoints to be challenged, and with tools such as Google Translate, it is easy to access newspapers in foreign languages.

Experiments

I was lucky to meet the team behind Encounter Edu early in my career, through being involved with the RGS. There are a range of excellent experiments that can be used to explore ocean issues, an area of geography in which it is easy to develop misconceptions.

Experiment 1: Ocean acidification

This experiment helps to challenge the misconceptions around ocean acidification.

Equipment:

- two clear glasses
- drinking straw
- pH indicator (this can be provided by the science department)
- tap water.

Steps:

1. Fill two glasses two-thirds with water.
2. Using a drinking straw, blow into the water in one glass. Explain that our breath contains carbon dioxide and this represents increased carbon being absorbed by our oceans from the atmosphere. You'll need to blow into the water for around three minutes (taking a break now and again!).
3. Use the pH indicator with the glass of water that hasn't been blown into.
4. Ask students to predict what will happen to the pH indicator when added to the glass of water that has been blown into. Then add the indicator to the glass.

This simple experiment demonstrates the impact of increased carbon dioxide when added to water. Visit: https://encounteredu.com/take-action/ocean-acidification-in-a-cup.

Experiment 2: Thermal expansion

This experiment considers rises in sea levels.

Equipment:

- two full tins of food, such as tinned peas (representing land)
- two clear containers slightly wider and higher than the cans, one labelled 'Arctic Ocean' and the other 'Antarctic Ocean'
- some ice, split into two equal quantities
- marker pen.

Steps:

1. Place the cans of food into the clear containers.
2. Pour a mixture of ice and water into the Arctic Ocean container until it is just below the top of the tin.
3. Pour water into the Antarctic Ocean container until it is at the same level as the Arctic Ocean, just below the top of the tin. Place the same quantity of ice on top of the tin. This represents the Antarctic ice sheet, which rests on land.
4. Mark the height of the water in each container with a marker pen.

5 Ask students to make predictions on what will happen once the ice has melted, justifying these using their existing knowledge.
6 Allow the ice to melt, which can take up to a couple of hours, depending on the temperature of the room.
7 Mark the level of water after the ice has melted.

Students can comment on the difference they see: the water level will remain the same in the Arctic representation whereas in the Antarctic representation the water level will rise. Visit: https://encounteredu.com/take-action/sea-level-rise-investigation.

Both these experiments are simple representations of the real world and need careful planning but can have an enormous benefits to learning.

Concrete comparisons

This simple idea to investigate the mouth of the Amazon uses the measuring tool in Google Maps. It can be easily adapted to many other locations and case studies. When investigating the Amazon, I navigated to its mouth; there, I could demonstrate to the class the difficulty in deciding where exactly it was. After measuring the river's mouth, I then navigated to Portsmouth, where the school was located. I first measured the distance from the coast of Portsmouth to the Isle of Wight, before navigating to Dover to measure the distance between there and Calais. A final measurement was taken between Portsmouth and the coast of France. This gives students a reference point and understanding of the distance.

> **Activity**
>
> Repeat this activity yourself. First, write a prediction. Is the mouth of the Amazon wider or narrower than the distance between Dover and Calais? Then use Google Maps and the distance tool to check. Write down some other applications of this technique.

A similar example is comparing the storm surge height reported during a tropical storm to the height of the classroom. In both cases, measurements that can appear vague to young people and difficult to visualise are given a concrete comparison. Students at Priory School had stood on the beach and looked at the Isle of Wight, which helped when they were in the classroom.

Geographical models

Geographical models are representations of the world. Models provide useful curriculum artefacts when combined with others and when we explicitly teach what they are for. The activity can be to critique the model, rather than simply describing or memorising it.

The library lesson

This idea was borrowed and adapted from my English teacher colleagues. I was lucky to have worked in schools that have valued libraries, with physical books and journals. After speaking to the librarian and booking the space, I took A level classes there. Their task was simple: to investigate enquiry questions around sense of place purely by looking at physical artefacts. They had to choose a place and then search for at least ten sources of information. I didn't ask them to evaluate and analyse them – just to find them.

The outcomes were always mixed, sometimes linking to the evaluation of the quality of books available. One thing was certain: the students were taught how to access the library for geography research and got to grips with the Dewey Decimal System. They also found resources ranging from music and art to guidebooks and novels for their selected place.

Fieldwork

It would be remiss not to include a section on fieldwork. Fieldwork is the observation of geographical phenomena and measuring and recoding primary data about such phenomena. The RGS (n.d.) says that fieldwork is the jewel in the crown of geography and argues that it should happen regularly. I totally agree. The simplest school site, rural outlook or suburban street can provide a wealth of opportunities.

There is progression here. First, fieldwork can be conducted on-site. It can then move further away but it does not have to be expensive or outside of walking distance from a school. This is because our curriculum should be contextualised. One purpose of fieldwork is to apply classroom learning to the real world, so there is no need to go far away.

Second, fieldwork begins as closed enquiries, with teachers dictating the data collection and parameters. This allows us to explicitly teach and model issues such as:

- Sampling techniques and why we need them. This in itself brings in issues of simplifying the world. Geographers select information and generalise.
- How we adapt the textbook technique with what we see in the real world. A good example involves groynes. It's very simple to devise a method of measuring them, but how do you identify the top of the groyne when there are boards missing? How does a class decide upon the top of a rock groyne that has an uneven surface? Again, this is an opportunity for students to learn that the real world is messy and not easily measured.
- Modelling and explaining variables and how we measure them. It may be mundane, but a simple pedestrian or traffic count is full of issues. Recording the time of day is important, as is the number of measurements we take.
- Ethical issues, which can be added at all stages of the collection of information.

Even at the NEA stage, and indeed my undergraduate degree, fieldwork was about applying knowledge to a different place and testing geographical theory with the real world. Therefore, the NEA and my own dissertation are guided enquiries. Even with the 'free' choice given at the NEA, the choice is guided by the taught curriculum of the previous five or six years, plus what is contained in the specification. Fieldwork is actually an open enquiry.

Consider the timeline shared with Year 12 students in Table 8.3.

Table 8.3: Year 12 fieldwork timeline

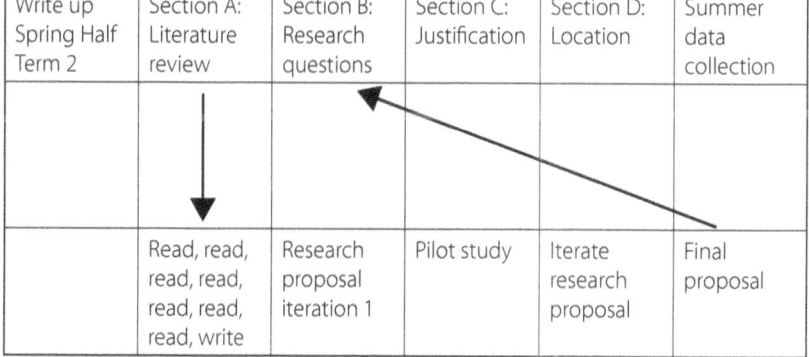

Write up Spring Half Term 2	Section A: Literature review	Section B: Research questions	Section C: Justification	Section D: Location	Summer data collection
	Read, read, read, read, read, read, read, write	Research proposal iteration 1	Pilot study	Iterate research proposal	Final proposal

The top section represents the four stages that need to happen during the spring and summer term *before* the main data collection over the summer break. Section A is expanded on the second line, demonstrating that reading, proposing, iterating and a pilot study need to be completed before the final research questions are solidified. It's not a simple case of going out and collecting data using some sheets from the internet: a lot of thought is needed *before* that happens.

I would also add the forgotten art of the field notebook. Eyes were invented before equipment. Ask students to spend ten minutes looking and noting down what they see:

- the location of everything
- general observations
- problems encountered and the solutions taken
- the time of day.

During a pilot study, staking out interpretation boards very soon demonstrates the feasibility of using them as a measure of engagement with the local area. Fieldwork should allow more time for sitting and observing. This is something that can be taught and honed on-site; remember, a geographer looks at places through different lenses. A quick 15 to 20 minutes of observation or measuring on-site can be invaluable.

I will end this section by saying that secondary 'desktop' studies should also be encouraged and valued. These form the literature review of A level studies, so should be introduced early on in Key Stage 3. This is important, as novice learners do not easily transfer domain-specific information (e.g. Margolis and Laurence, 2023) from one subject to another. Most students will not use what they know about the scientific method in geography. Literature reviews allow us to model and teach this, to create the opportunity for schemas to develop between what students know from other subjects. This also goes for maths. Just because a student has been to a maths lessons, that does not mean that they will transfer it over to geography analysis. Some of the tools we use are different, for a start.

On-site fieldwork microclimate and infiltration tables

With some simple equipment, it is possible to explore geographic phenomena on the school site. For example, with a section of drainpipe, a measuring jug and a stopwatch, different surfaces can be tested around the school site for their infiltration rates. Simply pour a predetermined amount of water into a drainpipe and then measure how much is left after a set period. This can be used to compare different surfaces.

At one school, we set up several thermometers in a secure area. The building happened to be aligned north–south, so we could measure the temperature at each cardinal point. In addition, we used simple handheld anemometers to measure the wind speed. Not only did this demonstrate the impact of the building on these weather variables, but we could also demonstrate how to scientifically take reliable information and sampling strategies.

Key takeaways

- The process of gathering information is foundational for enquiry-based geography and requires thoughtful planning.
- Curriculum artefacts can include anything from textbooks and digital resources to personal stories and fieldwork data, each offering different perspectives.
- Progression involves moving from teacher-selected resources to students independently sourcing and evaluating information.
- Critical evaluation of all resources, including awareness of their limitations and biases, is essential.
- A wide variety of artefacts – maps, books, experiments, images and more – enhances geographical learning and engagement.
- Fieldwork remains a vital and accessible way to connect classroom knowledge with real-world contexts.
- Explicit discussion of resource provenance with students helps develop their critical thinking and enquiry skills.

9 How do we develop critical evaluation of information?

In this chapter

In this chapter, we delve into the art and science of critically evaluating information within the context of geographical enquiry. We begin by expanding upon the enquiry model, exploring why developing these skills is vital for meaningful learning. The progression of critical evaluation is mapped out, followed by an examination of procedural knowledge and two key approaches – 'factfulness' and decolonisation –that shape how we interrogate sources. I present you with sets of questions to encourage a sceptical mindset, illustrate how statistics can be misleading and conclude with practical examples to demonstrate what critical evaluation looks like in the classroom. By the end, you'll be prepared to foster confident, questioning geographers who challenge the information they encounter and learn to see the world through a more nuanced, hopeful lens.

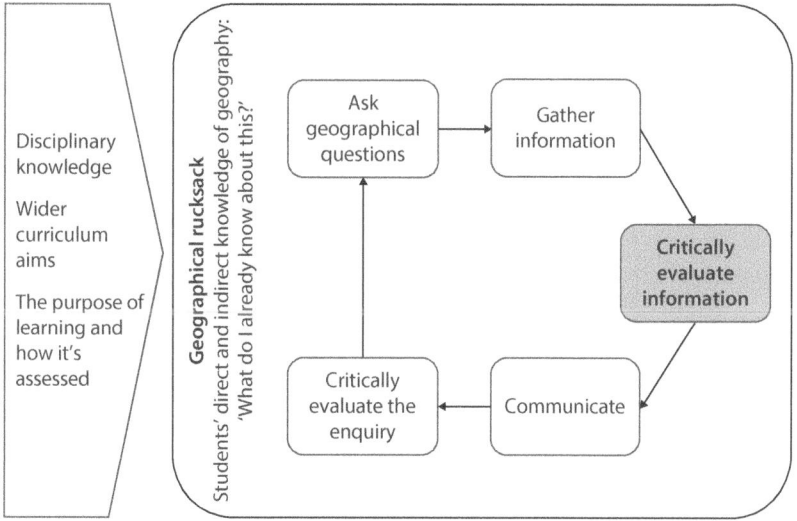

Figure 9.1: The simplified enquiry approach model: Critically evaluate information

So far, we have explored the first two stages of the enquiry model: asking geographical questions and gathering information. We have learned that most information presented to students is selected by their teachers. In this section, we look at one of the fundamental parts of thinking like a geographer: critically evaluating the information presented. The box below expands on the model presented in Chapter 2 (see Figure 9.1) by using a list of considerations. These are explored within the rest of this chapter.

Critically evaluate information

- What perspective(s) is this information from?
- Is this information representative? Reliable?
- How was this knowledge created and by whom? What values does it represent and are they the same as mine?
- What procedural knowledge is required to select, sort, classify and interrogate this information?
- Is this information representative of a single place or can it be applied everywhere?
- What are the similarities?
- When was this published?
- How do geography's key and organising concepts help me make sense of this information?
- Is this model/information too simple?

Why is critical evaluation important?

Arguably, the critical evaluation of information is one of the most important aspects of geographical procedural knowledge that we teach. Hans Rosling said that 'we should be teaching our children humility and curiosity' (2019, p. 249) and pointed out that what is learned about the world in our geography classrooms today will be outdated within a decade or so of leaving school. This is particularly relevant when we consider events such as Brexit and the pandemic, underlining the importance of teaching critical evaluation tools with an approach that is open to change. That is not to say that we can't teach the world as it is but also point out to classes that the world is constantly changing. In addition to this, geographical knowledge is always evolving.

Geography teachers also grapple with the conundrum of keeping our subject knowledge up to date. As two comedians said on the Bishop Exchange podcast, what we know about the world is stories, and those stories are not as solid as we think (Bishop and Bishop, 2025). They are versions of events, and these narratives change rapidly in the age of information. This means that, as geographers we need to hold on to our ideas lightly, consider them carefully and realise that solid, stationary 'facts' may not exist for many of the areas that we teach.

For this stage of enquiry, the procedural knowledge that young people need can be classified into two areas: data interpretation skills, and analytical and thinking skills. This section is about exposing students to these skills, which I can summarise as encouraging them always to ponder two previously mentioned mantras:

- So what?
- Prove it!

Whilst simplistic, getting classes into the habit of posing these two questions allows them to think. Indeed, in the secondary geography classroom, it matters very little what individuals think unless what they say and write is supported by data and evidence and considers different perspectives. As geography teachers, we should seek out the opportunity to have what we teach questioned by young people.

Progression

Ultimately, the end of the progression journey for this stage of enquiry means that students will question and evaluate all the information that they encounter, including information originating from us!

As students become more comfortable with the content and procedural knowledge of geography, the teacher can start to introduce a wider range of sources of information. To begin with, single sources (that are subject to our own critical evaluation) will be considered. This allows the development of the specific skills required to understand that particular resource. Over time, multiple sources of information will be given from an increasing range of perspectives: from a simple two viewpoints on the location of a new wind farm to multiple perspectives on climate change, moving from simple conflict in local spaces to complex global issues.

I would also encourage you to move from simple sources of information, such as bar and pie charts, to ever-more complex sources of information.

Data interpretation skills

Data interpretation skills allow students to make sense of information by understanding it and extracting meaning from the various types of data. A favourite classroom refrain of mine is that we should never trust raw data: we need to process it and make sense of it. All the clues are there on the resource, so check the key, axis labels, etc.

There are four areas of data interpretation in which geography students need to develop procedural knowledge, and these are shown in Table 9.1. I have included some examples, although this is not an exhaustive list.

Table 9.1: Data interpretation areas

Area	Skill	Examples
Map reading and interpretation	Understanding maps to locate and find out about places; understanding the relationships between different maps.	Physical maps: • topographic • relief • geological. Political maps: • country boundaries • location of selected cities and capitals. Thematic maps: • choropleth • dot distribution • proportional symbol • isoline • flow • cartogram.

Area	Skill	Examples
		Climate and weather maps: • digital and remote sensing maps • satellite imagery • GIS. Historical and cultural maps: • historic maps • ethnographic.
Graph interpretation	Reading and analysing graphs.	Graphs: • bar • line • pie • climate • scatter • population pyramid • histogram • flow line • isoline • box and whisker • pictogram.
Statistical analysis	Processing raw data, often collected in the field but also applicable to secondary information.	Descriptive statistics: • mean • median • mode • range • interquartile range. Measures of dispersion and distribution: • standard deviation • variance • frequency distribution. Graphical analysis: • line of best fit • box and whisker.

(*Continued*)

Table 9.1: Continued

Area	Skill	Examples
		Correlation and relationships: • Spearman's rank. Hypothesis testing: • chi-squared test • Mann-Whitney U test • t-test. Spatial: • nearest neighbour analysis • index of dissimilarity. Qualitative data: • coding of themes • word clouds • content analysis.
GIS	Using digital tools to analyse patterns and relationships.	Tools to analyse: • urban land use analysis • flood risk mapping • accessibility studies • environmental impact assessment • wildfire assessment • climate change • site suitability.

If geography teachers are curriculum-makers, we must ensure that students can encounter a wide range of data types and interpretation techniques. A note about GIS is that I always worked in schools with limited access to individual technology. Similarly, I could not assume equal access to devices outside the classroom or at home. This makes it a challenge, as GIS undoubtedly provides a powerful geographic tool for geographers. The way around this was to demonstrate from the front of the class using freely available GIS tools.

Similarly, statistics are scary to some colleagues. As a physical geographer, I became comfortable with large datasets, captured from data loggers, and applying statistical tests to them. At the time of writing, there are many excellent YouTube tutorial videos for the main statistical tests available, and a quick search yields worksheets and spreadsheet templates that can be completed. These are well worth encountering early on in Key Stage 3, and it's worth having a conversation with your maths colleagues to see whether they can also help.

> **Activity**
>
> How many of these interpretation areas will students encounter in your current curriculum? Look at one of your schemes of work and highlight the opportunities to develop and practise these skills. How does that compare with a textbook chapter? Are these skills repeatedly encountered or are they just a one-off?

Analytical and critical thinking skills

The main purpose of enquiry is to question, link different datasets and draw informed conclusions from the data. It takes more time to involve multiple sources of information and is more difficult to link them together. Table 9.2 lists analytical and critical thinking skills, with the more difficult at the bottom. Further examples are provided later in the chapter.

Table 9.2: Analytical and thinking skills

Skill	Example
Identifying patterns and trends	Using relief and population density to spot potential relationships between variables. This can also be done with other maps, such as the Parkrun map.
Comparative analysis	Comparing coastal erosion rates across different sites over time.
Cause and effect analysis	The differences between correlation (a statistical relationship between two variables) and causation (where one variable directly affects another).

(*Continued*)

Table 9.2: Continued

Skill	Example
Evaluating reliability and bias	Students being able to assess sources for accuracy and limitations, such as missing data or a single viewpoint. This can be explored through 'fact or fiction' activities. For example, give four articles to a class, one from the Intergovernmental Panel on Climate Change (IPCC), one from a tabloid newspaper, one from a political blog claiming that the threats are exaggerated and one from an Indigenous community (e.g. a diary written by a student from the Maldives). The class can assess and question each source.
Synthesising information	Combining multiple sources of information into a coherent argument. This is often the final question of GCSE decision-making papers and is certainly the main point of A level essays.

Factfulness is an approach and not just a book

There are two overarching approaches to critical evaluation that can be used to guide the process. The first is 'factfulness'. Hans Rosling's book *Factfulness* was published in 2019, and in it he encourages a fact-based world-view that is grounded in data and calm, critical thinking. In 2025, many of the examples contained within it are dated, but that ignores the fundamental importance of the book: its approach. Factfulness provides an approach that can be applied to geography classrooms. I used to display a poster that listed the ten 'instincts' of factfulness, ready to be referred to when teaching. The key is to adapt this approach to the geography in the secondary UK classroom, with the limited timescales that we have. Whilst the instincts and examples in *Factfulness* relate to economic development, they can be used in many other aspects of geography.

One of the advantages of taking a factfulness approach is that it offers hope to young people. The world can often feel awful. The main thread of factfulness is that the world is both much better than it was and can be much better than it is right now at the same time (Roser, 2018). It is important that we allow students access to data that tells them how the world actually is right now. At the same time, as geographers seek to understand the world so that we can make it better, we need to include hope that things can and will get better. Otherwise, we leave our students with the doom and gloom of the world without any mechanism by which the situation can get better.

A good illustration of this is explored by Roser (2018), using the example of child mortality:

- **The world is awful:** Globally, 4.4 per cent of all children die before the age of 15. This pattern is not evenly distributed.
- **The world is much better than it was:** Child mortality today is much better than any time in the past. In Niger, despite child mortality being the highest in the world in 2023, at 14.1 per cent, this rate has improved compared to two generations ago, when it was almost three times as high.
- **The world can be much better in the future:** The world's wealthiest places show extremely low child mortality (in the EU, child mortality is 0.47 per cent). This means that the knowledge exists to tackle this issue, although it – and the access to good healthcare – is not equally distributed.

Activity

In a geography department meeting, examine a set of current development statistics for a country of your choice. Critically evaluate that data by asking:

- How does this compare to other places in the world?
- Is this current situation better than it was in the past?
- Is there evidence in the world that this issue can be solved?
- Try repeating this approach with a class.

Definition

Hopeful education: David Alcock (2020) defines this as 'encouraging young people to understand progress, believe in humanity and help to create a better world'.

As the point of geographical enquiry is for geographers to understand the world so that they can make it better, I agree with the notion of hopeful geography. In a world where young people have increasing rates of climate anxiety (e.g. Hickman et al., 2021) and where the mental health of young people in schools is not OK (e.g. Ofsted, 2023b), due to a multitude of reasons such as global conflicts and the cost of living, geography can provide genuine hope, whilst maintaining a realistic world-view. We need to do more than get qualifications from young people and get them to remember more and do more. We can provide the inspiration for students in our classes to become active participants in shaping a better world in the future, although it's also OK if they decide not to. The main thing is providing the hope.

The ten 'instincts' of factfulness

Factfulness is based around ten 'instincts', which are summarised in Table 9.3. I will emphasise that this approach can be adapted to suit most geographical information explored in class, without using the examples contained in the book.

Table 9.3: The ten instincts of factfulness (adapted from Rosling, 2019 and Gapminder, n.d.)

Instinct	Summary	Questions to avoid this instinct	Example classroom application
1. The gap instinct	Beware of binary thinking (e.g. rich vs. poor). Reality is a continuum and not a split. Most people fall in the middle of the spectrum.	Is there really a gap? Where is the majority?	Start with the Brandt Line, which is based upon outdated information and was proposed in the 1980s. Ask students whether the world is split into rich and poor. Use a tool such as the Gapminder bubbles (GDP per capita vs. life expectancy) to explore this (see page 213). Use the slider to look at 1980 and explore the pattern. Compare with the latest data available and link to the country classification (for example, contained in your GCSE or A level specification). It is also possible to look at average values when looking at other datasets.

Instinct	Summary	Questions to avoid this instinct	Example classroom application
2. The negativity instinct	Bad news gets more attention but, overall, the world is improving in many areas, like education, health and poverty.	What is the trend and what is the variation?	Zoom out from the data to look at the long-term trend. Look at the trend vs. variation in the historical climate data. I start with a small section of the graph showing a decline, then zoom out to the day and explain diurnal differences in temperature. Depending on which section of the graph we look at, we can find sections that both support and do not support warmer temperatures. However, if we look at the graph as a whole, we can clearly see the difference. Applied to fieldwork, this instinct shows that any data collected can only describe one point in time, rather than a pattern or trend.
3. The straight line instinct	Not all trends continue in straight lines, and there is variation. For example, population growth will level off rather than increase indefinitely.	What has happened in the past? What will happen in the future?	See the earlier example on child mortality rates (page 201). Similarly, rates of coastal erosion differ between the seasons.
4. The fear instinct	Fear makes humans focus on dramatic dangers, such as terrorism or plane crashes, and not the most common or real risks, such as traffic accidents and disease.	What evidence is there?	Tropical storms and wildfires grab headlines and there is a link to climate change. Looking at the statistics, the IPCC's Fifth Assessment Report concludes that confidence remains low for detecting long-term changes in tropical cyclone activity, although it is clear that the frequency and intensity of the strongest tropical cyclones in the North Atlantic have increased since the 1970s (IPCC, 2014).

(Continued)

Table 9.3: Continued

Instinct	Summary	Questions to avoid this instinct	Example classroom application
			Forest fire evidence shows that, since 1983, approximately 70,000 wildfires per year have been documented in the USA (U.S. Environment Protection Agency, 2024), with the area burned by wildfires increasing since the 1980s and the ten largest areas being since 2004. This has been attributed to anthropogenic warming.
5. The size instinct	Big numbers can be misleading. Always look for comparison (such as using per capita) and context to understand their true significance.	How can I process this data to make a comparison?	In 2022, a UK National Park claimed to have rewilded 400 hectares of land, the equivalent to 100 football pitches. In 2024, this had increased to 6,082 hectares, an area bigger than Portsmouth or Worthing. These comparisons seem big and suggest that there has been great progress. However, when considered against the total size of the National Park, the 2022 figure represents 0.25 per cent of the total land area within the park and the 2024 figure 3.8 per cent. This isn't to say that the progress isn't good, but perhaps it could be even better?
6. The generalisation instinct	Avoid assuming that one group or country is homogenous. Recognise diversity and avoid stereotypes.	Does this view represent the world as it is?	A common misconception is that Africa is on homogenised land, rather than comprising 54 countries with eight major climatic zones and around 1.54 billion people. Using a range of maps and country statistics, ask students to fact-check their assumptions, looking for similarities and differences across the continent. This can be extended to any model – does this geographic model represent the world as it is or is it oversimplified?

Instinct	Summary	Questions to avoid this instinct	Example classroom application
7. The destiny instinct	Societies and cultures change over time. Assuming that countries are doomed to stay the same is misleading.	What evidence is there of change?	A common misconception is that an African country will always be poor and underdeveloped. Not only does this show an 'us' and 'them' mentality, but it is also incorrect. Share GDP growth, mobile phone ownership or literacy rates over the past 30 years and highlight the positive change in countries such as Ethiopia, Rwanda and Ghana. Include Indigenous voices by sharing real quotes and short video clips with community leaders, entrepreneurs and activists – for example, an Indigenous Maasai woman describing how education has transformed her village (Al Jazeera English, 2011).
8. The single perspective instinct	No single solution or viewpoint explains everything. Be open to multiple perspectives and disciplines.	What other perspectives are there? Is it really that simple?	Starting the lesson with a powerful image, such as the one from the *Guardian* (Schwartz, 2022) showing the Tuvalu foreign minister addressing Cop26 whilst knee-deep in the Pacific, provides an introduction to looking at different perspectives into climate change. Similarly, asking students whether someone can run along a river (Miles, 2025) introduces the impact of climate changes on the Wardaman in Australia and gives an insight into how climate change will disproportionately affect students (Australian Government, 2009; Nursey-Bray et al., 2019).

(Continued)

Table 9.3: Continued

Instinct	Summary	Questions to avoid this instinct	Example classroom application
9. The blame instinct	Avoid assigning blame to individuals or groups for complex problems. Look for systems and multiple causes.	What system made this possible? How has the past contributed?	Desertification in the Sahel is often attributed to simple local human and physical factors. However, colonisation had profound long-term impacts and contains the root causes of desertification, such as the disruption of traditional land use systems, forced cash crop agriculture and arbitrary colonial borders. For example, taxation policies led people to overuse land close to settlements, causing desertification. This is a good topic for examining the impact of colonisation on the present, before considering the post-colonial acceleration of desertification, due to multiple factors such as population growth and climate change.
10. The urgency instinct	Avoid panicking over urgent-sounding problems. Pause, get the data and think things through before acting.	What evidence-based solutions are there?	There is well-documented tension between individual, government and corporation responsibility on who takes action around climate change. Often, solutions, such as planting a tree instead of taking a medal at the end of a running race, lead people to think that they are making a positive impact. But where do those trees get planted and by whom? Take the example of National Highways, who pledged to plant an additional three million trees by 2030. In one road-building scheme, 850 thousand trees died because they were planted at the wrong time of year. These facts were discovered by accessing different sources of information. Does a pledge mean delivery? In addition, if we consider other sources, the UK has lost 15 per cent of its tree cover since 2000 (Global Forest Watch, n.d.).

There are some excellent examples of schemes of work shared by geography teachers around factfulness (including Alan Parkinson's collaborative scheme (2018) and work from Kate Stockings (2020) and Matt Podbury (n.d.)), although the data will constantly need updating and the authors acknowledge this. Rather than a one-off scheme of work, I recommend embedding this factfulness throughout the curriculum so that critical evaluation becomes embedded and a routine habit for young people.

> **Reflection**
>
> Choose one of the ten factfulness instincts. Reflect on how it may influence your teaching and your students' perceptions of the world.

Decolonising geography

The second overarching approach to critical evaluation is decolonising geography. Since 2020, there has been an increased discourse amongst geography teachers around decolonisation and lack of diversity in the curriculum. Some colleagues feel fearful of engaging with the discourse or, even worse, are left with a feeling that they are failing young people. For me, with a background as a director of inclusion, it is vital that we think carefully about the curriculum and, in particular, the 'human' aspects of our subject, including development and migration. Decolonisation, when applied to teaching and learning geography, encourages the inclusion of diverse voices and perspectives. We need to move beyond the Eurocentric narratives, explicitly addressing misconceptions and stereotypes that stem from an 'us' and 'them' view of the world.

Geography teachers can take positive action, as enquiry provides tools that enable students to critically engage with information and, in doing so, consider a range of viewpoints. Students should be actively questioning the origins and purpose of information. At the same time, teachers can recognise the importance of students' lived experiences by getting them to contribute observations contained within their personal geographical rucksacks in lessons. Teachers can value what is shared by including it within the taught curriculum.

Whilst much of the attention has been on textbooks and resources, systemic change is needed from the government in order for large-scale, lasting transformation. That doesn't mean that we should wait, as positive changes can be made by all geography teachers (Winter, 2023), and enquiry is the vehicle that helps us. Whilst I am no expert on the matter and can only speak from one perspective, and whilst these systemic changes may be beyond our direct power, we are not powerless.

Working in various schools over 20 years, it is clear that at least some of the points discussed here can also be applied to all nine protected characteristics that are law in the UK. Furthermore, our duty goes beyond the Teachers' Standards (DfE, 2011), which are limited in their scope; Standard 5 tells us that we need to respond to the strengths and needs of all students but does not explicitly mention specific protected characteristics. Intersectionality is the framework that says that people experience oppression and privilege in complex, interconnected ways. The different aspects of a person's identity, such as race, gender, class, sexuality and disability, interact to shape unique lived experiences. In the geography classroom, this means that we must be more inclusive and have nuanced understandings of discrimination and inequality, especially as large parts of our subject concern this directly.

It is also important that we do more than simply include the lives and experiences of the students in front of us, and also expose all students to decolonial thinking.

So what are some solutions? There are few examples of what this looks like in practice (Nayeri and Rushton, 2022). Whilst much has been written against textbooks, I would extend these issues to include any resource. We shouldn't include a resource without critically evaluating it and being explicit about this with our students. This is especially important because many of us do not have direct experience of the places and cultures about which we teach. Geography education also plays a critical role in shaping and developing a diverse world-view in our students, although there are other external factors that we may not be able to fully counter, with the personal lived experiential view (which includes parental views) being highly valued by young people.

Charlotte Milner (2020) and Nayeri and Rushton (2022) provide some excellent, practical classroom strategies to address this issue. I have summarised these in Table 9.4 and feel that they should be a key part of any enquiry classroom.

Table 9.4: Strategies to address decolonisation (based upon Milner, 2020 and Nayeri and Rushton, 2022)

Strategy	Example
Include racial aspects as a fundamental aspect of geographical understanding, to challenge misconceptions	Start with the impact of how colonialism in the past has shaped the geography of today, and how neocolonialism, through trade agreements, foreign aid, TNCs and strategic alliances, means that dominant cultures exert control over others. We must avoid the simplistic 'us' and 'them' comparisons. We can also challenge ideas of homogeneity on the African continent and highlight the colonial history of Britian.
Reconstruct the curriculum	Introduce curriculum artefacts and foci that have been left out of the curriculum, e.g. the impact of colonialisation on the countries being studied. Teachers as curriculum-makers make professional judgements on what to include in the curriculum and we do not need permission to include such items (Jankell et al., 2021).
Use students' lived experiences to diversify knowledge production in the classroom	As mentioned, a student's geographical rucksack of lived experience is valuable and can be considered part of their geographical knowledge. By embracing this and allowing opportunities for these to be brought into the classroom, the experiences of students with protected characteristics can be shared with all students.
Do not use single case studies	Enquiry means using one place to illustrate more than one aspect of geography. Whilst we shouldn't rely upon one single place for all examples and case studies, looking at a location from multiple topics and perspectives (including starting with the view from that place) encourages young people to move beyond a narrow world-view.
Use an enquiry approach	Encourage students to question authoritative sources of knowledge, such as books and teachers, and make connections between different aspects of geography and knowledge from other disciplines.

National policy reforms are required that will drive change in examination boards and the curriculum. This needs to be coupled with extensive teacher training and a purposeful effort to include Indigenous voices and update resources. Having said this, teachers have the power to both shape and contextualise their own geography curriculum and include a wider range of resources that present different viewpoints. Indeed, enquiry demands that we do.

I hope that by addressing this aspect directly, you leave with some confidence in what you may be doing already. Yes, there needs to be widespread structural change, but there is a lot that we can do as teachers. This can simply be starting with the impacts of colonialism or bringing authentic Indigenous sources into the classroom. Even sharing how research by Indigenous people is different from Western research (Louis, 2007) goes some way to addressing this issue and is all part of thinking critically as a geographer.

Questions that students can ask

Based on these two approaches, I refer you back to the list of questions I suggested the reader asks before selecting a source of information for inclusion in teaching (see pages 169–70). Ultimately, we want students to critically question any source of information, although we must balance this with ensuring that misconceptions and confusion do not develop. To do this, I would evaluate which areas of geography demand a more complex approach, moving from easy-to-understand, concrete ideas, such as the evidence for climate change, the world's climate zones or geomorphic processes, towards considering more complex, abstract ideas, such as how to solve the issues presented by climate change or development issues.

The main questions that I get students to ask are 'prove it' and 'so what?'. In addition, assuming that you are presenting information within discrete units, I suggest the following:

- Who produced this information and are they credible?
- What is the purpose of this information (e.g. to inform, persuade, sell)?
- Is the source biased or presenting a particular perspective?
- Is the information supported by evidence or data? Are there references?
- Are the methods used to collect the data reliable and clearly explained?
- Is the information up to date?
- How does this information relate to the topic I am studying?
- Whose voices or viewpoints are included or excluded?
- Does this information consider social, environmental, economic and political factors?
- Are there any patterns, trends or spatial relationships shown or implied?

Specific questions relate to the type of resource being studied. As mentioned earlier, I tell students that all the information they need should be on the source. For example, a map should have a scale and legend, make it clear whether it is real or a representation, detail who published it and be accurate for the purpose needed.

Practical examples

Having considered some of the overarching and fundamental issues when evaluating sources of information, what follows are a number of practical classroom examples.

Create the graph

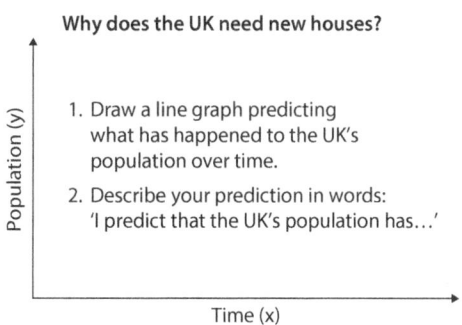

Figure 9.2: Incomplete graph example

We shouldn't always present the complete graph to students. The example in Figure 9.2 is a good way of exploring pre-existing knowledge and misconceptions, as well as linking to previously taught knowledge. Once students have grappled with this, revealing the actual pattern stimulates conversation. To add another dimension, graphs can be offered from different sources. How do they differ? Is this linked to the source? For example, do right-leaning newspapers select different information to display? In a world where the same facts are used to justify different arguments and courses of action, this is a very useful lesson to learn.

Mystery graph

After teaching how to interpret population pyramids, present students with a population pyramid with the name of the country missing. Ask them to describe the pattern, referring to information contained in the graph. Then, challenge the class to give some reasons for the pattern. This approach sparks curiosity and produces questions. This activity can also be used to provide context when looking at a country as a case study.

> **Activity**
>
> Use a website such as www.populationpyramid.net to source a few interesting population pyramids. Start with Qatar, Japan, Nigeria and the UAE.
>
> Present the pyramid to a class with the country name missing. Ask students to summarise the unusual pattern in three bullet points. Then, teach them the reasons why these exist. Using Qatar as an example:
>
> - The population is heavily concentrated in the 25–39 age bracket, accounting for over 50 per cent of the population.
> - Children and the elderly combine to make up less that 15 per cent of the population.
> - Qatar's working age demographic is significantly skewed toward males.

Instagram vs. reality

This is a simple technique designed to give a fresh perspective on places. Most people I know are bombarded by information through social media. In many cases, this has sparked interest in locations and an influx of visitors. Waterfall Country in South Wales is a great example of a place where economic benefits have been accompanied by the social drawbacks of increased visitor numbers. Similarly, the trend of visiting set locations of programmes such as *Game of Thrones* and then sharing the visit on social media can be looked at.

Present an idealised photography of the place, as well as one that represents a more typical view – for example, a view of Big Ben with empty streets, compared to one with many people (we assume tourists) taking the same photograph. Students can assess and evaluate why a 'clean' version may be used.

Cause and effect using Gapminder

A good way to explore correlation is to use the Gapminder bubbles (www.gapminder.org/tools). Keep the X axis at GDP per capita and change the Y axis. Ask students to write a prediction of the correlation beforehand. The default is life expectancy: where GDP increases, so does life expectancy. Try using carbon emissions, defence spending and fertility rate.

Causation can be explored by looking at the GDP per capita of countries by latitude. We can observe how countries closer to the equator have lower income, but that is not the cause, as we need to look at colonisation, climate impact and other factors. If we look at volcanic eruptions and global average temperature, the correlation is that there is short-term global cooling after eruptions, and this is caused by the volcanic eruption, as particles and sulphur dioxide are released into the atmosphere and reflect sunlight.

Who really said it?

If there is one thing for which the internet is useful, it is providing a huge range of feel-good cat memes! Quotes can heavily influence our perception around issues. Unfortunately, the internet is also full of misquoted, misattributed quotes. Many of these are liberally applied to classroom and corridor posters and assemblies. In the age of Google, we should be teaching students to correctly reference material as soon as we can.

Activity

Consider these quotations:

'Integrity is doing the right thing, even when no one is watching.'
C. S. Lewis

'You are never too small to make a difference.'
Greta Thunberg

> *'Think globally, act locally.'*
> Patrick Geddes
>
> Use the internet to assess them. Classify them into:
>
> - verified
> - misattributed
> - uncertain.
>
> Once done, which geographical concepts could they be used with? Does it matter who said them? Are some quotes oversimplified or taken out of context?

As well as understanding the true meaning and accurate source, students should:

- Check for accuracy – are they spreading false information?
- Think critically – do they agree with the quote? Why was that quote chosen for use in that context?
- Recognise bias or persuasion – quotes are used to inspire or influence opinions. Understanding the quote fully and its context allows students to understand whether it is being used to manipulate the audience or whether it is too simplified.
- Link to the real world so that they can connect to real places, people and issues.

Track your sources!

Whilst access to individual devices is always a lottery when teaching, and there is patchy access for students outside school, most young people can get access to an internet-enabled device. Teaching students how to attribute sources is important, as is teaching them about the correct use of images (looking for Creative Commons, for example). The increase of AI makes this even more relevant. We can teach students that using the tools available to us is useful and totally fine to do, within certain rules.

When in a computer room, give the class an enquiry question to research. They should aim to find three reliable sources. For each source, they should record:

- website name
- author or organisation (if available)
- URL
- date accessed
- one fact or quote that they will use.

These can easily be shared through online learning platforms. The next stage is to swap these mini reference lists and for another student to find them.

The activity can be concluded with a group discussion around why referencing is important. What problems could happen if students don't reference? In addition, did any students come up with a different viewpoint from their list?

Trends vs. variation

Students need to distinguish between long-term trends and short-term variations. Give the class two sets of real data. One shows the long-term trend of temperatures, showing a warming trend over time for the UK. Alongside this, give them a local temperature graph for the year that shows variations in temperature. Students evaluate the data to identify trends and variations.

Using geographical models

I have already mentioned models and their use in geography. Whilst I was fortunate to have a geography teacher in Carmarthen who routinely covered the limitations of such models, I also remember him saying just to learn this for the exam, as it would change as I progressed from lower to upper school. There is much discussion about whether or not they should be included in the geography classroom. I would argue that they provide a useful teaching point for students to understand their purpose, advantages and limitations. Certainly, they are good at summarising complex geographical processes in a simplistic way. For example, physical models that seek to emulate natural processes are very useful (e.g. Samingpai, 2023; Brady et al., 2023).

Before considering some examples, we should teach students to evaluate them, and therefore develop critical literacy. Steel (2023) suggests a few questions that students can use and I have summarised these in Table 9.5.

Table 9.5: Questions for evaluation models (based on Steel, 2023)

Question	Explanation
Why are we using this model?	What is its purpose? Is it aiming to explain, predict, simplify or explore a geographical concept? How does it link to the enquiry question? What will we learn from it?
Where does this model come from?	Does it present a Eurocentric viewpoint? Who is responsible for creating it? What was its original purpose? Whose experience and viewpoint does it reflect? What is the historical context of the model?
Is this model too simplified or too complex?	Real life is very messy and models are used in geography. How does it link to real-life examples? Will this model introduce more misconceptions?

Models should be a starting point for geographical exploration. For each question in Table 9.5, limitations are identified. This does not mean that models are not useful, as by simplifying real systems, the fundamental learning can be secured in students. I would add that all models should be linked to a real-world situation.

Let's take the Burgess model (Burgess, 1925), for example. This was produced in 1925, was based upon Chicago and was a theoretical diagram of a dynamic process. It does describe the growth of some American cities and went on to inspire further models of urban development. One hundred years later in the UK, cities such as Brighton (Rawdling, 2019) and Portsmouth do not fit the model at all – but that wasn't its original purpose. It was used to develop geographical understanding in a particular place and at a particular time. It is therefore how we use the model that is more important (Puttick, 2020). Burgess is a good model to use to introduce the purpose and critique of models with Key Stage 3 students.

As we encourage students to ask questions about models, rather than simply accept them, they will start to ask where the model comes from. Another widely used example is the Bradshaw model (Bradshaw et al., 1978), which appeared in a secondary school textbook in 1978, the year in which I was born, although it is loosely based upon earlier work by academic geographers (Redfern, 2023). The model is used in small-scale GCSE and A level studies.

The Bradshaw model, a theoretical model that describes changes in rivers between their source and mouth, is an oversimplification, and velocity is not supported by the earlier work upon which the model is based. It also does not consider human impact, such as channel modification, that leads to irregular changes. In short, the model is too simple and outdated, even though it presents a simple, visual tool. Again, this model is a great way to demonstrate the limitations of models.

The learning can be applied to models such as Lee's conceptual model of migration (itself produced in 1966), which explains why people migrate (Lee, 1966), or the Demographic Transition Model (Thompson, 1929), which describes how a country's population changes over time as it develops economically, which may be encountered later on in Key Stage 3.

The trouble is that in the time-starved geography classroom, this change takes a long time, especially if we are relying on old publications and websites that are based upon older models. AI can quickly give an accurate critique of the models used in the geography classroom, and by using an enquiry approach and considering the validity of models first, we are encouraging students to critically think.

In conclusion, when carefully used and when students are encouraged to actively critique them, simplified models can help students grasp complex concepts.

Floating topicality

Floating topicality – geography's secret weapon (Rogers, 2015) – is more than simply 'geography in the news', as it provides a well-thought-out and planned way to create curriculum opportunities that engage students in the world that is happening *now* – to apply their geographical knowledge to real-time events. I will stress that this is not the same as providing a knee-jerk reaction to current events, and following conflicts and natural disasters in real time must be done in a very sensitive manner. It is not OK to feel excited at the prospect of updated case study material during times of distress.

There are two types of floating topicality: the first is part of the planned curriculum (planned floating topicality) and the second is more reactionary, when major local or international events occur (reactionary topicality). Both require careful thought and consideration. There are three reasons why current events should feature in the geography curriculum:

1. What is the point of geography lessons if they don't help towards an understanding of the world as it is?
2. Geography teachers are in the ideal position to challenge media bias and editorial decisions.
3. Topical issues are an opportunity to reinforce and revisit prior learning.

Overall, whilst I give some examples below, it is up to the professional judgement of geography teams to decide upon the relevance and approach taken, tailored to your context and students.

Planned floating topicality involves sequencing units around the time at which events may occur in the news. For example:

- Tropical storms can be taught during the peak season for a chosen region. Not only does understanding the timing of tropical storms in different regions allow for better preparedness and risk mitigation, but teaching tropical storms during April to June or October and December (the two peak times in the North Indian Ocean) may result in such events happening in real time. Choosing a different region also provides the opportunity to move away from a Eurocentric view of the world.
- Teaching about Everest, including glaciated landscapes and the impact of climate change on mountain regions, can happen between April and the end of May. The peak climbing season is before the monsoon season.

Reactionary topicality is where current events feed into the curriculum. This needs to be done in a sensitive way.

- One example is tectonic events. For example, I remember cancelling a running trip to the High Atlas in 2023 as I didn't want to be a 'dark tourist' (a tourist who visits sites associated with death, tragedy or suffering), but it was a good opportunity to discuss with A level students whether tourists should go to earthquake areas to continue to help the economy or stay away. This is not using the event to follow real-time deaths and casualties. In addition, the international response to the event was examined.
- Brexit continues to impact on the UK economy, so it still makes a good unit to look at and is never far from the news. This could be included in a unit called 'Does the UK exist?', and Brexit still provides geography teachers with the chance to demonstrate the importance of our subject (Usher, 2019) and the unequal impacts on different regions of the UK and groups of people.

Tools such as Ground News allow students to quickly understand the bias behind news stories, presenting a useful analytical tool for looking at highly charged political issues such as migration. Table 9.6 gives an example.

Table 9.6: Looking at the bias behind news stories

Headline	Left	Right	Both
The UK could add an Edinburgh every year with net migration set to exceed forecast.	De-emphasises the headline and focuses on the nuances of migration and overlap with economic policies. Uses language like 'overestimate'.	Uses emotive and partisan language, such as 'spiralling out of control' and emphasises policy failure.	Concede migration's scale.

Generative AI also provides a snapshot into this. Pasting the URL of a news story and asking a chatbot to analyse the story for bias (Table 9.7) produces a useful summary, as well as alternative sources of information.

Table 9.7: AI bias summary of news stories

Story topic	Source	Summary
Migrants	*Daily Mail*	Bias against Kier Starmer and historical *Daily Mail* stance of being anti-immigration. The article downplays and omits viewpoints from positive sources.
View on green homes	*Guardian*	Reflects the publication's strong environmental advocacy stance.
Plans for new homes	*Worthing Argus*	The article provides a platform for opponents of development but offers limited insight into the developer's perspective or the broader context of rising housing needs. Suggests exploring alternative sources about the housing shortage in the area.

This could be used live in the lesson as a demonstration, after students consider the articles themselves.

Fieldwork

Fieldwork provides the ideal teaching opportunity to explore some of the limitations of geographical enquiry (see Table 9.8), as well as analysing and interpreting the data. Here, I want to consider the wider teaching points, as there are many excellent books on the analysis of data collection. This is important, as often students consider fieldwork (and enquiry) as a linear journey when in fact it is iterative, with methods being refined and tweaked. On-site fieldwork and small-scale investigations are ideal for this.

Table 9.8: Limitations of fieldwork

Limitation	Explanation
Bias	Is the study free of bias?: • confirmation • section • observer • overconfidence • hindsight • questionnaire • temporal • spatial.
Sources of error	• Was there human error in the data collection? • Were there equipment limitations? • Was the sample size too small or unrepresentative? • Did the site cause issues? • Were the time and location representative?
Does the data support the hypothesis?	• What other information is needed and what new questions have been identified? • Can I draw a valid conclusion?
Methods used	• Were the methods suitable for the aims? • Can this study be replicated?

Books

When leading behaviour, I quickly found that the typical student removed from class had a chronological reading age at least two years behind where it should be. When leading Pupil Premium, this was also the case. Books and our engagement as geography teachers in literacy are vital in attempting to address this, especially as communication in geography relies upon a good command of the English language.

Therefore, books have become commonplace in lessons. The first job is to get students to understand their limitations – for example, check the publication date at the front of the book and ask questions about the author.

The next stage is to get students to treat books as we would any resource: critically evaluate them. Sometimes, we may choose to explicitly share this with students and other times we might get them to do that work, depending on their stage and age in education. I would argue that we should not be using any resource in geography without some form of critical analysis.

Let's take Marshall's *Prisoners of Geography*, for example. We can start by asking the class to think about the claim of the subtitle of the 2025 version: *Ten maps that tell you everything you need to know about global politics*. Is this a realistic claim? Just like a geographical model, a book can present a simplistic view – and is it realistic that any book can teach us *everything* we need to know? Similarly, the idea of being a *prisoner* can also be pulled apart, especially as we can help students link to their English knowledge (it's well worth having a chat to the English team to find out how and mirror their techniques in geography).

Table 9.9: Critical evaluation of *Prisoners of Geography* (Marshall, 2025)

Strengths	Criticisms
Popularises geopolitics, as it is written in an accessible way to a general audience.	Takes a deterministic approach and links with ideas put forward by Mackinder (Trolley, 2020).
The 2025 version has 30,000 words of new content, covering Russia–Ukraine and China's growing influence.	Limited engagement with human geography and the interaction and interdependence of physical geography.
Strong physical geography narrative.	Tim Marshall is a journalist and is not writing with academic rigour.

Does this mean that we should avoid using such books? No – just that we need to be aware of their limitations and get students to read the information critically, combining it with other sources of information.

Maps

Maps can provide an immediate and effective visual stimulus with which to think about and debate geography (Vujakovic, 2019), as well as explore issues, but they cannot be used uncritically. Whilst the curriculum mentions Ordnance Survey maps, they are limited, as although they are great for navigation, they can be linked to the colonial use of maps to control conquered territories, and only present one representation of the world by including selected features. Maps, like many other aspects of geographical procedural knowledge, should be a matter of routine. In Table 9.10, I suggest some ways to investigate the issues with maps, plus some alternative activities based upon maps so that they can be used critically in geography classrooms.

Table 9.10: Using maps in the classroom

Question	Example	Classroom application
Who created the map? Why? For whom?	Look at the purpose and audience of the map – for example, colonial and Indigenous maps.	Explicitly teach this to the class and get them to ask the questions.
Is there political, cultural or economic bias?	How are borders drawn? What names are used and what is the map emphasising?	Examine maps of disputed territory or place names, such as: • Persian Gulf vs. the Arabian Gulf • Gulf of Mexico vs. the Gulf of America • Russian and Ukrainian maps • maps of Kashmir from India and Pakistan perspectives • Aboriginal songline maps and Inuit stick maps.
What is the projection being used?	Different projections distort the work.	Look at the differences between Mercator vs. Peters projection and the impact on places.
Is this map neutral?	Maps are created by people and are not neutral or objective reflections of reality.	Give students maps that are centred on different parts of the world or upside down. Get students to ask what isn't shown, emphasised or marginalised. Does this map consider the Global South perspective (a term itself not without its limitations)?
How do these maps connect with the historical and social context?	Maps should be viewed in their context.	Include the context in your teaching, e.g. evacuation maps for Grindavik, psychogeography maps focused on human emotions or the Native Land digital maps (https://native-land.ca).

If we use Ordnance Survey maps purely to locate places and be able to describe them, we miss fantastic opportunities for on-site and local fieldwork and nature connection (Richardson, 2024). The ideas in Table 9.11 are based upon the book *Local* (Humphreys, 2024) and can be done in one location within a grid square, with the class predicting what they will see for the map.

Table 9.11: Fieldwork suggestions (based on Humphreys, 2024)

Enquiry	Activity	Procedural knowledge
Local landscape investigation	Choose a green space and use an OS map to predict what will be found there. Then visit the site to observe the landscape.	• using OS map symbols • field sketching and observation • identifying human impact on the landscape.
Local sustainability walk	Plan a walk in the local area and plan to assess local sustainability features, such as green transport, waste management and biodiversity.	• field data collection • creating reports and proposals on the findings.
Accessibility and route analysis	Plan a walk using rights of way. Assess the accessibility of the route for signage, paths and terrain.	• route planning • comparing maps vs. actual access • evaluating human impact.

Adverts

Adverts provide a good way into encouraging students to question everything around them, although we need to be considerate and careful about what we use in the classroom to avoid sexist narratives that reinforce stereotypes, biases or discrimination based on gender. Table 9.12 details some claims in recent adverts.

Table 9.12: Claims in recent adverts

Claim	Caveat in the small print
The number one washing liquid	Based on an independent test
40 per cent more volume	Compared to untreated air
Better performance	70 per cent of 82 people agreed

Whilst not totally geographical, adverts are available in print or freely available online and are a good resource for spotting false and misleading claims.

When looking for adverts, we can also critique other sources from which students get information. For example, my son and his contemporaries get a lot of information from YouTube, but which videos cite their source material and references?

Key takeaways

The critical evaluation of information could easily fit into a volume on its own. There are several important points that I wish to make:

- It should be an embedded, integrated part of our normal teaching. All sources of information should be used critically.
- There are simple questions that enable students to do this.
- Fieldwork is an opportunity to teach about the pitfalls and biases of information.
- Much of the information used in classrooms is not created by geographers. Whilst this does not mean we cannot use it, we need to be mindful and communicate to students that this information has not been created by geographers.
- Geographical knowledge is socially created and changes. What we teach today will be out of date, sometimes by the time students leave school. Enquiry gives a mechanism with which we can tackle this.

10 How do we enable students to communicate their learning?

In this chapter

This chapter explores the central role of communication in geographical enquiry, showing how students move from simple description to critical evaluation as their confidence and knowledge grow. It highlights the importance of purpose and audience in shaping communication, whether through writing, oracy, visual outputs or digital media. The chapter stresses the importance of authenticity and students providing clarity in how they express their conclusions. Practical strategies are outlined that develop note-taking, oracy and extended arguments. By teaching the importance of communication, we not only support success in assessment outcomes but also help students learn to argue (positively!), question and disagree well – skills that allow them to participate meaningfully in debates about geographical issues and the wider world.

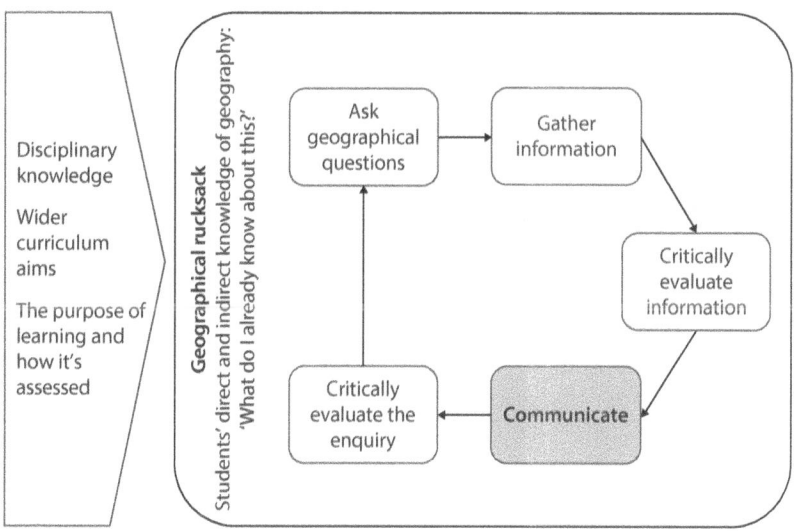

Figure 10.1: The simplified enquiry approach model: Communicate

In order to communicate, students need to write about their knowledge and understanding. Whilst there are other mediums available to us, we cannot escape the fact that the main method of assessment in the UK is through the written examination. During the enquiry process, students need to communicate at every stage. They need to draft their geographical questions, write their critical evaluation of information and then express their conclusions and thoughts.

Communicate

- So what? Prove it!
- Am I being asked to give facts or an argument?
- Who am I writing for?
- Synopticity: How does this link into other key concepts and parts of geography?
- Who is the audience?
- What are the limitations of my viewpoint and conclusions?
- What will happen in the future?
- How can I use this knowledge to change the world?
- What is the appropriate output? Examination, written argument, oral presentation, academic poster?

Progression

In essence, students' communication of enquiry should get more complex and use a greater range of evidence as they progress through secondary school. In addition, whilst most of the time the teacher will dictate how students communicate, some choice can be introduced once they have been taught the purpose and advantages and disadvantages of communication methods.

I will state strongly that when the majority of students get to Year 7, they are capable of far more than asking simple enquiry questions and communicating in simple sentences.

Progression in communication moves from students being able to write simple descriptions to presenting critical evaluations of issues that link multiple ideas and concepts together. Table 10.1 outlines what progression looks like.

Table 10.1: Progression in communication

Stage	Communication
1. Description Describing, observing and basic questions	• Verbal description of features and places. • Labelled pictures and simple diagrams. • Use basic geographical vocabulary and everyday language. • Begin to use structured sentence starters for explanation.
2. Explanation Comparative thinking and using data	• Write structured explanations using evidence. • Use geographical vocabulary confidently and accurately. • Use comparative language. • Use maps, diagrams and data in oral or written arguments.
3. Argument Analysis, interpretation and evaluation	• Write geographical arguments that are well structured (e.g., introduction, methodology, data presentation, conclusion). • Use more complex geographical vocabulary. • Begin to link to other interconnected parts of geography when considering an issue. • Begin to relate ideas to a single overarching concept. • Include spatial and temporal trends. • Use a wider range of data, including GIS and multimedia, to present findings. • Begin to reflect on bias and representation in sources of information.
4. Critical evaluation Synthesis, debate and nuanced understanding	• Construct extended evaluative written responses (essays and reports). • Use sophisticated geographical terminology and concepts. • Present a balanced viewpoint that reflects different scales and engages with critical and ethical dimensions.

At the end of their geographical journey, students need to communicate effectively and confidently on their own in examinations and with limited guidance in the NEA. The building blocks of success comes from Key Stage 3.

What is the communication for?

If students are to communicate their learning effectively, they must be able to understand why they are writing in the first place. This requires knowledge of who the audience will be, whether debate is expected, whether students are making notes to refer to in the future and whether that work is to be assessed.

Audience

It is important to share the audience of their communications to students. These should be authentic and not made up. There is very little point in writing a letter to a third party who will never read it. Most of the time, students will be writing for their teacher, but the purpose of enquiry is to eventually suggest improvements and make recommendations. In this case, the audience may well be their peers (in the case of an assembly or debate), the school's SLT (for on-site enquiries) or the wider community (e.g. online writing).

Pause and answer the enquiry question

There is little point in asking questions and developing sequences of lessons around overarching fertile questions if we don't pause and allow students to answer them. To this end, pause points should be built into units. The question is often best answered through extended writing, which most students from Year 7 are able to do, even if it is through scaffold.

Disagreeing well

Communicating allows students to develop the skill of disagreeing well. This means that they appreciate that there is more than one viewpoint on the same issue. Disagreeing well involves six aspects, shown in Table 10.2.

Table 10.2: Aspects of disagreeing well

Aspect	What it means	Why it matters in enquiry
1. Recognise and respect different perspectives	Disagreement doesn't mean one view is necessarily wrong; it can reflect different priorities, values or experiences. For example, a farmer might see flood management differently from an ecologist.	Many of the issues studied in geography affect people differently across the world.

Aspect	What it means	Why it matters in enquiry
2. Base arguments on evidence, not emotion alone	Opinions should be supported with facts, data, case studies and geographical reasoning from a range of sources.	Geography is based on understanding the real world.
3. Listen actively and respectfully	Teachers can model and expect active listening, not interrupting and not shutting down views.	Geography involves collaboration and hearing diverse voices.
4. Critique ideas, not people	Get students to challenge what is being said and claimed, not the people saying it. For example, the leader of the Reform party may make claims on migration and its impact on the UK. Are those claims based on fact?	Geography has many contested areas and involves sensitive subject matter, thus includes debate and different points of view. Doing so kindly builds better discussions.
5. Consider values and ethics	Help students understand that some geographical decisions involve moral choices (e.g. should the UK make a commitment to resettle climate refugees?). In addition, show that people's beliefs, priorities and lived experiences shape their views on issues.	Geography often deals with moral dilemmas like environmental justice or migration.
6. Reflect on one's own biases	Teach students to hold their ideas lightly and be open to changing their view. The media, background, education and other factors all shape opinion.	Great geographers stay curious and are willing to see things differently in order to make the world a better place.

Making notes

Over time, a student's exercise book becomes a geographical artefact. Whilst writing for assessment is likely to form a large part of their exercise books, note-taking encourages students to actively listen, process and communicate their learning. Notes also provide information with which to tackle future enquiries. In addition, teaching note-taking skills is very helpful for future stages of education, as well as making observations in the field.

There are several methods for taking notes, such as bullet points, the Cornell method (a way of organising notes into subheadings; see Cornell University, n.d.) and mind maps. In geography, the key features of note taking are as follows:

- summarising information
- organising content

- using geographical terms
- using diagrams and sketches
- recording case studies.

Assessment

Whilst not all Key Stage 3 students will go on to study geography at GCSE and beyond, it makes sense to start this work from lesson one in Year 7. That is not to say that we drill students in exam skills, but we subtly include these from the very start, including the skills-based questions that focus on analysing sources of information.

In addition, most communication by students in the geography classroom is for the teacher to assess – both summatively and formatively – their learning. It is more than OK to share this purpose with students.

Communication skills

When students communicate in geography, whether through writing or talking, they need a range of skills to be developed through explicit teaching. These skills allow young people to present and assess geographical issues clearly.

- **Structured writing:** Using a range of scaffolds, such as PEEL (point, evidence, explanation, link) or SEEP (social, economic, environmental, political) frameworks or structure strips and other pedagogical techniques. In general, it is important that the level of scaffolding meets the need, as assessed by teachers, and is gradually removed.
- **Justification:** The 'so what?' – being able to defend a conclusion or choice with reasoned arguments supported by data and links to geographical concepts and processes.
- **Balanced evaluation:** Being able to present advantages and disadvantages or giving different perspectives on an issue.
- **Decision-making:** Students need to make justified recommendations using multiple sources and viewpoints.

The problem with terminology

I have previously mentioned the issue with the terminology that we use, and there are issues around any labels. For example, the term 'Global South' is widely used in academic, political and development discourse but, like terms such as 'Third World' and the classifications listed by examination boards (e.g. 'Advanced Countries'), there are drawbacks. This doesn't mean that we shouldn't use them – just that we should at least be aware of the problems and explicitly teach students about them. This is important because we want to encourage those that we teach to communicate effectively and with a full understanding of the terms used. Issues include:

- **Overgeneralisation and homogenisation:** Any single label is going to mask the huge diversity both between and within countries, in terms of culture, politics, economy, development levels and historical experiences.
- **Geographical inaccuracy:** For example, Australia is not included in the Global South, and some Global South countries are in the northern hemisphere.
- **Historical and colonial legacy:** The term has roots in post-colonial theory and often replaces terms that preceded it, such as 'developing countries'. There is a danger that it maintains the 'us' and 'them' outlook on the world.

With a lack of nuanced alternatives, geography teachers can use these terms, whilst the enquiry approach, where we encourage curiosity and critical engagement, allows students to understand the advantages and disadvantages of using such contested terms in geography. This, I would argue, is part of our fundamental subject knowledge.

Activity

As part of a department meeting, discuss other terms in geography that are contentious and can lead to oversimplification. How can you communicate the pros and cons of using such terms to students and embed these in your curriculum?

Methods of communication

As already mentioned, most communication methods will be controlled by the teacher. Whilst the main method of enquiry is through persuasive writing or short-answer questions that demonstrate learning, in real life geographers use a diverse range of communication methods. In addition, if we are to develop qualifications *and* qualities in young people that reflect the ways in which geographers communicate in the real world, then we should use a wide range of relevant communication methods. In the short term, whilst we are within the assessment regime in which we find ourselves, using alternatives to essays ensures that we assess geographical thinking and knowledge and not just writing ability.

Table 10.3 summarises some of the ways in which students can communicate geographical knowledge, with some practical examples following in the rest of this chapter. One caveat I will add is that whilst curriculum artefacts such as song lyrics, poems and films are widely used in the geography classroom, if we are to assess the extent of the geographical learning taking place, then we need to have careful thought before getting students to use those methods. This is because their thinking can be limited to the nature of communication and the geography forgotten. There can also be a combination of communication types. For example, a script can be written to help support a presentation or debate and a fieldwork report would include a range of diagrams and maps.

Table 10.3: Ways to communicate geographical knowledge

Communication type	Examples	Skills developed
Written	<ul><li>Essays</li><li>Reports</li><li>Case study write-up</li><li>Reflective journals</li><li>Notes</li><li>Short answers</li></ul>	<ul><li>Structured argument</li><li>Use of evidence</li><li>Geographical thinking</li><li>Geographical vocabulary</li></ul>
Visual	<ul><li>Maps (hand-drawn or GIS)</li><li>Diagrams and flow charts</li><li>Infographics</li><li>Academic posters</li></ul>	<ul><li>Data interpretation</li><li>Spatial understanding</li><li>Synthesis of information</li></ul>

Communication type	Examples	Skills developed
Oral	• Presentations • Group discussions • Debates • Role-play	• Verbal reasoning • Persuasion • Listening and responding • Confidence in expressing views
Digital	• Podcasts • Videos • Blogs and vlogs • Story maps	• Digital literacy • Multimedia storytelling • Scripting • Audience awareness
Numerical	• Graphs and charts • Statistical analysis	• Data-handling • Interpretation and trend analysis • Linking data to place and process
Fieldwork	• Field sketches • Survey write-ups • Annotated photos • Field reports • Field notebooks	• Observation • Recording and analysis • Linking theory to real-world contexts

As always, the professional judgement of geography teams – as well as practical considerations, such as access to technology – is paramount. In most of the schools I taught in, it wasn't possible for students to routinely create their own GIS or story map. Another example is that we used to get students to write their script for a group presentation, a piece of writing that could also be assessed.

Practical examples

What follows are some practical examples of different teaching strategies that can be used to develop writing.

Understanding Tier 3 words

Definition

Tier 3 words: Tier 3 words are those that are specific to geography and use academic language. They are not commonly used in everyday language, and when they are used outside of a geography context, they often hold a different meaning. An understanding of Tier 3 words is vital in developing students' understanding of concepts and for success in assessments.

Central to successful communication is spelling, and an effective activity I used with all year groups was the simple low-stakes, high-impact vocabulary test. This involved three aspects:

- the spelling of the word
- the definition
- the word used in context three times.

I would use one of the aspects as the prompt and the class would complete the other two. Sometimes I would allow a bit of paired discussion before individuals committed to paper or a mini-whiteboard. For example:

- Erosion.
- The increasing interconnectedness of the world through trade, investment, communication and the movement of people, knowledge and ideas.
- Many people migrate to cities from rural areas to find employment. Birds often migrate to warmer areas during the winter. Migration can happen because people want to escape danger or find a safer home.

It is a legitimate homework activity for students to learn definitions, especially when there is widespread misuse and misconceptions.

Command words

> **Definition**
>
> **Command words:** Whilst command words are associated with external explanations, they are key verbs and phrases used in questions or tasks that indicate to students what kind of answer or response is expected.

In this capacity, command words guide how students should think about and communicate their geographical knowledge. As such, they should be a routine part of geography lessons and their meaning explicitly taught from lesson one of Year 7. I used the command words and definitions used in the GCSE and A level specifications throughout the school. This was to dispel their mystery and make them such a routine and low-threat part of geography lessons that when they were encountered in the high-stakes world of examinations, anxiety was reduced.

I found that the best way to illustrate the command words was to have the main examples on display on the wall. In addition, using everyday objects, such as classroom chairs or tables, helped. This went alongside the routine modelling of extended writing by teachers. Table10.4 illustrates a selection of command words in common use by UK exam boards.

Table 10.4: Commonly used command words

Command word/term	Meaning	Example using an everyday object: classroom chairs
Identify	Name the feature. What is it?	Students correctly call it a chair.
Describe	Give information on the characteristics of features or processes. What is it like?	Students give me details. What material is the chair made from? Does it have legs? How many? What colour is it?
Explain	Give reasons or causes for why something happens. What is it for? Why did that happen?	At the basic level, a chair is for sitting on. This can also become more complex if linked to the supply chain, manufacturing process and origin of materials, and the transport and selling of the product.
Assess	Make a judgement by weighing up the evidence. Is this any good?	This is where students comment on whether the chair easily tips up or the ease of cleaning and list some advantages and disadvantages. We can also compare it to the teacher's chair. They key is to encourage students to decide.
Evaluate	Make a reasoned, balanced judgement supported by evidence. Go beyond assessment by considering strengths, weaknesses and implications.	How does the chair perform in hot weather? Is it comfortable? What impact may that have on learning? What information would we need to test that hypothesis?
To what extent	Evaluate the degree to which something is true or effective.	'To what extent do you agree that all students would get better exam results if they were given padded chairs?' is a good example to get thinking going. Again, referring to the lack of empirical evidence, this also allows a teaching point about the use of evidence.

> **Activity**
>
> Make a list of the command words in use in your curriculum. When are they first introduced to students? What classroom objects could you use to explain these?

Banned words

> **Definition**
>
> **Banned words:** Banned words are words that students either are not permitted to use in their writing or can only do so with qualification.

This is a simple and effective idea for improving the standard of students' communication, both in writing and when taking part in whole-class questioning and discussions. The Banned Word Board (Rogers, 2006) is displayed in the classroom and is a list of words that are not permitted to be used.

After some feedback from colleagues, both online and face to face, I introduced semi-banned words, words that can be used as long as they are qualified. These include words such as 'polution'.

Table 10.5: Banned words and alternatives

Banned word	Alternatives
People	Name individual groups of people that are affected by the issue.
Stuff	Name the goods or specific phenomena being written about.
Thing(s)	State the actual object under discussion.
Up/right/down/left	Increasing, decreasing, cardinal compass points, trends.
Pollution	Explicit reference to the type of pollution being written about.
Affected	Positive or negative?
Effected	Positive or negative?

A further iteration was to ensure that some 'heavenly words' were also available. In my classroom, these were on the ceiling. These words included:

- urbanisation
- factors
- relief
- globalisation.

> **Activity**
>
> Have a look at some recent writing from your classes. Make three lists. What words would you ban? Which would be semi-banned? Which words would you love to see in your students' writing? Now display these often.

Defining geographical terminology

Geography, like many other subjects, has a wealth of subject-specific terminology. Part of the challenge of answering questions is first to understand what is being asked. Here, pausing to consider the etymological origins of words is useful. Have the standard enquiry questions 'Where does this word come from?' and 'What does it mean?'.

It should go without saying that we should use geographical terminology from lesson one of Year 7 in a secondary school. Let's consider two examples.

- **Saltation:** This comes from the Latin verb *saire*, meaning 'to leap'. Armed with this knowledge, it now makes sense why this transportation process is named such.
- Similarly, let's break down the word **geomorphology**. This often stumps young people when faced with a question such as 'List the geomorphological processes that may occur in the photograph'.
    - **geo:** Earth
    - **morph:** changes
    - **ology:** the study of or branch of knowledge.

When we break down the word, it is clear that geomorphology is the study of how the earth changes. This makes it easy for students to understand the term and subsequently use in it their writing.

Scaffolding extended writing

A range of scaffolds can be used to support extended writing and, together with modelling, scaffolding has been proved to have a positive effect on learning and an even larger impact for students with learning disabilities (Belland et al., 2017, cited in EEF, 2023). It is best used when we pause to consider the overarching enquiry question. This is where students can think hard, include multiple perspectives and connect their learning to other parts of geography. Just as the enquiry has a number of iterative stages, extended writing does not just happen and also has an iterative approach. This needs to be modelled and taught.

- **Stage 1:** understanding the question.
- **Stage 2:** planning – organising ideas, gathering relevant knowledge and examples.
- **Stage 3:** drafting – producing the first draft.
- **Stage 4:** reviewing and editing – checking that the argument flows and makes sense, clarity in spelling, grammar and geographical accuracy.
- **Stage 5:** submitting the work to a teacher for assessment.

Some fertile questions could include:

- Is Freiburg a model for sustainable urban living?
- Why do Niger and Mali continue to face deep development issues despite global aid and efforts?
- How does the Mexico–USA border affect people's lives?
- Did Cop28 in Dubai decide what happens to our planet?
- Should people in the UK stop flying and 'staycation'?
- Is water a right or a commodity in Cape Town?

VCOB (vocabulary, connective, opener, banned) was a technique introduced to me by a literacy lead, and I later adapted it for use in the geography classroom. A VCOB sheet (Table 10.6) is a useful scaffold when developing geographical writing. It can be used in a number of ways in the classroom, either providing it for all learners or using it in a targeted way.

Table 10.6: Example VCOB sheet: What are the challenges and opportunities of living in Rocinha and how do they compare with those in Brighton?

Vocabulary	Connective
Favela	In addition to
Rocinha	On the other hand
Environment	Whereas
Urban	However
North, south	Because
Infrastructure	Therefore
Sprawling	Likewise
Pride	Unlike
Steep	Which is similar to
Communications	Contrasting with
Change	Despite
Crime	So as to
Openers	**Banned**
Rocinha is located in…	Stuff
The *favela* is most famous for…	Things
The similarities to Brighton are…	It
There are mixed feelings about Rocinha…	People
Evidence to support my view includes….	Poor
Some people may agree/disagree because…	Shantytown
	Slum

This framework can also be adapted to VCOP, where the P stands for 'perspectives'. This is a good way of ensuring that students include a range of viewpoints. These viewpoints would have been provided through the data collection and evaluation stages of the unit. For example, on the topic of climate refugees, we could include the choices of:

- climate refugees displaced people
- marginalised and Indigenous communities

- host-country governments
- local communities in host country
- international organisations and NGOs
- environmentalists
- climate scientists
- policymakers
- nonmigrants in the source country.

There is a wide range of scaffolds that can be used to support extended writing. Many great books and articles cover these (Selmes, 2016, is a useful start for a review of geography-specific examples), and I have summarised some of the best examples in Table 10.7. They are included because if geographers seek to understand the world to make it better, students must be able to communicate well. It is also worth using whole-school literacy initiatives. Like everything, it is your professional judgement that will dictate what you use. I would advocate using a smaller selection of methods throughout your curriculum, rather than many. In this way, students will build up their procedural knowledge of the technique. These are different from sharing and teaching tactics around the mark scheme. Whilst that is important, if we teach geography well enough, good exam results will follow.

Table 10.7: Examples of scaffolds

Scaffold type	Why use	Example
PEEL paragraph structure	A classic structure to help students build clear, well-supported paragraphs. Great for short-answer questions.	P: Make a clear point. E: Support with facts, data, examples. E: Say why this is important. L: Link back to the question or bigger picture.
Command word sentence starters	Gives students a way to respond to command verbs.	Describe: 'The feature is…' Explain: 'This happens because…' Assess: 'One benefit is…', 'However…', 'Overall…' To what extent: 'I disagree/agree a little/agree a lot…', 'On one hand…', 'On the other hand…', 'Overall…'

Scaffold type	Why use	Example
Graphic organisers	These help to plan extended answers, including fieldwork projects.	Spider diagram: Used in the ideation phase for recording ideas and examples. T-charts: For comparing to places, perspective or outcomes. Flow charts: For sequences and processes such as coastal erosion. Case study grids: With boxes for location, cause, effects and responses. Mind maps: Generate a web of ideas to make associations between ideas and concepts.
Essay planning frame	A useful ritual for longer questions, such as 6–9 marks at GCSE or A level essays.	Splitting the essay into four or five parts: • introduction • main point 1 • main point 2 • optional main point 3 • conclusion/judgement.
Connectives for cohesion	These improve the flow and connect ideas.	Adding: 'In addition…', 'Another example is…' Contrasting: 'However…', 'In contrast…', 'On the other hand…' Explaining: 'This is because…', 'As a result…' Concluding: 'In conclusion…', 'Overall…', 'This shows that…'
Questions to encourage thinking hard	These encourage deeper thinking before writing.	What is the main cause of this issue? Who is affected most and why? What are the short-term and long-term impacts? What are the disadvantages and advantages of this solution? Which is more effective and why?

Oracy

There has been much debate around oracy and its place in the classroom recently, since the Oracy Education Commission's report in 2024. For the enquiry classroom, oracy is essential in securing academic success. However, I would argue that it is nothing new for geography, as well as modelling the process of disagreeing well and creating a positive classroom climate where all views are respected (with geography tackling a multitude of perspectives and views, this is vital!). The techniques in Table 10.8 can help students to think geographically, improve their ability to express complex ideas clearly and engage critically with others' perspectives.

Table 10.8: Strategies for including oracy in geography

Oracy strategy	What it involves	Benefit for geographical enquiry
Class discussions and debates	Students discuss issues.	Introduces multiple perspectives. Encourages using evidence and formulating balanced arguments.
Think-pair-share	Students pause and think about their answer individually, then talk about it with a partner before whole-class feedback.	Builds confidence. Allows the rehearsal of geographical vocabulary.
Presentations	Individuals or groups talk on case studies, research or fieldwork.	Develops structured thinking and precise use of geographical language. This could also include giving weather forecasts.
Geographical storytelling	The journey of a specific river, migrant or tectonic event (for example) is narrated.	When based upon real-world examples, helps sequence ideas and connect human and physical processes.
Explanation tasks	Students explain aloud using a diagram, map or process, such as longshore drift.	Reinforces understanding and improves clarity of explanation.

Key takeaways

- Students are assessed through the written word, so communication is central to enquiry and progresses from description to critical evaluation.
- The purpose and audience of their writing shape how students communicate their geographical knowledge.
- Authentic outputs and varied modes of communication affect how students learn and what they remember: they need to focus on the geography.
- Tasks like presentation, storytelling and explanation build clear thinking and the use of precise language, and encourage students to make connections between geographical units.
- Time spent on developing effective communication is valuable. Allowing sufficient time for extended writing is essential for success.

11 How do we critically evaluate the enquiry process?

In this chapter

This chapter highlights the role of critical reflection as the final stage of the geographical enquiry process. Reflection moves students beyond simply completing tasks and helps to question methods, weigh up evidence and reconsider conclusions. This culminates in better learning. I will distinguish critical reflection from self-assessment and metacognition, whilst demonstrating how all three complement one another in classroom practice. By embedding reflection, teachers create space for students to connect geographical learning to their own lives, challenge assumptions and build more rigorous enquiry questions to build better schemas. The chapter includes a progression framework for reflection and presents several practical strategies for implementation. Effective reflection results in better learning, strengthens disciplinary knowledge, nurtures metacognition and helps students think like geographers.

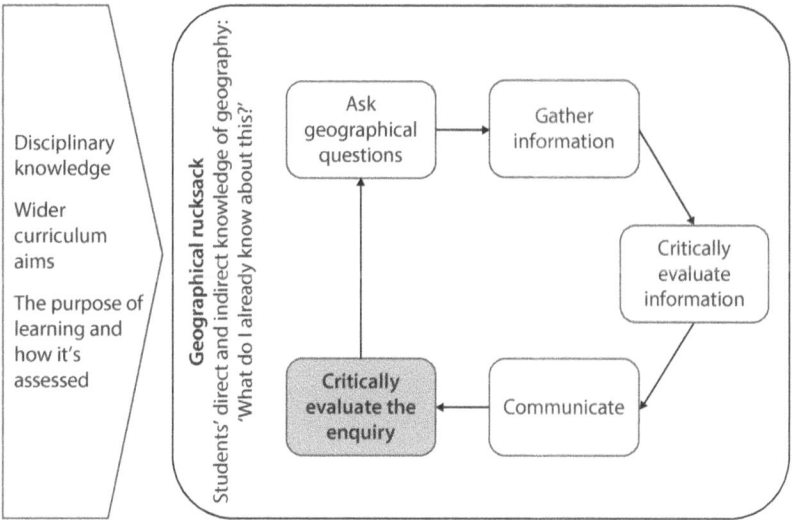

Figure 11.1: The simplified enquiry approach model: Critically evaluate the enquiry

The final stage of the enquiry process is to critically evaluate it (Figure 11.1). This refers to the process and the conclusions made. The box below expands upon this stage of the enquiry process. This stage also includes metacognition.

Critically evaluate the enquiry

- What do I already know about this?
- What gaps are there?
- What else do I need to know?
- How does this change my thinking?
- Is this knowledge contested or agreed upon?
- Is this a single story?
- Does it represent the world as it is now or in the past?

Reflection

Read the following scenario and reflect on how you would tackle this as a geography teacher:

In my geography teaching career, I have encountered the sweeping conclusions of students many times. For example, based upon a small sample of 20 people, students have regularly concluded that their findings were representative and reliable. On another occasion, Year 7 students were adamant, based on one local newspaper source, that they had decided the best thing for Stonehenge was to build a massive road tunnel.

But it's not in the curriculum!

This is a refrain that I often heard from my line manager as a head of geography. Time and space for reflection are squeezed out, as it's not content on the curriculum. This argument is also used when trying to connect students' lived experiences to what is being taught. The argument is false, as the National Curriculum does demand time for reflection. I have summarised this in Table 11.1.

Table 11.1: National curricula reflection requirements

Nation	Curriculum expectation	How reflection in geography aligns to the curriculum
England (DfE, 2013b)	How might someone in your community experience this issue differently? Would people in other countries or cultures see this differently? Why?	• Encourages students to connect learning with their identity, background and context. • Supports SMSC (spiritual, moral, social and cultural) development and empathy. • Enables diverse, multimodal reflection and deeper critical thinking.
Northern Ireland (DfE NI, 2007)	Students should have opportunities to… appreciate how places and people interact. Express opinions and support with evidence. Explore local and global issues.	• Encourages students to link enquiry topics to their own lives and communities. • Builds evaluative skills through reflective justification. • Makes global issues locally relevant and personally meaningful.
Scotland (Education Scotland, 2018)	Develop an understanding of the natural environment and our place in the world. Evaluate the impact of human activity and decision-making from different perspectives. Reflect upon my learning using feedback.	• Personal reflection on geographical issues promotes understanding of place and identity. • Encourages examining diverse perspectives and moral judgement. • Aligns with metacognitive goals of reflection and self-awareness.
Wales (Welsh Government, 2022b)	Develop an understanding of identity, heritage and cynefin [sense of place]. Explore and express different perspectives… consider the impact of their actions and those of others.	• Lived experience reflection honours students' *cynefin* – personal and cultural roots. • Builds understanding of difference and shared responsibility. • Supports integral cross-cutting themes: equity, voice, and wellbeing.

As geographical knowledge is not just a body of facts but a way of thinking about the world, we must also include the lived experiences of students. There are also wider curriculum requirements that are met through reflection, whilst the accountability frameworks contain the need for reflection in building schemas and supporting personal development.

Of course, all geographers will realise that even if we consider a single geographical concept – that of place – it is impossible to gain a full understanding of the concept *without* linking to personal experiences.

Critical reflection, self-assessment and metacognition

All three of these are closely related concepts, although they each have a distinct meaning and purpose. In practice, they often overlap, although distinguishing between them helps in planning pedagogy or developing student rubric. All three approaches need careful planning and space for students to reflect. All three can be explicitly taught and modelled by teachers.

> **Definition**
>
> **Critical reflection:** The process of analysing one's experiences, actions and outcomes. The purpose is to challenge assumptions, gain insights and improve future practice. In the case of enquiry, for example, students may come to realise that they need to include more than one perspective about migration into the UK.

Critical reflection focuses upon:

- understanding why something happened.
- evaluating the quality and impact of decisions and information available.

> **Definition**
>
> **Metacognition:** Thinking about one's own thinking. It involves being aware of the cognitive processes before, during and after learning tasks. Metacognitive approaches are more effective when they are applied to challenging tasks rooted in the usual curriculum content (EEF, n.d.), which makes geographical enquiry an ideal vehicle. Teachers modelling their own thinking is one strategy for this.

Students would focus on three questions:

- **Planning:** How will I approach this?
- **Monitoring:** Am I understanding this?
- **Evaluating:** How well did I do and why?

> **Definition**
>
> **Self-assessment:** The act of evaluating your own performance against a set of criteria, learning objective or standards. This is helpful, as students:
>
> - judge how well they have met learning goals
> - identify strengths and areas for improvement
> - match their work to their expectations.

In summary:

- **Critical reflection** encourages students to think like geographers. It focuses on the geographical content needed and how their procedural knowledge can be improved.
- **Metacognition** encourages students to think about and understand how they learn more effectively.

- **Self-assessment** encourages student to focus on the task and how to get better at assessment – the tactics.

This chapter focuses on critical reflection and its relation to the enquiry process in geography.

Progression

Table 11.2 shows four stages of critically evaluating the enquiry process. As with other stages, the procedural knowledge needs to be explicitly taught within the context of enquiry teaching. The descriptors here should be applied in a best-fit way at the end of an enquiry unit, when students have had the opportunity to answer the big question. They can be applied to any enquiry, whether an entirely closed, teacher-led unit of work, an independent piece of fieldwork or a guided enquiry.

Table 11.2: Four stages of critically evaluating enquiry

Stage	Description	Key procedural knowledge	Example student reflections
1. Emerging awareness	Describe what was done, with support.	• Describe what the enquiry was about. • Identify basic strengths and weaknesses with help. • Begin to distinguish fact from opinion.	'I found out that…' 'I think I did well at…' 'Next time, I might try to…'
2. Developing understanding	Begin to evaluate own decisions.	• Explain choices (e.g. methods or source choice). • Identify simple problems or challenges. • Begin to consider the reliability of findings.	'I chose this method because…' 'One problem was…' 'I could improve by…'

Stage	Description	Key procedural knowledge	Example student reflections
3. Competent evaluation	Reflect with reasoning and evidence.	• Justify choices made during the enquiry. • Identify bias and limitations. • Suggest improvements or future research based on analysis. • Link reflection to wider reading and other, interdependent geographical content.	'This approach helped me because…' 'The evidence was limited by…' 'Next time, I need to…'
4. Critical and independent evaluation	Evaluate the process and impact independently.	• Critically assess the whole enquiry. • Weigh alternatives and justify choices. • Reflect on significance and implications. • Connect learning to self and society.	'Although my conclusion was supported, a different method might have…' 'This enquiry changed how I think about…' 'I recognised bias in the sources, which affected…'

To implement reflection, time needs to be devoted to it at the end of a unit, when the students have created a longer piece of work. To support this, these stages can be developed into a rubric, or a mini reflection journal could be developed as a routine feature of the time preceding the main work.

Practical examples

Like all aspects of geographical enquiry, expert teachers need to spend time making the curriculum and planning in critical reflection. This section will consider how to implement critical evaluation.

Have students been able to answer the enquiry question and can they apply this knowledge to a new situation?

If enquiry is not to be a bolt-on but an embedded part of lesson sequences, then it's vital that young people arrive at an answer to the question posed at the start of the unit. The implication on planning for teachers is that the unit provides this opportunity.

Most enquiries will be controlled and guided by teachers through well-thought-out sequences of lessons. This ensures that the knowledge is secured, and this can be tested though assessment. From a teacher's perspective, it is important that we know whether students know more and remember more as the result of our teaching. This may be for internal data-tracking and external assessments, but it should also be to help identify misconceptions and whether our teaching is making an impact. I always remember encountering the phrase 'feedback is a gift' from colleagues, and one of the other purposes of assessments was made clear through the realisation that I had done such a bad job of teaching the unit that students had remembered very little or remembered incorrectly. This was often the result of rushing through content, rather than slowing down to make students think hard and think about what I wanted them to learn.

We also have the curse and blessing that most aspects of geography are interconnected and interdependent on other parts. Concepts overlap and some issues, such as climate change and level of development, underpin the entire curriculum. This means that end-of-unit tests should always include the full range of knowledge encountered throughout the curriculum until that point, even if this means using a range of data presentation or adding in a short question. Restricting questions to the issues just studied not only gives a false sense of the progress made by young people, but also goes against the nature of geography as a subject – it is synoptic, where most units link to one another in some way.

Providing an end-of-unit test with a selection of synoptic questions, as well as some data-response and knowledge-recall questions from earlier units, allows us to reflect upon the impact of learning. Doing so not only encourages thinking hard about geography but also gives us reliable assessment information that can feed into whole-school systems. It is my argument that end-of-unit tests should take the form of some sort of extended writing. Most students can handle this.

It also allows teams to reflect upon the gaps in knowledge that are developing in young people and, more importantly, provide time for action to be taken. I always looked upon marking as an assessment of my teaching. If there were similar gaps around a particular piece of knowledge, then that was on me to address.

As young people progress though our geography department, we want them to become independent. By that, I mean creating their own enquiry to apply their own knowledge to a new situation. To do this, students must have the time to reflect upon the enquiry. What are the main aspects that they have learned? To do this, you could provide the following ten questions, or a selection, at the end of each unit:

Understanding and thinking

1. What is the most important thing I learned in this enquiry?
2. How did my understanding of the topic change during the unit?
3. Did I have any misconceptions at the start? How did I correct them?

Research and enquiry process

4. What sources of information were most useful and why?
5. Were sources of information representative, unbiased and inclusive?
6. How well did I organise and communicate my ideas?

Judgement and improvement

7. What part of my work am I most proud of?
8. If I did this enquiry again, what would I do differently and why? How can I apply this to future enquiries?
9. What skills did I develop?

Wider connections

10. How does what I learned in this enquiry help me understand the wider world or current issues?

These questions show that it is OK to be wrong or to misunderstand. It also makes it routine to reflect upon perspectives.

Has my view changed?

We have repeatedly mentioned the idea of students' own geographical rucksacks: their experiences of geographical concepts outside the classroom. One way to explore this pre-existing knowledge is to allow students to record it at the start of a unit, perhaps through a concept map or mind map. At the start of a unit, this can be used to recall previously taught knowledge, as well as students' own experience. The concept map can be revisited at the end of the unit. Is there anything else to add? Were there any misconceptions, or ideas and thoughts that are different now? Had they remembered all the information? Concept maps have the added advantage of quickly becoming revision tools.

Another example is to ask students to write down the enquiry questions that they would like answered throughout a unit. Before teaching tectonic hazards, I asked students to do this and share them. Of course, as the expert teacher, I had carefully crafted a well-sequenced unit of work; however, now and again there were questions posed by students that I included. At the end of the unit, we revisited these questions to see how many of them could now be answered.

A psychologically safe classroom space is needed to embed the lived experience of students in geography. For this, there are a range of questions that can be incorporated, as illustrated in Table 11.3.

Table 11.3: Creating a psychologically safe classroom space

Strategy	Teacher prompts	Examples
Create a safe and inclusive classroom	• Establish that all reflections are valid and valued. • Remind students that there are no 'right' answers. • Encourage honesty and reassure students that it's the geography that will be judged for opinions and not their work. • Do not assess reflections against performance-based assessment. • Allow for private reflection, with sharing optional.	'We all bring different experiences to our learning. Your reflection is a chance to show how this enquiry meant something to *you*.'

Strategy	Teacher prompts	Examples
Model reflection using diverse voices	• Share sample reflections and stories from students of diverse backgrounds. These can be anonymised and built up over the years. • Use short quotes or videos showing how real people connect geographical topics to lived experience. • Invite guest speakers and community members into the classroom. • Use case studies from a wide range of perspectives.	'Here's how others have related to this topic. What's your connection?'
Include identity-aware prompts	Use reflection prompts.	'How did your background influence the way you understood this enquiry?' 'Did anything in this enquiry challenge your own views or assumptions?' 'Did your identity shape how you experience the enquiry or response to the evidence?' 'Were any parts of the topic challenging to your beliefs and experience?'
Use culturally responsive scenarios	Frame questions in ways that acknowledge diverse backgrounds.	'How might someone in your community experience this issue differently?' 'Would people in other countries or cultures see this differently? Why?'
Prompt personal connections	Use reflection questions that invite students to connect learning to their own lives and communities.	'What does this topic mean to you personally?' 'Have you seen or experienced something like this in real life?' 'Did anything we studied remind you of your own community or culture?'

Metacognition and reflection

I have already mentioned that the three types of reflection overlap. Being able to reflect upon an enquiry or individual project is important if young people are to understand the limitations of data and information. However, metacognition is different from refection.

It is beyond the scope of this book to explore metacognition fully and, if we remain focused upon enquiry, critical reflection is more important to consider. When considering enquiry, reflection must be critical. Yes, students must retain and retrieve knowledge about geography, but we also want them to think about the nature of what they have found out. Geography, like other subjects, should not simply be a series of activities loosely bound together around a topic.

Reflection need not be restricted to discussion. In fact, I have found it more useful to get students to write reflections, where there is also opportunity for them to explain the reasons behind their conclusions and thoughts, which is a useful source of data when tackling misconceptions.

> **Activity**
>
> Look at a unit of work in your department. Answer the questions contained in the box at the start of this chapter (page 244) about it. Would this change how you teach the unit in future? Would you ask students to answer the same questions? Are they similar?

Going beyond the curriculum, classroom and specification

As we aim for our students to leave with qualifications and qualities, it is important that they go on to do more with the information found out in class. Geography curriculum time is limited, as is the scope of what we set out to achieve. However, we can plant the seeds for future thought. If students leave our classrooms questioning why a particular type of knowledge is included, then we have started to develop young people who think geographically.

For example, whilst the Burgess model (Burgess, 1925) is not mentioned in many – if any – GCSE specifications, it remains a prevalent feature of online and published resources. Why? Of course, students can easily remember the model, but do they know where it came from? Does it match their own world?

A simple transect when walking through most UK towns and cities will quickly illustrate that the model bears little in common with reality:

- High streets have started to see residential land use, as big department buildings close and landlords need to secure an income.
- Some streets start with number '8' rather than '1'. Why is this?
- Shops selling low-order goods are becoming more common on the high street as people go online to compare deals.

As teachers, *we* need to be aware of these limitations, as well as our students.

Reflection gives the opportunity for students to understand the limitations of geographical models whilst acknowledging that they have a place. It also allows them to suggest improvements and consider the implications of models: our understanding of some geographical concepts is incomplete, and if we are to have any chance at all, we need to simplify the real world.

'Then and now' learning log

Give students time to write down what they think they know about the topic before starting. This also allows teachers to assess prior knowledge and identify any common misconceptions that apply to that group of students. Encourage them to look back at this at the start of each lesson to see whether anything has changed. Allow time at the end of the enquiry, once the assessment is complete, to reflect once more. Use the following prompts:

- What did I believe at the start of the unit?
- What changed my thinking?
- What do I think differently about at the end of the unit?

'Whose view?' perspective mapping

At the end of the unit, students look back and identify different groups of people that have different perspectives on an issue. They then create a mind map about how the issues, such as deforestation or tourism, impact on that group. After the mind map is complete, use the following prompts:

- Who is affected most?
- Whose voices have been heard and whose are missing?
- How does my own perspective compare?

You could also use the template in Table 11.4, which could be used as part of the planning process ahead of answering a fertile question.

Table 11.4: Considering different perspectives

Group of people	What they value or want	How they are affected	How their view differs from mine
Local farmer	Wants crops for land	Livelihood at risk from conservation laws	I hadn't considered farming impacts
NGO	Wants forest protected	Campaign for biodiversity and rewilding	I agree with them more

'Mistaken assumptions' activity

Sometimes I present the class with a common misconception or stereotype about a place. For example:

- Africa is one country with one culture.
- All LICs (low-income countries) are poor and underdeveloped in every way.
- Deforestation only happens in the rainforest.
- Migrants are a burden on host countries.
- We can't do anything about natural disasters; they are completely unpredictable.
- Maps are neutral and always show the truth.
- All rural areas are peaceful, slow and disconnected from modern life.
- Globalisation means everyone is becoming the same.
- Climate change will mostly affect faraway places like polar regions or small islands.

The idea is to be provocative and allow students to respond at the end of a unit and then challenge and reflect. You can use the following prompts with students after the activity:

- What was your first assumption? What did you believe or think about this place or issue at first?
- What did you discover? What evidence challenged or disproved the view?
- What does it matter in geography? How do stereotypes and misconceptions change how I see places, people or the world?

Local to global reflections

This is where we ask students to connect what they have learned to something in their own local community or personal experience. This allows us to connect sometimes vague concepts with their lived experiences. You could use the template in Table 11.5.

Table 11.5: Example connecting local to global reflections

What we learned	What is happening in my local area	How this topic relates to my life
Climate change is leading to greater frequency and severity of flooding.	The river flooding the park last winter stopped me taking part in Parkrun with my family.	I can begin to understand how it feels to have life disrupted by flooding, although the impact on me and my family wasn't too severe.

Other prompts could be:

- Have I seen this issue before?
- Would people in my area care about this?
- How has this topic changed how I see my own community?

'One change I'd make' exit ticket

At the end of the unit, students write one change they'd make if they did the enquiry again and justify that point of view. Consider giving the following prompts:

- If I answered this enquiry question again, I would…
  - choose different sources of information because…
  - ask a better question, like….
  - think more about…
- Why?
  - What I learned from making mistakes.
  - What would lead to a stronger conclusion?
  - How my thinking has changed.
  - What other perspectives I would include that I hadn't thought about before.

Key takeaways

- Critical reflection is an essential stage of the enquiry process and should not be ignored.
- It strengthens geographical thinking by refining questions, getting students to use data and communicate effectively.
- Reflection differs but overlaps with self-assessment and metacognition.
- A safe, inclusive classroom culture is key to encouraging honest and thoughtful reflection.
- Reflection allows time for students to connect what they have learned to their own lived experiences and identities.
- Progression supports development from simple awareness to independent evaluation.
- Embedding reflection results in better learning.

12 Conclusion: How does enquiry enable great geographers to change the world?

> **In this chapter**
>
> This chapter draws together the central argument of the book: that geographical enquiry is the subject's signature pedagogy and the most powerful way to teach geography. We have considered what enquiry is and why its place in the curriculum is justified. We have tackled the common misconceptions about enquiry and looked at how enquiry can be structured for progression and sequenced in our curricula. We have systematically examined each stage of the process.
>
> There are many powerful reasons to use enquiry, as both a pedagogy *and* a way to structure the curriculum. Enquiry leads to better learning of geography. In addition, it provides space for thinking hard, critical reflection, hope and action, encouraging young people to gain knowledge and understanding of the world so that they may change it for the better, even if that is through small, simple and sustainable actions.
>
> Perhaps more importantly, enquiry creates a better world by equipping young people with the qualifications – through external examinations – and qualities needed to engage in the wider world in order for future success.

If I haven't done a good job of convincing you of the power of geographical enquiry and its place at the heart of a geography school curriculum, I am hoping that this chapter will tip the balance. For me, geographers seek to understand the world so that they can make decisions to make the world better. This is what geographers *do* and they need geographical knowledge and skills to do so. This journey starts at school, and whilst this book has focused on secondary school, students arrive already having a geography education. They already have lived experience of geography. They can write well. They are full of curiosity and hope.

The educational landscape in the UK is no doubt challenging. There are many people, many of whom are not geography experts, telling us how to teach. Teaching and planning is a small part of what teachers are expected to do, and time for collegiate campfire conversations about geography teaching and geography learners is limited. I refuse to give up the belief that geography makes a difference, though. Geography is far more than a body of knowledge, which in itself shifts as we understand more and find out more. It is a way of thinking about the world and how we interact with it. Enquiry is a powerful lens with which to approach our beautifully frustrating, dynamic subject.

This chapter will summarise a hopeful geography, an approach that demands that we show how geographers are making the world a better place. I will then present five core arguments that demonstrate that great geographers change the world, giving examples at the classroom scale.

Hopeful geography

The Covid-19 pandemic and climate crisis begun a discourse around hopeful geography. This is based on the premise that there can be a better tomorrow, and recent research suggests that those who have high levels of hope experience greater academic success (Chang, 1998). Whilst this hope should not be blind, enquiry enables us to introduce 'critical hope' (Kidman and Chang, 2021).

> **Definition**
>
> **Critical hope:** Where students find out and acknowledge some of today's challenges but remain hopeful that things can improve in both the short and long term. This is demonstrated by exploring data that shows improvement.

David Alcock (2020) has been a leading voice in hopeful geography, proposing three strands that can present a balanced view of human progress and challenges. These are summarised below:

1. **Evaluating progress** encourages students to assess both achievements and setbacks. Through enquiry, we can allow classes to explore a range of information from different perspectives. Enquiry also deals with the past and the future, looking at trends over time.
2. **Believing in humanity** fosters a collective belief that people can address and solve global issues. Geographers enquire about the world so that they can make decisions to make it better. Enquiry allows us to develop agency and self-efficacy in students, even if this is at the classroom or school scale. Small changes can result from the enquiry process. In addition, enquiry allows students to critically assess solutions, and they can acknowledge that some solutions impact on different groups of people in different ways.
3. In **striving for a better world**, the purpose of geography education is for young people to gain qualifications for their next stage of life *and* develop the qualities that will motivate them to help create sustainable and equitable futures. Enquiry allows us to ask questions and look at different scales. Improving life in a community, street or classroom is possible. If that is possible, then so is helping the world.

The approach aligns to national education goals:

- It enhances climate literacy by framing environmental issues within a context of human agency (Brace, 2024b).
- It promotes equity and inclusion, as hopeful geography encourages discussions around social justice, enabling students to consider solutions and how geographical factors intersect with issues of race, class and inequality (Puttick and Murrey, 2020).
- It fosters engagement, as we can highlight positive case studies and examples such as community-led conservation projects. Enquiry at the classroom and local scale, coupled with nature connection fieldwork, can connect young people with their locale, motivating them to participate in civic life (Griffiths, 2024).

Hopeful education isn't anything new, but it does provide geography teachers with a pause point. Are lessons full of doom and gloom? Do case studies on migration and natural disasters focus too much on the negative impacts and not enough on positive progress and mitigation? Enquiry allows us to integrate hopeful geography into our curriculum by balancing critical analysis with constructive optimism. Enquiry demands that we look at issues from different perspectives, and hopeful geography demands that we ask, 'How can this be better in the future?'

> **Activity**
>
> How hopeful is your geography curriculum? Discuss with your colleagues or carry out an audit of your current curriculum. Does it provide opportunities for 'critical hope?'

Why we should use enquiry in the geography classroom – five core arguments

Puttick argues that we should be 'geographers in education' (2023, p. 1), which means that we are great geographers. Put simply, great geography teachers change the world by securing strong educational outcomes for young people. We can also expose them to different perspectives and ways of critically engaging with the world around them. Here, I present five core arguments that – when implemented and embedded throughout the curriculum as our subject's signature pedagogy and approach – enquiry empowers young people to change the world. This may be in the future. This may be at a smaller scale because you are working within a restrictive system. But it can be done. I have provided some examples of enquiry in Appendix 1 and I encourage you to adapt and use them in your setting.

First, using an enquiry approach builds powerful disciplinary thinking and literacy. Enquiry is a vehicle to teach students how to think like geographers. That means weighing up evidence from different sources and perspectives, analysing patterns and understanding complex systems. This fosters a deeper disciplinary understanding in students, allowing them to engage with the contests and provisional nature of geographical knowledge (Ofsted, 2023a). Disciplinary literacy recognises that literacy skills are both general and subject-specific (EEF, 2018). Enquiry supports students in developing the reading and writing skills necessary to engage with geographical texts and concepts.

Second, an enquiry approach supports deep learning through retrieval and reflection, as connecting knowledge to other concepts and units is encouraged. Geographical enquiry is full of desirable difficulties (Bjork and Bjork, 2020), fosters long-term transferable thinking and introduces cognitive conflict. In addition, as enquiry allows room to pause and connect with other aspects of geography, retrieval practice, spacing and elaboration can easily be baked into the curriculum (Willingham, 2009b). Enquiry embeds these naturally as students revisit core concepts, apply them to new contexts and reflect critically on their learning.

Third, the enquiry approach promotes curiosity and agency and helps to improve motivation. As young people progress through enquiry, moving towards having more choice in the evidence they consider and the questions they ask, coupled with an approach that harnesses critical hope, learners have more of a chance to feel autonomous, competent and connected to the world around them. Introducing the opportunity for students to be guided through and lead enquiry at the appropriate point nurtures autonomy and ownership, helping them to see geography as meaningful, personal and socially relevant. Self-determination theory (Deci and Ryan, 2020) suggests that students are more motivated when they feel like this, and enquiry allows students to take increasing ownership over their learning.

Fourth, enquiry empowers students to engage with real-world issues and to see the world as it is, and encourages them to act, even if that is personal in scale. The GA's Young People's Geographies project demonstrates that geographical enquiry approaches enable students to connect personal experiences with global issues, which in turn enhances their critical thinking and feelings of social responsibility. This is because enquiry allows students to make connections between the local and the global. Encouraging geographic enquiry, such as asking deep geographical questions or critically engaging with sources of information to understand gaps, is more likely to lead to informed action.

Finally, far from not fitting into the modern way of approaching teaching, geographical enquiry allows geography teaching to be high-quality, which means that it is responsive, reflective and rigorous. A core aspect of enquiry is understanding and then responding to students' geographical rucksacks, part of how they see the world and influencing what they need. Adaptive teaching (Mould, 2021) and enquiry approaches complement each other. Enquiry also aligns with Rosenshine's (2012) principles of asking lots of questions and checking for understanding. Enquiry and great teaching in geography are the same thing.

In summary, the changes can be at a personal level and rely upon solid knowledge of geography as it is now. Geographical enquiry can be led and guided by teachers to control the knowledge and skills that are learned and to avoid misconceptions and the development of a single story. Enquiry empowers students to think, question and act like geographers. Enquiry draws on cognitive science to secure learning, supports high-quality teaching and fosters critical, informed learners who are equipped to understand and shape the world.

> **Activity**
>
> Go on an obstacle hunt with colleagues. This means identifying all the obstacles and potential negatives about adopting an enquiry approach. What are all the barriers in using enquiry? Once done, go through them one by one and back each up with evidence.

Enquiry belongs in the geography classroom

Consider today's headlines. They will all be geographical in nature. In this book, I have argued that enquiry is school geography's signature pedagogy; it helps to structure the curriculum and provides a lens through which to critically look at abstract geographical concepts and connect them to the real world. I have outlined my own blend of enquiry, shaped in the classroom, which is not discovery learning.

Geography teachers must be able to defend enquiry to non-specialist leaders and understand that what we know about cognitive science is compatible with enquiry. Whilst school geographers do not set out to create new knowledge, they do develop the habits of scholarship in our classrooms, and we should aim to embed these by the end of compulsory geographical study at 14.

Enquiry allows students to take what they have been taught and apply it to new situations and problems. Taking an enquiry approach from lesson one of Year 7 develops synoptic thinking, which is essential to securing good grades at GCSE and beyond.

Enquiry is what makes geography geography. Communicating to students that geographers understand the world so that they can go on to change it, hopefully for the better, is important. It provides hope and agency that they can be part of shaping their world.

Enquiry provides the mechanism where students leave with qualifications and the qualities to be able to move from being passive consumers of knowledge towards people who are critically engaged in the world around them.

Finally, enquiry allows us to bring a rich and varied range of perspectives and knowledge into the classroom in a safe way. It helps teachers identify misconceptions, whilst allowing room for young people to hold their own viewpoints, informed by their experiences *plus* the geography that we teach them.

Through enquiry, we develop the great geographers of the future. They can use the enquiry knowledge that we teach them to understand the world and make it better. These changes may be small in nature or global in scale.

Geographical enquiry is more than a teaching method to be consigned to the occasional foray outside the classroom. It secures the knowledge and skills that students need whilst at the same time nurturing curiosity, criticality and hope. In a world of shifting knowledge, urgent challenges and competing voices, enquiry offers both academic rigour and relevance. By teaching through enquiry, we develop young people who can question, reflect and act. Not only that, but they become more effective learners, gaining success in external examinations and the future. In other words, by using enquiry, we help create geographers who not only understand the world but are ready to make it better.

Key takeaways

- Enquiry is geography's signature pedagogy.
- We should be using the enquiry approach because it:
  - builds powerful disciplinary thinking and literacy
  - supports deep learning through retrieval and reflection, as connecting knowledge to other concepts and units is encouraged
  - promotes curiosity and agency and helps to improve motivation
  - empowers students to engage with real-world issues and see the world as it is and encourages them to act, even if that is personal in scale
  - allows geography teaching to be high-quality, which means that it is responsive, reflective and rigorous.

Afterword

One day or day one?

I have one professional regret, which is that I stopped behind a head of geography far too soon. It truly was – and is – the best job there is. If there has ever been a time for great geography teaching, then it is now, when data and information are freely available and the latest fake news travels so fast around the world that it becomes the headlines. Great geography leverages its signature pedagogy: enquiry. Enquiry is how geographical knowledge is created and it is how it is learned. In this often crazy and beautiful world, geographical enquiry gives hope. Geographical enquiry gives belief.

Enquiry gives us a framework to challenge the nature of the subject and its knowledge. It enables us to safely manage misconceptions and preconceptions and to carefully consider moral challenges. Enquiry gives a framework for young people's voices to be legitimately heard and incorporated into the curriculum.

Enquiry demands that we question the world, question perspectives, and seek, welcome, integrate, critically review and respect the views of everyone. Enquiry exposes us to information from different perspectives and gives us the time to reflect upon how that changes us and how we view and act in the world. Geographical enquiry is more important now than ever.

Great geography teachers secure the content needed to gain qualifications, but also ensure that the procedural knowledge is there, so that students are aware and can begin to cope with their ever-changing world.

> **Reflection**
>
> Look at the examples of enquiries contained in Appendix 1 (page 281). Which of these can you adapt for your context? Which will excite young people?

Activity

One day or day one? Come up with an action plan based on this book. It could look like this:

1 **Your vision for geographical enquiry in your context:** *In one or two sentences, describe what you want enquiry to look and feel like in your context.*
2 **Enquiry priorities – what do you want to focus on?**
    - *focus area, e.g. improve real-world context for procedural knowledge*
    - *rationale – make geography more relevant to the world as it is*
    - *where we are now – topics feel abstract*
    - *where we want to be – use local case studies and issues.*
3 **Strategies to try, adapt or bin:**
    - *strategy/idea*
    - *page number/aspect of enquiry*
    - *how we will adapt it*
    - *when we will try it.*
4 **What will improvement look like?** *Better geographical extended writing, considering a range of perspectives and linking concepts to local examples.*
5 **Reflection schedule**
    - *date*
    - *what we will reflect on*
    - *evidence we will use*
    - *next steps.*
6 **Support and collaboration:** *Who will support us? Are there colleagues, mentors or networks we can share progress with or learn from?*

Bibliography

References

Abbey, E. (1968) *Desert Solitaire: A season in the wilderness*. Toronto: Random House Publishing Group.

Adichie, C. N. (2009) 'The danger of a single story', *TED*, www.ted.com/talks/chimamanda_ngozi_adichie_the_danger_of_a_single_story

Alcock, D. (2020) 'Hopeful education', *Alcockblog*, https://alcock.blog/2020/09/18/hopeful-education

Al Jazeera English (2011) 'Maasai women's quest for an education', YouTube, www.youtube.com/watch?v=c-sxE5V9aPk

Allaway, R. (2024) 'It is not just the staff that need training! Getting everybody at school to use AI positively'. *Practical Pedagogies Conference 2024*, session resources, www.gatw.tech/It-is-not-just-the-staff-that-need-training-Getting-everybody-at-school-to-use-AI-positively-12bd928cb634809ab88dd9cd4d080736

Al-Momani, F. (2019) 'Qualitative study: An analysis of pre-service science teachers' understanding about scientific inquiry and their confidence in inquiry-based science pedagogy'. *Journal of Education and Practice,* 10, (5), 76–91.

ap Dafydd, M. (2005) *The Faithful Dog Gelert*. Translated by S. Lewis. Llanrwst: Gwasg Carreg Gwalch.

AQA (n.d.) 'A-level geography specification 3.2.4.5: Principles of population ecology and their application to human populations', www.aqa.org.uk/subjects/geography/a-level/geography-7037/specification/subject-content/human-geography

Arden, K. (2024) *The Warm Hands of Ghosts*. London: Penguin.

Askew, J. (2024) 'One man's campaign against his "anti-fun" city'. *BBC News*, 13 October, www.bbc.co.uk/news/articles/crkd7861xgro

Attenborough, D. (2008), 'My Places – David Attenborough'. *Teaching Geography*, 33, (2), 86.

Atterton, G. and Dixson, I. (2009) 'Going round in circles'. *The Geographical Association Magazine*, 13, 24–25.

Australian Government (2009) 'Risks from climate change to Indigenous communities in the tropical north of Australia', https://library.sprep.org/sites/default/files/5_23.pdf

Barton, C. (2018) 'Why we should ban all displays in the classroom!', *SecEd*, www.sec-ed.co.uk/content/best-practice/why-we-should-ban-all-displays-in-the-classroom

Bishop, D and Bishop, J. (2025) '#010: Conversations on Mortality'. *The Bishop Exchange*. www.globalplayer.com/podcasts/episodes/7DrpPK7

Bjork, R. A. and Bjork, E. L. (2020) 'Desirable difficulties in theory and practice'. *Journal of Applied Research in Memory and Cognition*, 9, (4), 475–479.

Bonnett, A. (2008). *What is Geography?* London: SAGE Publications.

Brace, S. (2024a) 'Is your classroom plagued by "zombie" resources?', *Tes Magazine*, 6 March, www.tes.com/magazine/teaching-learning/secondary/the-problem-of-outdated-teaching-resources-schools-geography

Brace, S. (2024b) 'Why geography lessons are the key to climate awareness', *Guardian*, 3 November, www.theguardian.com/science/2024/nov/03/why-geography-lessons-are-the-key-to-climate-awareness

Bradshaw, M., Abbott, A. J. and Gelsthorpe, A. P. (1978) *The Earth's Changing Surface*. London: Hodder and Arnold.

Brady, B., Suter, K., Lamb, R. and Scott, A. (2023) 'Using physical models to improve geographical learning'. *Teaching Geography*, 48, (2), 72–75.

Brooks, C. (2013) 'How do we understand conceptual development in school geography?' In: Lambert, D. and Jones, M. (eds) *Debates in Geography Education*. Abingdon: Routledge, pp. 75–88.

Burgess, E. W. (1925) 'The growth of the city: An introduction to a research project'. In: Park, R. E., Burgess, E. W. and McKenzie, R. D. (eds.) *The City*. Chicago: Chicago University Press, pp. 47–62.

Butler, R. W. (1980) 'The concept of a tourist area cycle of evolution and implications for management of resources'. *The Canadian Geographer*, 24, (1), 5–12.

Campbell, N. (2020) *Fifty Words for Snow*. London: Elliott and Thompson.

Campbell, R. and Bokhove, C. (2021) 'Building learning culture through effective uses of group work'. *Impact*, 5, https://my.chartered.college/impact_article/building-learning-culture-through-effective-uses-of-group-work

Chang, E. C. (1998) 'Hope, problem-solving ability, and coping in a college student population: Some implications for theory and practice'. *Journal of Clinical Psychology*, 54, (7), 953–962.

Cinner, J. (2018) 'How behavioral science can help conservation: Leveraging cognitive biases and social influence can make conservation efforts more effective'. *Science*, 362, (6417), 889–890.

Coe, R. (2019) 'Does research on "retrieval practice" translate into classroom practice?', *EEF Blog*, https://educationendowmentfoundation.org.uk/news/does-research-on-retrieval-practice-translate-into-classroom-practice

Cornell University (n.d.) 'The Cornell note taking system', https://lsc.cornell.edu/how-to-study/taking-notes/cornell-note-taking-system

Council for Curriculum, Examinations and Assessment (CCEA) (2007) 'Key Stage 3 curriculum: Geography', https://ccea.org.uk/key-stage-3/curriculum/environment-society/geography

David, D. (2018) *The Almighty Dollar: Follow the incredible journey of a single dollar to see how the global economy really works*. London: Elliott and Thompson.

Deci, E. L. and Ryan, R. M. (2000) 'Self-determination theory and the facilitation of intrinsic motivation, social development, and well-being'. *American Psychologist*, 55, (1), 68–78.

Department for Education (DfE) (2011) 'Teachers' standards', www.gov.uk/government/publications/teachers-standards

Department for Education (DfE) (2013a) 'Geography programmes of study: Key Stage 3', https://assets.publishing.service.gov.uk/media/5a7b8699ed915d131105fd16/SECONDARY_national_curriculum_-_Geography.pdf

Department for Education (DfE) (2013b) 'National curriculum in England: Geography programmes of study', www.gov.uk/government/publications/national-curriculum-in-england-geography-programmes-of-study

Department for Education (DfE) (2014) 'Promoting fundamental British values as part of SMSC in schools', https://assets.publishing.service.gov.uk/media/5a758c9540f0b6397f35f469/SMSC_Guidance_Maintained_Schools.pdf

Department for Education (DfE) (2024) 'Factors influencing secondary school pupils' educational outcomes: A literature review supporting the Growing Up in the 2020s study', https://assets.publishing.service.gov.uk/media/66e4006e3f1299ce5d5c3e11/Factors_influencing_secondary_school_pupils__educational_outcomes.pdf

Department for Education (DfE) (2025) 'Curriculum and Assessment Review: Interim report', https://assets.publishing.service.gov.uk/media/6821d69eced319d02c9060e3/Curriculum_and_Assessment_Review_interim_report.pdf

Department of Education (Northern Ireland) (DfE NI) (2007) 'The Education (Curriculum Minimum Content) Order (Northern Ireland) 2007', www.legislation.gov.uk/nisr/2007/46/pdfs/nisr_20070046_en.pdf

Department for Environment, Food & Rural Affairs (DEFRA) (2024) 'Policy paper: Criteria for 30by30 on land in England', www.gov.uk/government/publications/criteria-for-30by30-on-land-in-england

Department for Environment, Food & Rural Affairs (DEFRA) (2025) 'The Habitat Target: Creating and restoring habitats across England', Blog: Environment, https://defraenvironment.blog.gov.uk/2025/02/05/the-habitat-target-creating-and-restoring-habitats-across-england

Dove, J. (1999) *Theory into Practice: Immaculate misconceptions*. Sheffield: Geographical Association.

Downing, E. (2021) *Coasting: Running around the coast of Britain – life, love and (very) loose plans*. London: Summersdale.

Education Endowment Foundation (EEF) (n.d.) 'Teaching and Learning Toolkit: Metacognition and self-regulation', https://educationendowmentfoundation.org.uk/education-evidence/teaching-learning-toolkit/metacognition-and-self-regulation

Education Endowment Foundation (EEF) (2018) 'Improving literacy in secondary schools: Guidance report', https://d2tic4wvo1iusb.cloudfront.net/production/eef-guidance-reports/literacy-ks3-ks4/EEF_KS3_KS4_LITERACY_GUIDANCE.pdf?v=1758012020

Education Endowment Foundation (EEF) (2021) 'Cognitive science approaches in the classroom: A review of the evidence', https://d2tic4wvo1iusb.cloudfront.net/production/documents/guidance/Cognitive_science_approaches_in_the_classroom_-_A_review_of_the_evidence.pdf?v=1744624056

Education Endowment Foundation (EEF) (2023) 'The "five-a-day" principle: Scaffolding', https://d2tic4wvo1iusb.cloudfront.net/production/eef-guidance-reports/send/5-a-Day_Reflection_Tool_2023.pdf?v=1747670888

Education Endowment Foundation (EEF) (2024) 'Using research evidence: A concise guide', https://d2tic4wvo1iusb.cloudfront.net/production/documents/using_research_evidence_-_a_concise_guide.pdf?v=1

Education Scotland (2018) 'Curriculum for Excellence: Experiences and outcomes', https://education.gov.scot/media/wpsnskgv/all-experiencesoutcomes18.pdf

Enser, M. (n.d.) 'Applying Rosenshine to the geography classroom', My College Early Career Hub, https://my.chartered.college/early-career-hub/applying-rosenshine-to-the-geography-classroom

Fiorella, L. (2023) 'Making sense of generative learning'. *Educational Psychology Review*, 35, 50.

Freeman, D. (2024) 'Advocacy for geography'. Geographical Association newsletter, autumn 2024, pp. 6–7.

Gapminder (n.d.) 'Factfulness', www.gapminder.org/Factfulness

Gardner, D., Coles, J., Hopkins, E., Lyon, J. and Owen, C. (2024) *Progress in Geography: Key Stage 3* (2nd edn.). London: Hodder Education.

Gaw, M. (2020) *Under the Stars: A journey into light*. London: Elliott and Thompson.

Geographical Association (GA) (2008) 'Young Geographers: A living geography project for primary schools', https://geography.org.uk/curriculum-support/projects/project-archive/young-geographers

Geographical Association (GA) (2022) 'A framework for the school geography curriculum', https://geography.org.uk/wp-content/uploads/2023/07/GA-Curriculum-Framework-2022-WEB-final.pdf

Geographical Association (GA) (2024a) 'Response to review of curriculum and assessment', https://geography.org.uk/wp-content/uploads/2024/11/Geographical-Association-Response-to-Review-of-Curriculum-and-Assessment-Nov24.pdf

Geographical Association (GA) (2024b) 'Episode #74: James Esson – Viewing the world through a geographical lens', *GeogPod*, https://geogpod.podbean.com/e/episode-74-james-esson-viewing-the-world-through-a-geographical-lens

Geographical Association (GA) (2025) 'Geography for everyone?', https://geography.org.uk/geography-for-everyone

Gilbert, I. (2007) *The Little Book of Thunks: 260 questions to make your brain go ouch!*. Carmarthen: Crown House Publishing.

Global Forest Watch (n.d.) 'Dashboard: United Kingdom', www.globalforestwatch.org/dashboards/country/GBR

Grenell, A., Ernst, J. R. and Carlson, S. M. (2024) 'Preschool children's science learning: Instructional approaches and individual differences'. *Early Education and Development*, 35, (8), 1891–1919.

Griffiths, A. (2024) 'Hopeful geographies in 2024', *Tutor2u*, www.tutor2u.net/geography/blog/hopeful-geographies-in-2024

Halliwell, J. (2020) 'Applying social media research methods in geography teaching: Benefits and emerging challenges?'. *Journal of Geography*, 119, (3), 108–113.

Hamill, A. (2023) 'Time for a seismic shift in teaching of plate tectonics?' *Teaching Geography*, 48, (2), 50–53.

Hattie, J. (2003) 'Teachers make a difference, what is the research evidence?'. In: *Building Teacher Quality: What does the research tell us ACER Research Conference*, Melbourne, Australia, https://research.acer.edu.au/cgi/viewcontent.cgi?article=1003&context=research_conference_2003

Hickman, C., Marks, E., Pihkala, P., Clayton, S., Lewandowski, R. E., Mayall, E. E., Wray, B., Mellor, C. and van Susteren, L. (2021) 'Climate anxiety in children and young people and their beliefs about government responses to climate change: A global survey'. *The Lancet Planetary Health*, 5, (12), 863-873.

Hickman, J. and Ghosh, R. (2024) 'ChatGPT: Are geography teachers redundant?'. *Teaching Geography*, 49, (1), 18–21.

Humphreys, A. (2024) *Local: A search for nearby nature and wildness*. Much Wenlock: Eye Books.

IPCC (2014) 'Climate Change 2014: Synthesis Report. Contribution of Working Groups I, II and III to the Fifth Assessment Report of the Intergovernmental Panel on Climate Change' [Core Writing Team, R.K. Pachauri and L.A. Meyer (eds.)]. IPCC, Geneva, Switzerland, 151.

Jackson, P. (2006). Thinking geographically. *Geography*, 91 (3), 199–204.

Jankell, L. D., Sandahl, J. and Örbring, D. (2021) 'Organising concepts in geography education: A model'. *Geography*, 106, (2), 66–75.

Jian, M. (2001) *Red Dust: A path through China*. London: Random House.

Jones, K. (2024) 'Conversations about cognitive science in the classroom', Evidence Based Education, https://evidencebased.education/conversations-about-cognitive-science-in-the-classroom

Jusslin, S., Korpinen, K., Lilja, N., Martin, R., Lehtinen-Schnabel, J. and Anttila, E. (2022) 'Embodied learning and teaching approaches in language education: A mixed studies review'. *Educational Research Review*, 37, (1), 100480.

Kidman, G. and Chang, C. H. (2021) 'Hope and its implication for geographical and environmental education'. *International Research in Geographical and Environmental Education*, 30, (1), 1–3.

Kirschner, P. A. and Hendrick, C. (2020) *How Learning Happens: Seminal works in educational psychology and what they mean in practice*. London: Routledge.

Lambert, D. and Morgan, J. (2010) *Teaching Geography 11–18: A conceptual approach*. Maidenhead: Open University Press.

Leat, D. (2001) *Thinking Through Geography*. London: Chris Kingston Publishing.

Lee, E. S. (1966) 'A theory of migration'. *Demography*, 3, (1), 47–57.

Louis, R. P. (2007) 'Can you hear us now? Voices from the margin: Using Indigenous methodologies in geographical research', *Aboriginal Policy Research Consortium International (APRCi)*, 175, https://scispace.com/pdf/can-you-hear-us-now-voices-from-the-margin-using-indigenous-3vzp5x0ner.pdf

Map Men (2024), 'The phantom island of Google Maps', YouTube, www.youtube.com/watch?v=PVemGumEEgo

Margolis, E. and Laurence, S. (2023) 'Making sense of domain specificity'. *Cognition*, 240, 105583.

Marshall, T. (2025) *Prisoners of Geography: Ten maps that tell you everything you need to know about global politics*. London: Elliott and Thompson.

Massey, D. (2006) 'The geographical mind'. In: Balderstone, D. (ed.) *Secondary Geography Handbook*. Sheffield: Geographical Association, pp. 46–51.

Matthews, J. A., & Herbert, D. T. (2008). *Geography: A very short introduction*. Oxford: Oxford University Press.

Mccrea, P. (2025) 'Planning expertise: Knowledge for designing learning', *Evidence Snacks*, https://snacks.pepsmccrea.com/p/planning-expertise

Miles, B. (2025) 'The world's oldest river has a big problem', YouTube, www.youtube.com/watch?v=BbC5ZmaFiRo

Milner, C. (2020) 'Classroom strategies for tackling the whiteness of geography'. *Teaching Geography*, 45, (3), 105–107.

Moorhouse, T. (2021) *Elegy for a River: Whiskers, claws and conservation's last wild hope*. New York: Doubleday.

Morgan, J. (2013) 'What do we mean by thinking geographically?'. In: Lambert, D. and Jones, M. (eds) *Debates in Geography Education*. Abingdon: Routledge, pp. 115–125.

Mould, K. (2021) 'Assess, adjust, adapt – what does adaptive teaching mean to you?', *EEF Blog*, https://educationendowmentfoundation.org.uk/news/eef-blog-assess-adjust-adapt-what-does-adaptive-teaching-mean-to-you?utm_source=chatgpt.com

Naish, M., Rawling, E. and Hart, C. (2002) 'The enquiry-based approach to teaching and learning geography.' In M. Smith (Ed.) *Teaching Geography in Secondary Schools*. London: Routledge.

National Geographic (n.d.) 'Learning tool: Exploring multiple perspectives', https://education.nationalgeographic.org/resource/exploring-multiple-perspectives

Nayeri, C. and Rushton, E. A. C. (2022) 'Methodologies for decolonising geography curricula in the secondary school and in initial teacher education'. *London Review of Education*, 20, (1), 4.

Newsround (2020) 'BBC Bitesize: Sir David Attenborough gives geography lessons', www.bbc.co.uk/newsround/53048939

Nursey-Bray, M., Palmer, R., Smith, T. F. and Rist, P. (2019) 'Old ways for new days: Australian Indigenous peoples and climate change'. *Local Environment*, 24, (5), 473–486.

Office for National Statistics (ONS) (2023) 'Ability to speak Welsh by NS-SEC', www.ons.gov.uk/datasets/RM151/editions/2021/versions/3

Ofqual (2017) 'GCSE, AS and A level assessment objectives', www.gov.uk/government/publications/assessment-objectives-ancient-languages-geography-and-mfl/gcse-as-and-a-level-assessment-objectives

Ofsted (2011) 'Geography: Learning to make a world of difference', www.gov.uk/government/publications/geography-learning-to-make-a-world-of-difference

Ofsted (2019) 'Education inspection framework 2019: Inspecting the substance of education', www.gov.uk/government/consultations/education-inspection-framework-2019-inspecting-the-substance-of-education/education-inspection-framework-2019-inspecting-the-substance-of-education

Ofsted (2021) 'Research review series: Geography', www.gov.uk/government/publications/research-review-series-geography/research-review-series-geography

Ofsted (2023a) 'Getting our bearings: Geography subject report', www.gov.uk/government/publications/subject-report-series-geography/getting-our-bearings-geography-subject-report

Ofsted (2023b) 'The annual report of His Majesty's Chief Inspector of Education, Children's Services and Skills 2022/2023', www.gov.uk/government/publications/ofsted-annual-report-202223-education-childrens-services-and-skills/the-annual-report-of-his-majestys-chief-inspector-of-education-childrens-services-and-skills-202223

Oracy Education Commission (2024) 'We need to talk: The report of the Commission on the future of oracy education in England', https://oracyeducationcommission.co.uk/wp-content/uploads/2024/10/We-need-to-talk-2024.pdf

Owens, J. (2023) *Dust: The modern world in a trillion particles*. London: Hodder & Stoughton.

Oxford, Cambridge and RSA (OCR) (2018) 'OCR GCSE (9–1) in Geography A (Geographical Themes) J383', www.ocr.org.uk/Images/207306-specification-accredited-gcse-geography-a-j383.pdf

Pace-Humphreys, S. (2022) *Black Sheep: A story of rural racism, identity and hope*. London: Quercus.

Parkinson, A. (2018) 'Factfulness: A collaborative scheme of work', *Living Geography*, https://livinggeography.blogspot.com/2018/05/factfulness-collaborative-scheme-of-work.html

Parkinson, A. (2020) *Why Study Geography?* London: London Publishing Partnership.

Parkinson, A. (2022) 'Everyday geographies: The power of the quotidian'. *Teaching Geography*, 47, (2), 53–55.

Perry, T. (2022) 'What we don't yet know about cognitive science in the classroom'. *Impact*, 16, 77–79.

Podbury, M. (n.d.) 'The "dream team"', Geographypods, www.geographypods.com/g6-Factfulness.html

Pryke, M. (2024) 'Learning from the Global South', OpenLearn, www.open.edu/openlearn/learning-the-global-south

Puttick, S. (2020) 'Taking Burgess out of the bin'. *Teaching Geography*, 45, (1), 6–8.

Puttick, S. (2023) *The Geography Teaching Adventure: Reclaiming exploration to inspire curriculum and pedagogy*. Abingdon: Routledge.

Puttick, S. and Murrey, A. (2020) 'Working towards anti-racist school geography in Britain', Oxford University blog, https://medium.com/oxford-university/working-towards-anti-racist-school-geography-in-britain-8b16a94e25ba

Raven-Ellison, D. (2012) 'Guerilla geography' (video), National Geographic, https://education.nationalgeographic.org/resource/daniel-raven-ellison-guerrilla-geography

Rawdling, C. (2019) 'Putting Burgess in the bin'. *Teaching Geography*, 44, (3), 94–96.

Redfern, D. (2023) 'Why it is time to ditch the Bradshaw model', *A Level of Geography*, https://dredfern.substack.com/p/why-it-is-time-to-ditch-the-bradshaw

Richardson, M. (2024) *The Blackbird's Song & Other Wonders of Nature: A year-round guide to connecting with the natural world*. London: New River Books.

Ritchie, H., Rodés-Guirao, L., Mathieu, E., Gerber, M., Ortiz-Ospina, E., Hasell, J. and Roser, M. (2023) 'Population growth', Our World in Data, https://ourworldindata.org/population-growth

Robbins, C. (2007) *In Search of Kazakhstan: The land that disappeared*. London: Profile Books.

Roberts, M. (2003) *Learning Through Enquiry: Making sense of geography in the Key Stage 3 classroom*. Sheffield: Geographical Association.

Roberts, M. (2013) 'The challenge of enquiry-based learning'. *Teaching Geography*, 38, (2), 50–52.

Roberts, M. (2023) *Geography Through Enquiry: Approaches to teaching and learning in the secondary school* (2nd edn.). Sheffield: Geographical Association.

Rogers, D. (2006) 'Banned word board', *David Rogers*, https://daviderogers.blogspot.com/2006/12/banned-word-board.html

Rogers, D. (2012) 'Simple but effective ideas: Iceland does not exist', *David Rogers*, https://daviderogers.blogspot.com/2012/10/simple-but-effective-ideas-iceland-does.html

Rogers, D. (2015) 'Planning your Key Stage 3'. *Teaching Geography*, 40, (2), 67–68.

Rosenshine, B. (2012) 'Principles of instruction: Research-based strategies that all teachers should know'. *American Educator*, 36, (1), 12–19, 39.

Roser, M. (2018) 'The world is awful. The world is much better. The world can be much better', Our World in Data, https://ourworldindata.org/much-better-awful-can-be-better

Roser, M. and Ritchie, H. (2023) 'Two centuries of rapid global population growth will come to an end', Our World in Data, https://ourworldindata.org/world-population-growth-past-future

Rosling, H. (2010) 'The magic washing machine', *TEDWomen*, www.ted.com/talks/hans_rosling_the_magic_washing_machine

Rosling, H. (2019) *Factfulness: Ten reasons we're wrong about the world – and why things are better than you think*. London: Sceptre.

Rosling, H. (2021) *How I Learned to Understand the World*. London: Sceptre.

Rostow, W. W. (1959) 'The stages of economic growth'. *The Economic History Review*, 12, (1), 1–16.

Royal Geographical Society (RGS) with IBG (n.d.) 'Fieldwork', www.rgs.org/schools/resources-for-schools/guidance-and-support-in-developing-high-quality-primary-geography/fieldwork

Samingpai, B. (2023) 'Modelling the coastline: using physical models to aid student understanding'. *Teaching Geography*, 48, (3), 124–126.

Sammar, I. (2024) 'Decolonial and anti-racist pedagogy through personal geographies'. *Teaching Geography*, 49, (1), 22–25.

Sayers, J. (2013) 'Questioning', *John Sayers Geography Blog*, https://sayersjohn.blogspot.com/2013/01/questioning.html

Schwartz, G. (2022) '"It was like an apocalyptic movie": 20 climate photographs that changed the world', *Guardian*, 5 November, www.theguardian.com/environment/2022/nov/05/20-climate-photographs-that-changed-the-world

Scottish Government (2010) 'Curriculum for excellence', https://education.gov.scot/media/wpsnskgv/all-experiencesoutcomes18.pdf

Selmes, I. (2016) 'From the archives: Extended writing in geography'. *Teaching Geography*, 41, (2), 68–69.

Sethi, A. (2021) *I Belong Here: A journey along the backbone of Britain*. London: Bloomsbury.

Shrubsole, G. (2024) *The Lie of the Land: Who really cares for the countryside?* London: William Collins.

Smith, K. (2007) *The Guerilla Art Kit: Everything you need to put your message out into the world*. New York: Princeton Architectural Press.

South Downs National Park (n.d.) 'Help nature to ReNature', www.southdowns.gov.uk/renature

Steel, H. (2023) '"All models are wrong… but some are useful" – George E.P. Box', https://geogsteel.wordpress.com/2023/03/13/all-models-are-wrong

Stockings, K. (2020) 'Teaching geography through books' (Part 2), *Kate Stockings*, www.katestockings.com/geographycurriculum/teaching-geography-through-books-part-2

Stockings, K. (2023), Tweet, 7 November, @kate_stockings, https://x.com/kate_stockings/status/1721954113745817624

Taylor, L. (2021) 'Think piece: Concepts in geography', Geographical Association, https://geography.org.uk/wp-content/uploads/2023/05/Think_Piece_Concepts_in_geography.pdf

Teach the Future (2024) 'GCSE geography students let down by outdated textbooks teaching inaccurate climate science', www.teachthefuture.uk/blog/gcse-geography-students-let-down

Thompson, W. (1929) 'Population.' *American Journal of Sociology*, 34, (6).

Tomlinson, B., Black, R. W., Patterson, D. J. and Torrance, A. W. (2024) 'The carbon emissions of writing and illustrating are lower for AI than for humans'. *Scientific Reports*, 14, 3732.

Trolley, S. (2020) '*Prisoners of Geography*? How contextualising a book can develop students' understandings of geography'. *Teaching Geography*, 45, (2), 72–74.

UNESCO (n.d.) 'World Heritage List', https://whc.unesco.org/en/list

UNICEF (1989) 'UN Convention on the Rights of the Child', www.unicef.org.uk/wp-content/uploads/2017/09/Our-rights_UNCRC.pdf

Usher, J. (2019) 'Brexit and borders: Topical geography'. *Teaching Geography*, 44, (3), 111–114.

U.S. Environmental Protection Agency (EPA) (2024) *Climate Change Indicators: Wildfires*. www.epa.gov/climate-indicators/climate-change-indicators-wildfires

Vujakovic, P. (2019) 'World maps in a time of crisis'. *Teaching Geography*, 44, (3), 101–104.

Wainwright, A. (1986) *A Pennine Journey: The story of a long walk in 1938*. Biggleswade: The Wainwright Society.

Welsh Government (2022a) 'Curriculum for Wales: Humanities', https://hwb.gov.wales/curriculum-for-wales/humanities

Welsh Government (2022b) 'Curriculum for Wales: Humanities – Statements of what matters code', www.gov.wales/sites/default/files/publications/2023-06/curriculum-for-wales-statements-of-what-matters-code.pdf

West, H. (2021) 'Taking the first steps towards bringing GIS into the classroom'. *Teaching Geography*, 46, (1), 14–16.

Wiliam, D. (2006) 'Assessment for learning: Why, what and how?', talk for Cambridge Assessment Network at the Institute of Education, London.

Wiliam, D. (2012) 'How do we prepare our students for a world we cannot possibly imagine?' Keynote speech. In: *SSAT National Conference*, AAC Liverpool, UK, 4–5 December 2012.

Willingham, D. T. (2009a) *Why Don't Students Like School? A cognitive scientist answers questions about how the mind works and what it means for the classroom* (2nd edn.). San Francisco: Jossey-Bass.

Willingham, D. T. (2009b) 'Ask the cognitive scientist: What will improve a student's memory?'. *American Educator*, 32, (4), 17–44.

Windrush Foundation (n.d.) '7 Windrush education resources', https://windrushfoundation.com/news/7-windrush-education-resources

Winter, C. (2018) 'Disrupting colonial discourses in the geography curriculum during the introduction of British Values policy in schools'. *Journal of Curriculum Studies*, 50, (4), 456–475.

Winter, C. (2023) 'The geography GCSE curriculum in England: A white curriculum of deceit'. *Whiteness and Education*, 8, (2), 313–331.

Wood, P. (2006) 'Developing enquiry through questioning'. *Teaching Geography*, 31, (2), 76–78.

World Commission on Environment and Development (WCED) (1987) *Our Common Future: World commission on environment and development*. Oxford: Oxford University Press.

Ying Chua, C., Wong, J., Chang, J. and Hagen, R. (2021) 'Virtual fieldwork in a time of COVID-19'. *Teaching Geography*, 46, (2), 64–67.

Further reading

Allen, J., Amin, A., Featherstone, D., Gunaratnam, Y., Jazeel, T., McDowell, L., Skelton, T., Wainwright, H. and Lisiak, A. (2022) 'Full of power', *Spatial Delight* podcast, https://thesociologicalreview.org/podcasts/spatial-delight/full-of-power

Arden, K. (2024) *The Warm Hands of Ghosts*. London: Penguin.

Arnold, M. (2006) *Culture and Anarchy*. Oxford: Oxford University Press.

Ashman, G. (2018) *The Truth about Teaching: An evidence-informed guide for new teachers*. London: Sage.

Bradford, T. (2004) *The Groundwater Diaries: Trails, tributaries and tall stories from beneath the streets of London*. London: Flamingo.

Bromley, M. (2024) 'Learning objectives and success criteria', *SecEd*, www.sec-ed.co.uk/content/best-practice/learning-objectives-and-success-criteria

Caudrey, G. (2010) 'The hazards of enquiry learning'. *Teaching Geography*, 35, (1), 15–17.

Didau, D. (2012) 'Learning objectives and when we need 'em', *Learning Spy*, https://learningspy.co.uk/learning/learning-objectives-why-we-need-em-2

Downs, J. and Campbell, T. (2024) 'Using AI to transform adaptive teaching at A level'. *Teaching Geography*, 49, (3), 102–104.

Doyle, A. C. (2020) *A Scandal in Bohemia*. Dorset: Solis Press.

Geocapabilities (n.d.) 'Into practice: Training materials', www.geocapabilities.org/training-materials/module-2-curriculum-making-by-teachers/into-practice

Geographical Association (n.d.) 'From intent to implementation: Curriculum making', support for trainees and ECTs, https://geography.org.uk/ite/initial-teacher-education/geography-support-for-trainees-and-ects/learning-to-teach-secondary-geography/geography-subject-teaching-and-curriculum/curriculum-and-curriculum-planning/from-intent-to-implementation

Griffiths, A. (2023) 'OK computer? Using artificial intelligence for teaching and learning about climate change'. *Teaching Geography*, 48 (2), 68–71.

Hawley, D. and Lyon, J. (2017) 'Plate update: Refreshing ideas for teaching plate tectonics'. *Teaching Geography*, 42, (1), 30–32.

Hopkin, J. and Owens, P. (2015) 'Progression in global learning'. *Teaching Geography*, 40, (2), 60–61.

Hughes, H. (2024) *Plays, Prose, Pieces, Poetry: Presented by Richard Ayoade*. London: Faber & Faber.

Jackson, E. and Lisiak, A. (2025) 'You'll never walk alone: Theorising engaged walking with Doreen Massey'. *The Sociological Review*.

Kraemer, M. U. G., Tsui, J. L. H., Chang, S. Y. et al. (2025) 'Artificial intelligence for modelling infectious disease epidemics'. *Nature*, 638, 623–635.

Massey, D. (1991) 'A global sense of place'. *Marxism Today*, 38, 24–29.

McPartland, M. (1998) 'The use of narrative in geography teaching'. *The Curriculum Journal*, 9, (3), 341–355.

Mills, L., Mills, O., Tait, G., Tait, T. and Witt, S. (2024) 'Geography from the ground up: Baby geographies'. *Primary Geography*. Spring 2024, 113, 8–9.

Myatt, M. (2018) *The Curriculum: Gallimaufry to coherence*. Woodbridge: John Catt Educational.

Rawling, E. (2020) 'How and why national curriculum frameworks are failing geography'. *Geography*, 105, (2), 69–77.

Rogers, D. (2007) 'Look up for inspiration', *Tes Magazine*, 30 March, www.tes.com/magazine/archive/look-inspiration?amp

Rogers, D. (2009) *Citizenship Through Geography for KS3*. Haddenham: Folens.

Sittner, T. (2021) 'A case for the curriculum: Health geography'. *Teaching Geography*, 46, (1), 21–24.

Star (n.d.) 'Geography primary curriculum progression map', www.olivehackney.com/wp-content/uploads/2022/03/Geography-Primary-Curriculum-Progression-Map-FINAL-21.02.22.pdf

Sullivan, K., Thompson, H. and Willis, H. (2021) 'Note making: It's just writing stuff down… isn't it?'. *Teaching Geography*, 46, (2), 72–75.

Tarisayi, K. S. (2024) 'Integrating Indigenous knowledge in South African geography education curricula for social justice and decolonization'. *E-Journal of Humanities, Arts and Social Sciences*, 5, (7), 1195–1206.

Teacher Tapp (2024) 'No excuses, no Sats and no photocopying...', https://teachertapp.com/articles/no-excuses-no-sats-and-no-photocopying

Widdowson, J. and Lambert, D. M. (2006) 'Using geography textbooks'. In: Balderstone, D. (ed.) *Secondary Geography Handbook*. Sheffield: Geographical Association, pp. 146–159.

Winn, R. (2018) *The Salt Path*. London: Penguin.

Yan, V. X., Sana, F. and Carvalho, P. F. (2023) 'No simple solutions to complex problems: Cognitive science principles can guide but not prescribe educational decisions'. *Policy Insights from the Behavioral and Brain Sciences*, 11, (1), 59–66.

Appendix 1: Example enquiries that lead to change

In geography, we are often concerned with scale and we adeptly move from the local to the global. Scale influences how geographers study phenomena and shapes how we think about them. As we aim for students to leave with great educational outcomes, we must accept that change can occur at the personal scale. It may not be possible to change the entire world, but it is possible to get students to contribute to local plans, decide to spend the Duke of Edinburgh Award service section on an environmental task or provide input into local plans.

Here are a range of example enquiries that can be used where a change is made. For each, I provide a brief description of the outcomes. The change can be very small in scale, and that is OK. Some of these enquiries could span an entire unit, whilst others are more suited to mini units. These ideas are outlined so that they can be contextualised for your area. The enquiries can be adapted for any stage and age, and linked to any specification or curriculum. The best way to do it is by talking to your team around the curriculum campfire.

How do stories of witches and fairies shape the way people understand and value their landscapes?

Context
• The South Downs is a landscape rich in chalk hills, ancient trackways, burial mounds and Neolithic sites.
• Worthing sits between the costal urban fringe and a countryside steeped in stories such as the Devil's Dyke legend, tales of smugglers' caves and the folklore of Chanctonbury and Cissbury Rings.
• The area is part of a living cultural landscape, where stories contribute to how some people perceive and engage with this place.

(Continued)

Big ideas/concepts
- Place identity
- Cultural landscapes
- Memory and oral history as a source of information
- Human interactions
- How landscapes are valued and protected
Sequence of enquiry
1 **What is folklore and why do people tell stories about places?**
- *Introduce the concept of folklore and its links to landscape, memory and culture.*
- *Discuss why certain places inspire myths and legends.*
- *Opportunity to consider myths and legends from other places, e.g. Welsh, Indigenous Australian and Mexican folklore.*
2 **What stories are told about the South Downs around here?**
- *Explore local legends: Why was Devil's Dyke believed to be dug by the Devil? Who planted the trees at Chanctonbury Ring?*
- *What do these legends say about how people once viewed the landscape?*
- *Perspective of the unknown is magic.*
3 **Where in the landscape do these stories live and why there?**
- *Using maps to find evidence of legends and looking at different maps that locate folklore.*
- *Map stories to physical features.*
- *How does the physical geography influence the folklore?*
- *Would the story work somewhere else or is it rooted in this land?*
4 **How do these stories affect how people value and protect places today?**
- *Consider how folklore shapes place identity, tourism and interpretation, and conservation efforts.*
- *Does a story make a place feel more important or 'special'?*
5 **What would happen if we lost these stories?**
- *Explore what is at stake when cultural heritage fades.*
- *Can we understand a landscape fully without its stories?*
- *Can we feel that we belong in a place without knowing its stories? Links to personal stories of places: place is location plus meaning, and different people see and experience places in different ways.*
6 **What stories could we create today that reflect how we see this place?**
- *Students create their own myth or narrative linked to a local place.*
- *How might future generations understand Worthing through our stories?*
- *Are our stories more urban than in the past?*

Potential fieldwork/nature connection activities (can be adapted for on-site or virtual)
• Story walks, visiting folklore sites to tell stories in situ. • Getting outside the classroom on-site to tell stories. • Sensory mapping of a place with real stories layered on.
Data sources
• South Downs National Park Authority cultural heritage pages • Sussex Past/Heritage Gateway • Ordnance Survey maps and historic overlays • Local oral history archives from the local museum • British Library Sounds Archive – folklore collection.
Possible outcomes
• Student-created myths and landscapes map of the South Downs • Extended writing: How has this place shaped stories and how do stories shape our view of this place?

Why are the UK, Ireland, Denmark and Iceland fighting over a rock the size of a standard swimming pool?

Context
• Rockall is a remote islet in the North Atlantic. • Though uninhabitable, it is contested by four nations due to its potential implications for Exclusive Economic Zones (EEZ), fishing rights and mineral resources. • The enquiry explores how sovereignty, natural resources, the United Nations Convention on the Law of the Sea (UNCLOS) and environmental concerns interact in a seemingly insignificant place.
Big ideas/concepts
• Geopolitics and sovereignty • Place significance and scale • Power and perception of space • Natural resources and conflict
Sequence of enquiry

1 **What and where is Rockall? Why does it seem so insignificant and yet so important?**
    • *How big is Rockall compared to places we know (e.g. school hall, field)?*
    • *Where is it located in relation to the UK, Ireland, Iceland and the Faroe Islands?*
    • *What does it look like and who has ever visited it?*

(*Continued*)

2. **Who currently claims Rockall and what are their reasons?**
   - *What is the UK's legal claim to Rockall?*
   - *Why do Ireland, Denmark and Iceland contest the claim?*
   - *How do different countries utilise international law?*
3. **What makes a small rock in the middle of the sea so politically and economically valuable?**
   - *What is an EEZ?*
   - *What potential resources are nearby?*
   - *How does controlling Rockall extend control over surrounding waters?*
4. **What laws govern the ocean and how are they interpreted differently?**
   - *What is UNCLOS and how does it define an island versus a rock?*
   - *Can a place with no fresh water or people still give a country rights to the sea?*
   - *How are maritime borders decided?*
5. **What role do environment, sustainability and Indigenous knowledge play in this dispute?**
   - *What maritime life and ecosystems exist near Rockall?*
   - *How do conservation concerns affect the area?*
   - *Who benefits and loses from exclusive access to these waters?*
6. **Should Rockall belong to anyone or everyone?**
   - *Is it right to claim ownership of ocean space around a rock?*
   - *How do different perspectives conflict or align?*
   - *What might a fair or sustainable solution look like?*
7. **What does this dispute teach us about how humans perceive space, place and power?**
   - *Why are some places worth fighting for?*
   - *How do stories, symbols and strategic interests shape geography?*
   - *Does Rockall change the way I think about borders, oceans and territory?*

Data sources

- United Nations Convention on the Law of the Sea (UNCLOS)
- Marine Scotland or Irish Department of Foreign Affairs
- BBC Bitesize or *Newsround* features on Rockall
- British Geological Survey – seabed resources
- EEZ maps from Marineregions.org
- Articles from *The Conversation* or academic blogs on micro-territories
- Google Earth and satellite images of Rockall.

Possible outcomes

- A digital story map of Rockall's political history.
- A decision-making essay: Who has the best case and why?

What do everyday signs and notices reveal about how people use and value local spaces?

Context
• Public and unofficial signs are a powerful but often overlooked feature of our everyday geographies, from 'no ball games' to hand-painted welcome signs or poetry pinned to fences.
• These texts reflect how spaces are controlled, protected or shared.
• This enquiry helps students decode the hidden messages of signs.
• Many of these activities can be applied to on-site fieldwork.
Big ideas/concepts
• Place and meaning
• Power in space
• Informal vs. formal geography
• Private vs. public space
• Representation and voice
• Social and cultural landscapes
Sequence of enquiry
1 **What is a sign and what does it tell us about a place?**   • *Where do we see signs and notices in our everyday life?*   • *What are signs for? Who makes them and why?*   • *How can a sign influence how people behave, feel or value a space?*   • *Can signs make places 'anti-fun' (Askew, 2024)?*
2 **Who gets to speak in a public space and who is silenced?**   • *What kind of language is used in public signs?*   • *Who is the intended audience of different signs?*   • *What do the signs say about who 'belongs' in a space?*
3 **What do signs tell us about how people value nature or place?**   • *How do some signs reflect respect or emotional connection to places? (e.g. 'Please do not climb the trees – they are older than you.')*   • *How can humour, art or poetry shift the tone of a space? Looking at the work of informal artists in public spaces.*   • *What would the environment say if it could write its own signs?*
4 **What can we learn from the signs in our own community?**   • *What types of signs exist in our school/local area/town centre?*   • *What stories, conflicts and values do these reveal?*   • *Are there any missing voices or messages?*

(Continued)

5 **How can we reimagine our space through our own signs?**
• *This is a potential on-site guerrilla geography task, but the signs can easily be created and left as artefacts in exercise books.*
• *What messages do we want to share about our space? What are we proud of? What makes us stop in our tracks? What makes us look away? What makes us joyful? What makes us sad?*
• *How can our notices influence how others think and behave?*
• *How do we create 'little notices' that reflect care, inclusion and connection?*
Potential fieldwork opportunities
• Sign-spotting walk: photograph, sketch or log every sign in a specific area – around the school or micro-fieldwork on the way to school.
• 'Little notice' design – write positive or poetic messages to post in places.
• Quiet mapping: observe where there are no signs. What does this silence suggest?
Data sources
• Photographs of real signs from the local area, school or online collections
• Keri Smith (2007) – 'Sound Little Notices' (short excerpts or visual examples)
• Examples from public spaces (e.g. churchyards, National Parks, community gardens)
• Google Street View for remote sign-spotting, having a go at GeoGuesser
• Local authority by-law signage (e.g. 'No cycling', 'Respect our space')
• Student-created surveys on how signs make them feel in different spaces
• Examples of 'nudge' behaviour, e.g. example of Cornwall (https://behaviourchangecornwall.co.uk/signs-to-stop-plastic, based on Cinner, 2018).
Possible outcomes
• Annotated fieldwork maps.
• Critical reflection: What does the signage in my area say about us?
• A proposal to the headteacher with ideas for more inclusive/positive signage.

Is north always up? How do maps reflect power, perspective and cultural bias?

Context
• Maps are not neutral: they are cultural artefacts that reflect the values, purposes and power structures of their creators.
• Standalone map units, whilst having some merit, are usually detached from geographical context.
• Many students are taught that north is 'up' or the 'top of the map' and maps are objective.
• This enquiry reveals how mapping can be deeply subjective, political and shaped by world-views and the purpose of the finished map.
• This enquiry explores different cultures.

Big ideas/concepts
- Perspective and representation
- Power and Eurocentrism
- Decolonising geography
- Indigenous knowledge systems
- Orientation and spatial literacy
- Cartographic skills
- Critical evaluation
Sequence of enquiry
1 **Does Iceland exist?**
- *What do we already know about Iceland?*
- *Can countries just appear and disappear?*
- *What are phantom islands and why did they exist?*
- *Can we prove that Iceland exists using a range of sources?*
2 **What do maps really show?**
- *What makes something a map?*
- *Who decides what goes on a map?*
- *What is 'north up' on most maps we use in the UK?*
3 **What perspectives do different maps show and why do they matter?**
- *What is the difference between Mercator, Peters, Robinson and 'south-up' projections?*
- *What might these choices say about who holds power?*
- *What are the consequences of using distorted maps in education and the media?*
4 **How do Indigenous cultures map space differently?**
- *How do Indigenous peoples represent and navigate their landscapes?*
- *What do Indigenous maps tell us about relationships to land, water and ancestry?*
- *What makes Indigenous mapping relational rather than territorial?*
5 **How do Indigenous maps change what we think maps are for?**
- *Use Inuit spatial memory maps, Yolngu songlines, Marshall Islands stick charts and Māori pūrākau and carved representations.*
- *What is similar and different to Eurocentric maps?*
- *How do different cultures pass down knowledge using maps?*
6 **How do maps shape what we value and what we ignore?**
- *What places are often left off or marginalised on maps?*
- *How do maps influence tourism, funding, protection of places or political control?*
- *Can maps create invisibility?*

(Continued)

- *Use examples such as Palestine–Israel border maps from difference sources, First Nations maps of Canada, map of the colonial world vs. map of land acknowledgements.*

7 **What would a fairer or more honest map look like?**
- *How can we reimagine maps to be more inclusive or just?*
- *What do we want people to understand or feel when looking at a map?*
- *How would we map our own place differently?*
- *Create a counter-map of a familiar area using south-up orientation, Indigenous perspective, sensory or emotional experiences, non-Western symbols or storytelling methods.*

Potential fieldwork opportunities
- Creating a relational map of the school grounds.
- Explore how direction feels, e.g. Where does the sun rise? What path do birds follow? What natural signs can be used for navigation?

Data sources

Indigenous and decolonial mapping examples:
- Native Land Digital – interactive map of Indigenous territories globally
- First Nations map of British Columbia
- Yolngu songlines (ABC Education Australia)
- Marshall Islands stick charts (British Museum, Google Arts & Culture)
- Canadian First Nations cartography (Assembly of First Nations)
- UK-based Indigenous-inspired mapping, e.g. deep mapping of Dartmoor.

Alternative projections and critical maps:
- South-up world map (ODT Maps)
- Peters projection (UNESCO resources)
- MapFight or TheTrueSize.com for comparisons
- Colonial world maps for visual critique
- Decolonising map library resources (e.g. Radical Cartography, Decolonial Atlas).

Possible outcomes
- A critical map.
- An academic poster showing 'what maps don't show'.
- A persuasive letter to a textbook publisher suggesting more inclusive map use.

Is a river still a river without water?

Context
• The Finke River (Larapinta in Arrernte) is often cited as one of the oldest rivers in the world, only flowing intermittently through the dry heart of Australia.
• Though it holds little or no surface water most of the year, it remains a cultural, ecological and geographical presence.
• The enquiry asks students to consider the identity of rivers beyond just flowing water and to consider climate impacts, tourist use and the river's role in Indigenous knowledge systems.
• The unit also allows an examination of the colonial history of Australia and how the UK is connected to that.
Big ideas/concepts
• Place identity and cultural meaning
• Ephemeral landscapes and environmental rhythms
• Climate change and hydrological systems
• Human–physical interaction
• Tourism and sustainability
• Indigenous ecological knowledge and relational world-view
• What defines a natural feature? Function, form or meaning?
Sequence of enquiry
1 What makes a river a river?
• *Must a river always flow?*
• *How does our lived experience shape our picture of a river and what assumptions does that reveal?*
• *Where do we find rivers with no water?*
• *Compare perennial, intermittent and ephemeral rivers globally (e.g. Thames vs. Finke vs. Wadi Derna).*
2 Why is the Finke River so important even when it's dry?
• *What makes the Finke River the 'oldest river'?*
• *How does it shape the Central Australian landscape?*
• *What is the Arrernte name for the river and why is it different?*
• *What do the Arrernte people believe about the river's story and identity?*
3 What happens when tourists come to places like this?
• *Why do people visit dry rivers and desert landscapes? Instagram vs. reality.*
• *What are the cultural and environmental impacts of tourism?*
• *How are land rights, heritage sites and sacred spaces protected – or not?*
• *Case study of tourism at Tjoritja and the Larapinta Trail.*

(Continued)

4. **How is climate change affecting rivers that already struggle to flow?**
   - *How is the Finke River and its surrounding ecosystem responding to a hotter, drier climate?*
   - *What role does water scarcity play in ecosystem health and Indigenous culture?*
   - *Are ephemeral rivers disappearing or adapting?*

5. **What can we learn from Indigenous views of rivers and water?**
   - *What is greenwashing and how can it mislead people?*
   - *How do power and privilege shape environmental messaging?*
   - *Does offsetting and planting trees work?*
   - *Who gets to speak for nature and who is often silenced?*
   - *How can we recognise and challenge climate narratives that centre on white, wealthy voices?*

6. **How do different knowledge systems help us understand and protect places?**
   - *How do Aboriginal people understand rivers as part of a living system, even when dry?*
   - *What does it mean to have kinship with the land and how is that different from the UK idea of stewardship?*
   - *How can Western science and Indigenous knowledge work together?*

7. **What is threatening our rivers here? The case of Afon Teifi.**
   - *How is the Afon Teifi affected by environmental pressures?*
   - *What role do invasive species play in shaping (or damaging) local river ecosystems?*
   - *How does a flowing river like Afon Teifi compare to the Finke River in meaning, vulnerability and use?*

8. **What do we value more – presence or meaning?**
   - *Can a river be 'real' without water?*
   - *Should outsiders get to define the meaning of a place?*
   - *What responsibilities do we have to protect rivers we may never see flow?*

Fieldwork/nature connection ideas

- Map an ephemeral or seasonal water flow in or near school.
- Sensory observation walk: how does the landscape feel different when dry vs. wet?

Data sources

- Geoscience Australia
- Central Land Council – Aboriginal land rights and tourism guides
- ABC Education – Indigenous stories and environment
- Australian Bureau of Meteorology – river flow and rainfall data
- NASA Earth Observatory – satellite imagery of dry rivers
- First Nations Media Australia – interviews and documentaries.

Possible outcomes
• Extended writing: Is a river more than just water? • ArcGIS StoryMap: If a river could speak, what would it say? • A GIS map of the Finke River showing visible and invisible layers (cultural, ecological, seasonal).

How can human activity impact remote environments we rarely see or visit?

Context
• Remote and fragile environments, such as highland areas, islands, polar regions and arid landscapes, are often perceived as untouched or unaffected by people. Yet these places are deeply vulnerable to global human activity, particularly climate change. • The enquiry explores indirect impacts and fosters a sense of global interconnection and responsibility. • There are opportunities to encourage empathy for Indigenous and marginalised people. • There is some hopeful geography, showing how students can act. • Case studies include the Scottish Highlands, Iceland's glaciers, Pacific islands, Australian Outback.
Big ideas/concepts
• Climate change and vulnerability • Interdependence • Remote does not equal untouched • Political literacy • Indigenous knowledge systems
Sequence of enquiry

1 **What makes a place remote and why do these places matter?**
  • *What do we mean by 'remote'?*
  • *Are remote places really disconnected from our lives?*
  • *Why should we care about distant landscapes?*
2 **How is climate change reshaping remote places around the world?**
  • *What does sea level rise mean for the Pacific islands?*
  • *How is Iceland's landscape changing with glacial melt?*
  • *What are the visible impacts in Scotland's uplands?*

(Continued)

3 **What's happening to the Australian Outback and who is affected?**
   - *What are the climate impacts in Australia's interior (e.g. droughts, fires, biodiversity loss)?*
   - *How is this affecting Indigenous communities and culture?*
   - *What do Aboriginal perspectives teach us about living with the land?*
   - *Who is telling the stories of Indigenous communities and what perspective do they have?*

4 **How do our everyday lives impact these distant places?**
   - *How does our carbon footprint affect remote regions?*
   - *What roles do consumption, travel and energy use play?*
   - *How connected are we through our lived experience to the Outback or Pacific?*

5 **Who tells the climate story and who gets left out?**
   - *What is greenwashing and how can it mislead people?*
   - *How do power and privilege shape environmental messaging?*
   - *Does offsetting and planting trees work?*
   - *Who gets to speak for nature and who is often silenced?*
   - *How can we recognise and challenge climate narratives that centre on white, wealthy voices.*

6 **How do different knowledge systems help us understand and protect places?**
   - *What does Indigenous knowledge offer that science might overlook?*
   - *How do traditional stories and land-based practices guide sustainability?*
   - *Can science and Indigenous wisdom work together?*

7 **What can we do from here?**
   - *What actions can we take locally to reduce our impact globally?*
   - *How can we use our voice in school, the community and democracy to call for systemic change?*
   - *What are some real-world examples of young people making a difference at different scales?*

8 **What future do we want for remote places?**
   - *How can we express solidarity with people we'll never meet?*
   - *What messages or pledges would we send to future generations or impacted communities?*
   - *What will we commit to change?*

Data sources
Climate and remote impact:
- IPCC regional reports
- NASA Earth Observatory
- Climate Council of Australia
- NatureScot
- Icelandic Met Office.
Indigenous voices and case studies:
- Indigenous Knowledge systems in Australia
- Yolngu or Anangu Country stories (ABC Education)
- Red Desert Dreamings
- Voices from Tuvalu – UN Stories.
Hopeful geography and youth agency:
- Teach the Future UK
- Global dimension (sustainability and citizenship)
- Zero Carbon Britain.
Possible outcomes
- Comparative impact map: Places my carbon touches.
- Extended writing: To what extent do remote places matter to people living in the UK?
- Youth voice letters to MPs and local councils.

How do different ways of seeing shape our understanding of landscapes?

Context
- Landscapes are not neutral.
- They are shaped by how people see, represent, value and use them, whether through myths, maps, art or protest.
- This enquiry could fit well with a more traditional look at geomorphology. It invites students to explore how diverse world-views express relationships with place through art, symbols and cultural artefacts.
- In 2020, Rio Tinto legally destroyed Juukan Gorge, a 46,000-year-old sacred Aboriginal site in Western Australia, to extract iron ore. For the Puutu Kunti Kurrama and Pinikura (PKKP) peoples, the caves were not just ancient but alive with ancestral meaning. To Rio Tinto, the site was a resource location with documented cultural heritage that was less valued than economic output.

(Continued)

Big ideas/concepts
- Multiple ways of knowing and seeing
- Cultural landscapes
- Place identity and connection
- Colonial legacies and perspective
- Art as geographical interpretation
- Decolonising representation
- Public art and protest
Sequence of enquiry
1 **What makes a landscape and how do we know what it means?** 　- *What is a landscape?* 　- *Who decides what a landscape means?* 　- *Can art or stories change the way we see a place?*
2 **How do Indigenous artists see and show their land differently?** 　- *How is land represented in Aboriginal Australian art?* 　- *What is a 'Dreaming' painting or songline?* 　- *How do you map relationships and not just terrain?* 　- *Example: Emily Kame Kngwarreye.*
3 **What stories are told through artefacts and objects?** 　- *What do artefacts tell us about relationships with place?* 　- *How are land and ancestors connected?* 　- *Examples: Dogon people of Mali, San rock art in Botswana/Namibia, Inuit carvings and storytelling from Arctic Canada, Malagasy tomb carvings in Madagascar.*
4 **What happens when Western perspectives erase Indigenous landscapes?** 　- *How did colonial maps and museum displays change the story of land?* 　- *Compare Indigenous and Western maps of the same spaces, e.g. Yolngu Sea Country map vs. political map of Australia.*
5 **How are landscapes reimagined in our own communities?** 　- *What stories does local graffiti or mural art tell us about our place?* 　- *Who gets to paint their version of the landscape and who doesn't?* 　- *Local fieldwork.*
6 **Whose story survives in the landscape?** 　- *How can a place hold meaning for one group and be invisible to another?* 　- *What does the destruction of the Juukan Gorge reveal about conflicting world-views?* 　- *Can landscapes be protected if they are seen through different eyes?*

Possible fieldwork
• Local sacred landscape investigation: Visit a local ancient site, graveyard or natural monument. Students document who uses it, how it's maintained and whether its meanings are layered or contested.
• Create a 'heritage layering map' showing overlapping uses/values of a local space.
Data sources
• British Museum Indigenous collections
• Google Arts & Culture Indigenous art projects
• Inuit Art Foundation
• Decolonising Geography
• *The Conversation* – articles on Aboriginal art, San rock art and Malagasy beliefs
• Local authority street art trails or community arts groups
• ABC News Australia – Juukan Gorge
• PKKP Land Council public statements
• The Australian Institute of Aboriginal and Torres Strait Islander Studies (AAIATSIS).
Possible outcomes
• Extended writing: Should sacred land ever be up for negotiation?
• Reflective writing: The most powerful way to see a place is…
• Fieldwork – annotated maps showing graffiti.

How has migration shaped the cultural landscape of west Wales?

Context
• West Wales is often associated with strong Welsh cultural identity, including language and rural traditions. Yet from the twentieth century onwards, it has been shaped by waves of inward migration: post-WW2 resettlement and evacuees, in-migration from England for a rural lifestyle or retirement, EU migrants working in hospitality and agriculture, asylum seekers and refugees (including from Syria, Afghanistan and Sudan), return migration of Welsh speakers reclaiming cultural roots.
• These movements have influenced the cultural landscape, seen in languages spoken, shops, religious buildings, food, festivals, schools and social tensions and integration.
Big ideas/concepts
• Cultural landscape
• Migration
• Place and identity
• Global–local connections

(Continued)

Sequence of enquiry
1 **What is a cultural landscape and how can we read it?** • *What does 'culture' look like in a landscape?* • *What evidence of migration might appear in a town, village or rural area?* • *Possible virtual fieldwork using Street View* 2 **Who has come to west Wales and why?** • *What are some of the main migration patterns in west Wales since 1945?* • *What are the reasons for people moving to the area?* • *How does west Wales compare to other UK regions?* 3 **How has migration shaped everyday life here?** • *What is my lived experience of migration in this area?* • *How do migrants contribute to food, faith, music, festivals and schools?* • *What celebrations, integrations and tensions exist around migration?* 4 **What stories do local people tell about migration?** • *How do migrants describe their sense of belonging?* • *What do longer-term residents think about change?* • *Can we see places of cultural exchange or exclusion?* 5 **What does the future cultural landscape of west Wales look like?** • *How is the region likely to change with future migration?* • *What role can young people play in shaping inclusive places?*
Potential fieldwork
On-site (school grounds or local urban/rural community): • Cultural landscape walks: Students identify shops, buildings, signs, languages and features that reflect migration (e.g. Eastern European food shops, places of worship, fusion cuisine). • Interviews or surveys: Speak with local business owners, students or teachers from different backgrounds (respecting consent and ethics). • Photo voice: Students take photos of 'evidence of migration' and annotate their meanings. **Off-site:** • Visit a town like Haverfordwest, Carmarthen or Aberystwyth to explore food markets, religious sites and community centres. • Partner with local refugee support charities or community integration projects.

Data sources
- Census data (Office for National Statistics (ONS), Nomis) for local ethnicity and language trends
- Local authority migration reports (e.g. Pembrokeshire, Ceredigion)
- Welsh Government refugee and asylum data
- Voices from Wales: www.peoplescollection.wales
- British Red Cross or Ethnic Youth Support Team (EYST) Wales
- Local newspapers or community radio
- Interviews or oral history projects with migrants or host communities.
Possible outcomes
- Extended writing: What migration means to west Wales today.
- Fieldwork: mapping the cultural landscape.

Activity

For one of these enquiries:

1 Where would it fit within your current curriculum?
2 Do you have the expertise and resources to be able to develop this?
3 How would you adapt it to fit into your context?
4 What prior knowledge would students need to access this enquiry?
5 How could we tie this into the lived experiences of students in our context?
6 What misconceptions and preconceptions may surface and how could these be found and corrected?

Index

Abbey, E. 175
Alcock, D. 201, 261
algorithms 16, 23, 127
Al-Momani, F. 104
analytical skills 195, 199–200
anti-racist geographies 68–71, 125
artificial intelligence (AI) 16, 214, 219
    chatbot 177
    geography teaching 177–8
    questions 157–8
Attenborough, D. 183
audio 181–2

balanced evaluation 230
Banned Word Board 236
banned words 156
    alternatives 236–7
    definition 236
Black Sheep: A story of rural racism, identity and hope (Pace-Humphreys) 176
Blue Planet (documentary) 183
Bonnett, A. 108
books 175–7, 188
    critically evaluate information 220–1
    information 175–7, 188
Brace, S. 79
Bradshaw, M. 216
Brooks, C. 28, 111
Burgess, E. W. 84–5, 216, 254
Butler, R. W. 128

Coasting: Running around the coast of Britain – life, love and (very) loose plans (Downing) 176
cognitive load theory 27, 37, 95
    definition 91–2
    enquiry classroom 92–3
    learning process 92
cognitive science 11, 19, 55, 83–4, 86, 92, 264
    embodied learning 96
    in geography classroom 87
    and psychology 97–8
    research studies in 85

cognitive theory of multimedia learning (CTML) 95
Coles, J. 110
command words 160
    definition 234
    uses 235
communication 83, 90, 94
    assessment 230
    audience 228
    balanced evaluation 230
    banned words 236–7
    books 220
    command words 234–6
    decision-making 230
    disagreeing well 228–9
    enquiry approach model 220
    geographical inaccuracy 231
    geomorphology 237
    historical and colonial legacy 231
    homogenisation 231
    justification 230
    methods of 232–3
    notes 229–30
    oracy 241–2
    overgeneralisation 231
    pause and answer, enquiry question 228
    progression 226–7
    saltation 237
    scaffolds 238–41
    structured writing 230
    Tier 3 words 233–4
constructivism 47
contested, geographical knowledge 127
Cornell method 229
Covid-19 pandemic 39, 52, 260
critical evaluation, enquiry 243
    critical reflection 246
    curriculum, classroom and specification 254–5
    local to glo`bal reflections 257
    metacognition 247
    misconception 256
    National Curriculum 245

perspectives 255–6
progression 248–9
psychologically safe classroom space 252
questions 250–1
self-assessment 247–8
critical evaluation, information
adverts 223
analytical and critical thinking skills 199–200
books 220–1
data interpretation skills 196–9
decolonising geography 207–10
enquiry approach model 193
factfulness 200–7
fieldwork 219–20
floating topicality 217–9
Gapminder 213
geographical models 215–7
graph 211
importance of 194–5
Instagram *vs.* reality 212–3
maps 221–3
mystery graph 212
progression 195–6
questions by students 210–11
reliable sources 214–5
trends *vs.* variation 215
critical hope 260
critical reflection 247, 249, 254
definition 246
metacognition and 254
critical thinking skills 199–200
curriculum artefact
cartographic skills 170–1
definition 164
maps, types of 171
types of 165–9

data interpretation skills 195–9
decision-making 53, 98, 105, 129, 149, 230
decolonial school geography 68–71
decolonising geography 207–10
Demographic Transition Model 217
disagreeing well, skill of 228–9
disciplinary knowledge 25, 44
discovery learning 47–50, 264
definition 11
diversity, equity and inclusion (DEI) 24

documentaries 182–4
dual coding 94–5

educational research 10, 14–5, 19, 53–4, 83–5
cognitive load 91–3
cognitive science 87
embodied learning 96
enquiry 96–8
geographical model 84
instruction 96–8
interleaving 88–90
multimedia learning 94–5
retrieval practice 91
schemas/mental models 93–4
secondary students' outcomes 99
spaced learning 87–8
teacher agency 85–6
Education Endowment Foundation (EEF) 86–7, 93–5
Elegy for a River (Moorhouse) 74, 176
embodied learning 96
England 31, 245
enquiry approach 15, 28, 35–6, 47, 96–8
communication 225
critically evaluate information 193
definition 10, 11, 33
geographical question 141–2
geography classroom 36–8
information 161
lenses of 42
model 36
organisational tool 43–4
pedagogy 32
type of 106
enquiry curriculum 117–8, 299
challenging, inspiring and driven by expert teachers 121
datasets 131
diverse and representative 122–3
features of 121
'floating topicality' 123–4
Hampstead School geography 132–3
living and flexible 126
messy and contested 127
moral and ethical aspects 127–8
physical and human geography 128–9
physical environment 130
scheme of work 136

sequence of lessons, questions 124–5
shared resources 129
skills and knowledge 129
teaching vs. knowledge 119
time-pressured curriculum 125
unified curriculum 122
unit of learning 133–4
Esri's Digimap 131
Esson, J. 70, 125
Eurocentric approach 70, 207
examination specifications 21, 38, 44, 107
external 22
National Curriculum and 28
progression 112–13
expert teachers 15, 45–6, 50, 54
challenging and inspiring 121
decisions of 19
professionalism of 19
qualifications and qualities on 19
explicit instructional guidance 48

factfulness 200
child mortality 201
instincts of 202–6
Factfulness (Rosling) 200
fieldwork 52, 56, 73, 124, 151, 163
critically evaluate information 219–20
desktop studies 190
notebook 190
progression 188
teach and model issues 189
Fifty Words for Snow (Campbell) 176
Fiorella, L. 95
floating topicality 217–19
'floating topicality' 123–4
Full Circle (documentary) 182

Game of Thrones 212
Gapminder 202, 213
Gardner, D. 109
generative AI 219
generative learning 95
GeogPod 42, 70, 125
Geographical Association (GA) 13, 27–8, 33, 35, 118
Centre of Excellence 45
curriculum framework 29
geographical enquiry 45–6
discovery learning 47–50

educational research 53–4
fieldwork 52
group work 50
hypothetical/fictional situations 53
instruction, principles of 97–8
knowledge 51–2
signature pedagogy 51
geographical inaccuracy 231
geographical knowledge 8, 21–2, 35, 39, 51–2
disciplinary 25
substantive 26
geographical models 25, 188, 215–17, 221, 255
definition 84
use of 25, 215–17
geographical questions
AI 157–8
definition 141
development 143–4
'Do now' task 155–6
enquiry approach model 141
everyday experience 154–5
grid 156–7
guerilla geography unit 151–2
image of week 159
progression 144–9
sequences of 149
teacher invites questions 158–9
understanding 159–60
Year 8 unit of work 149–50
young people with emotion of place 152–4
geographical rucksack 15, 37, 75
geographic information systems (GIS) 25, 28, 182–3, 198
geography classrooms 14, 19, 24–5, 37
cognitive science 87
curiosity and agency 263
disciplinary thinking and literacy 262
enquiry model for 36–8, 264–5
GIS 28
retrieval and reflection 263
geomorphology 175, 237
Gilbert, I. 180
globalisation 72, 77, 127, 176, 237, 256
Global South 231
Google Maps 125, 182, 187
graphs 92, 171, 211

Grenell, A. 48
Ground News 218
group work 50
Guardian (newspaper) 159
'guerilla geography' 149, 151–2

Hamill, A. 28
Hampstead School geography curriculum 132–3
Hattie, J. 85, 98
Herbert, D. T. 109
historical and colonial legacy 231
homogenisation 231
hopeful education 201
Humphreys, A. 73

I Belong Here: A journey along the backbone of Britain (Sethi) 176
information 13, 23, 69, 74, 86, 109
    AI 177–8
    audio 181–2
    books 175
    cognitive load 91–2
    curriculum artefacts 164–71
    documentaries 183–4
    embodied learning 96
    enquiry approach model 161
    experiments 185–7
    fieldwork 188–90
    geographical models 188
    GIS software 182–3
    Google Maps 182, 187
    infiltration tables 190–1
    interleaving 88
    library lesson 188
    maps 162–3
    multimedia learning 94–5
    never off duty 172–3
    news 185
    on-site fieldwork microclimate 190–1
    personal stories as 184
    photos 179–80
    principles 96
    progression 163–4
    retrieval practice 91
    sources of 11
    textbooks 173–4
    thunks 180–1
Instagram *vs.* reality 212–3

instruction, principles of 12, 47, 96–8
interconnectedness 72, 111, 234
interleaving
    definition 88–9
    Key Stage 3 learning sequence 89
    shared classes, planning 90

Jackson, P. 109
Jones, K. 87
justification 15, 230

knowledge curriculum 25, 32
    disciplinary 25
    procedural 25–6
    rise of 27
    vs. skills debate 45
    substantive 26

Lambert, D. 127
landscapes 26, 74, 175–6
language 39–40
learning process 92, 96
Leat, D. 94
Lee, E. S. 217
lesson sequence 59
    planning expertise 70
    Year 7 students 60–3
    Year 8 students 64–7
library lesson 188
The Lie of the Land: Who really cares for the countryside? (Shrubsole) 176
Living Geography 126
Local: A search for nearby nature and wildness (Humphreys) 73

maps 25, 92–4, 120, 159, 170, 175, 256
    in classroom 222
    communication 232
    critical evaluation of information 221–3
    curriculum artefacts 165
    fieldwork suggestions 223
    information 162–3
    notes 229
    progression 113–16
    types of 171
    visualisation tools 182–3
Marshall, T. 221
massed learning 88

Massey, D. 151
Matthews, J. A. 109
Mccrea, P. 70
messy, geographical knowledge 127
metacognition 94, 244
    definition 247
    and reflection 254
migration 39, 49, 64–7, 131, 184, 217, 234, 262
Milner, C. 184, 208
minimally guided instruction 48
Moorhouse, T. 74
Morgan, J. 108, 127
multimedia learning
    definition 94–5
    enquiry classroom 95
mystery graph 212

National Curriculum 28, 56, 59
National Geographic 41
National Hurricane Center (NOAA) 181
Nayeri, C. 208
news 113, 124–5, 175, 185, 217–9
non-exam assessment (NEA) 48, 103–4, 107, 143, 157–8, 189, 227
Northern Ireland curriculum 31
notes 64, 229–30

Ofsted 25, 32, 56, 105, 118, 124
oracy 241–2
Oracy Education Commission 241
Ordnance Survey maps 73
organisational tool 32, 34, 43–4
overgeneralisation 231
Owens, J. 79

Palin, M. 182
Parkinson, A. 10, 109
Parry, B. 183
pedagogy 11, 32, 35, 51, 86–7, 100, 109, 131, 246, 265–6
    quality of learning 49
A Pennine Journey: The story of a long walk in 1938 (Wainwright) 176
perception 43, 111–2, 213
Perry, T. 84
personal geography 71
    of teachers and students 38, 46
personal stories 176, 184

photos 179–80
physical and human geography 78–9, 128–9
place, concept of 41, 111–3, 151
Planet Earth (documentary) 183
point, evidence, explanation, link (PEEL) 230
Prisoners of Geography: Ten maps that tell you everything you need to know about global politics (Marshall) 221
procedural knowledge 15, 25–8, 36, 44, 51–2, 64, 107, 113, 121, 266
    analytical skills 91
    automaticity of 30
    cognitive load 91
    critical reflection 247
    data interpretation 196
    development of 30, 58
    enquiry curriculum 121
    evaluation of information 194–5
    information 162
    maps 221
    myriad of 143
    progression 163, 195, 248
    scaffolds 240
    spaced learning 88
progression 15, 19, 33, 47, 92, 103–4, 143
    communication 226–7
    critically evaluating enquiry 248–9
    enquiry, type of 106
    evaluation of information 195–6
    examination specifications 112–3
    fieldwork 188
    geographical concepts 111–2
    geography curriculum 105–7
    maps 113–6
    model of 104
    own information 163–4
    qualifications 107–8
    qualities 107–8
    in questions 144–9, 157
    thinking geographically 108–11
psychology 19, 83, 96
    cognitive science and 97–8
Puttick, S. 22

qualifications and qualities 16, 19, 46, 86, 107–8, 118, 232, 254, 265

Raven-Ellison, D. 151
Red Dust: A path through China (Jian) 176
representation 53, 112, 125, 187–8, 211
   maps 221
   of spaced learning *vs.* massed learning 88
retrieval practice 32, 56, 91, 263
Roberts, M. 8, 33, 37–8, 86, 93, 104, 113
Rosenshine, B. 33, 263
   principles of instruction and enquiry 96–8
Roser, M. 201
Rosling, H. 200
Royal Geographical Society 13
Rushton, E. A. C. 208

saltation 237
Sammar, I. 71, 75
Sayers, J. 156
scaffolds
   examples of 240–1
   PEEL 230
   range of 238
   SEEP 230
   VCOB 238–9
schemas 15, 46, 76, 89
   cognitive conflict 94
   definition 93
   enquiry classroom 93–4
school geography
   aims of 23
   and curriculum 21–2
   GA framework 27–9
   knowledge, types of 25–6
   nature of 23
   state of 56
   in UK classrooms 31–4, 68–9
science of learning 86–7
Scotland 30, 245
Search of Kazakhstan: The land that disappeared (Robbins) 176
self-assessment 247–8
self-determination theory 263

senior leadership team (SLT) 45, 118, 130, 228
social, economic, environmental, political (SEEP) 230
spaced learning 111
   definition 87
   enquiry classroom 88
   interleaving 88
   vs. massed learning 88
state-funded education 40
Steel, H. 216
structured writing 230
student self-direction 105
substantive knowledge 15, 26–8, 30, 47–9, 64, 68, 110
   abstract concepts 75
   interleaving 88
   physical and human geography 128
sustainability 72, 180
   definition of 78–9

Taylor, L. 111, 149
teacher agency 15, 85–6
Teaching Geography (Attenborough) 99, 183
textbooks 68, 163, 165, 173–4
thinking geographically 108–11
thinking skills 195
Thinking Through Geography (Leat) 94
Third World 173, 231
thunks 180–1
Tier 3 words 233–4
time *vs.* content 56–8
trends *vs.* variation 215
Tribe (documentary) 183

UK 13, 41, 44, 58, 124, 215, 238, 260
   classroom 83
   school geography 31–3, 68–9
Under the Stars: A journey into light (Gaw) 176

Wales 31, 245
Why Study Geography? (Parkinson) 109
Wiliam, D. 46